The NAFTA Puzzle

The NAFTA Puzzle

Political Parties and Trade in North America

EDITED BY

Charles F. Doran
and Gregory P. Marchildon

Westview Press

BOULDER, SAN FRANCISCO, & OXFORD

Published in 1994 in the United States of America by Westview Press, Inc., 5500 Central Avenue, Boulder, Colorado 80301-2877, and in the United Kingdom by Westview Press, 36 Lonsdale Road, Summertown, Oxford OX2 7EW

Library of Congress Cataloging-in-Publication Data
The NAFTA puzzle : political parties and trade in North America /
    edited by Charles F. Doran and Gregory P. Marchildon.
        p.   cm.
    Includes bibliographical references.
    ISBN 0-8133-8872-4
    1. Free trade—North America.   2. North America—Commerce.
3. North America—Commercial policy.   4. Political parties—North
America.   I. Doran, Charles F.   II. Marchildon, Gregory, 1956–   .
HF3211.N34   1994
382'.917—dc20
                                                                94-10540
                                                                     CIP

Printed and bound in the United States of America

∞ The paper used in this publication meets the requirements
   of the American National Standard for Permanence of Paper
   for Printed Library Materials Z39.48-1984.

10   9   8   7   6   5   4   3   2   1

Contents

Acknowledgments

The editors would like to thank the Donner Foundation, the Draeger Foundation, and the Government of Canada for their timely and generous support of this study. The study was initiated by the editors as part of the research program of the Center of Canadian Studies at the Paul H. Nitze School of Advanced International Studies, The Johns Hopkins University, Washington, D.C., and the emerging affiliated program in North American Studies. Particular appreciation goes to Dr. Barbara G. Doran for the final editing of the entire manuscript. In addition to the individuals acknowledged in each of the chapters, the editors thank those scholars who helped guide the project at various times with constructive criticism and discussion: Tom Barnes, Robert Bothwell, Reuven Brenner, David Calleo, Colin Campbell, Benjamin Ginsberg, Judith Goldstein, Peter Katzenstein, Allan Kornberg, Jonathan Lemco, Seymour Martin Lipset, Charles Lipson, Charles Pearson, Richard Rosecrance, and Sidney Weintraub.

Charles F. Doran
Gregory P. Marchildon

1

Introduction: The Trade and Political Party Flip-Flop

Charles F. Doran

On November 17, 1993, a Democratic president passed a Republican initiative on trade and commercial regionalism in North America over the heads of the reluctant members of his own party. Is this the end of political party in the United States? Does this mean that government can make trade policy without taking political party into account? Or is there a more fundamental and complex relationship between trade and political party underlying this result? How, for instance, did each party come to adopt the outlook on free trade that goes with the party label? And when?

Three large puzzles confront the origin of the North American Free Trade Agreement (NAFTA). This book attempts to provide background material necessary to answer these puzzles.

The initial puzzle concerns the reason why the North American trade agreement ever was conceived in the first place. For those who may presently take NAFTA as an article of faith in terms either of its utility or of its inevitability, reference need only be made to the abortive North American Accord idea. Leading candidates in both the Republican and Democratic parties during the 1980 election campaign, including the eventual winner, proposed a far-reaching trade agreement with Canada and Mexico. The idea got nowhere. Indeed, the trade proposal was dropped from the campaign platforms largely because it met an extremely cool response in both Ottawa and Mexico City.

Moreover, as the essays in this volume reveal, North American trade liberalization historically has often experienced a bad reception in each of the three countries. This historical antipathy provides all the more justification for questioning why a regional trade agreement should come into existence. Deep suspicion of U.S. motives often shaped Canadian and Mexican foreign policy toward their larger neighbor, all but ruling out a trade initiative, especially one so restrictive in scope yet so demanding in terms of depth as NAFTA. Under both Diefenbaker and Trudeau, for example, Canada sought a North Atlantic trade pact with Europe to lessen trade dependence upon the United States; and President Salinas of Mexico first sought association with the European Community. For its part, the United States frequently discounted the significance of more formalized trading rules with its two smaller partners.

Strong protectionist lobbies and interest groups operate in each of these polities. At any time in the twentieth century perhaps a majority of the populations could be counted on to oppose free trade. In fact, the historic defeat of the Laurier government (1911) on the issue of free trade with the United States rang in the ears of Canadian government leaders and served to illustrate how few votes trade liberalization was likely to garner for any head of government courageous enough to propose the notion. Thus, alike for policy-maker and analyst, the puzzle concerning why NAFTA happened, why in the early 1990s and why in this format, remains a mystery worth examining.

A second puzzle, cutting in something of the opposite direction to the first, is why in the spring and summer of 1993 NAFTA began to run aground politically. What slowed its advancement, and why of all places did this loss of momentum occur in the United States? The two long-standing opponents to regional free trade, Mexico and Canada, had already put in place the legislation to make the agreement reality. A measure of the lack of anticipation for U.S. recalcitrance was the way the treaty had been drafted. According to the treaty, if one of the partners dropped out—and the architects had in mind Canada because of the unpopularity of further regional free trade agreements there beyond the highly criticized Canada-U.S. Free Trade Agreement (FTA)—the other two partners could go ahead with the arrangement. Without the United States, the agreement made no sense. Little did anyone suspect that the United States, the principal partner to the agreement, would be the country with "the coldest feet."

Arguments against the treaty discussed in the United States were easily enough identified. Environmental fears of a "pollution haven" in Mexico for foreign and U.S.-based industry on the one hand, and "unfair labor practices" linked to child-labor, unsatisfactory working conditions, and low wages on the other, were the most commonly asserted complaints. Behind these complaints lay the deeper anxiety of loss of U.S. jobs to Mexican industry. But what makes these "explanations" unsatisfactory is the fact that corresponding anxieties could be heard, and were heard, in both Mexico and Canada, albeit with slightly different slants. At base, the same refrain in each country was trepidation over "investment diversion" and "trade diversion." Was this consternation more severe in the United States than in Canada or Mexico? To assume so automatically, because the United States became the laggard in signing the treaty, is potentially a mistake of causal inference. Deeper structural differences between the governments may be at work. Similarly, the arguments of tactical timing inside the Clinton agenda can be overplayed as to explanation, since the issue of timing was more a response to a difficult situation than itself a cause.

Hence the second puzzle as to why, in the principal trading partner, where leadership is normally expected on most trade matters, there was instead hesitance and even back-sliding, is a perplexing question that goes beyond mere personality of leadership, bureaucratic style, or political happenstance. The answer, if it is to be found, must come from both careful comparative assessment and thorough historical examination of the interplay between politics and economics in each polity, in brief, in terms of the assessment of international political economy and of how it actually shapes trade policy. This study is an essential backdrop to a fuller understanding of the internal determinants of foreign trade policy in the modern state.

Why did passage of the North American Free Trade Agreement become such a *cause celeb*? Why was the opposition to it so virulent? How did free trade contribute to the bringing down of a government in Canada, and to the virtual destruction of the Conservative Party, leaving it with only two parliamentary seats after the 1993 elections? Why did President Clinton have to rely more on the Republican Party for Congressional votes for NAFTA, and to confront more opposition votes from within his own party? Why, indeed, did the Democratic president choose to support this initiative of the opposition party when it was so unpopular within his own? In short, is the nature of the relationship between trade and political party in North America changing?

According to the thesis of this book, the history of free trade and party politics in the United States, Canada, and Mexico reveals the third and most important political economy puzzle, a puzzle of far wider and deeper reach than those involving the specific trade agreements. That so much trade liberalization could occur in so short an interval is surely a story that has a political foundation, for it is within the leadership of governments and of political parties that the hard decisions were first made to put the trade negotiators to work. To answer the first puzzle, how and why trade took a front seat in foreign policy conduct for these three countries in a way that was politically unthinkable a decade prior, the analyst must also assess this political dynamic within each country. Therein the analyst will discover the surprising pattern of change that prompted this study.

The third and largest puzzle is that, on matters of trade liberalization, party politics appears to have flip-flopped in each of these countries. It is the chief theoretical contention of this volume that the major political parties in these polities have not only reversed their historical positions on trade. Each party has adopted the position of its principal contender. By exchanging positions on foreign trade, these parties have created one of the great conundrums of trade politics.

Historically, the Democratic Party, supported by labor, favored free trade because consumers benefitted from it and because protectionism, favored by Republicans, gave business a "monopoly rent" which had to come out of the consumer's pocket. Contemporaneously, the Republican Party favors free trade because multinational corporations need open markets everywhere, starting at home, and the Democratic Party tends to oppose it because organized labor favors protectionism in the attempt to "save jobs." In Canada, the Liberal Party favored free trade at the turn of the twentieth century while the Conservative Party opposed it. In the 1980s the Liberal Party opposed free trade with the United States because free trade supposedly threatened jobs and undermined nationalism, while the Conservative Party, supported by business, sought a free trade deal with the United States so as to safeguard access to the U.S. market.

What explains these historic flip-flops in which political parties in each country have taken the position of the other party regarding whether trade liberalization was or was not a good idea? In Canada, why has the Liberal party taken the Conservative's old outlook, and vice-versa? In the United States, why has the Republican Party taken the old position of the Democrats, and vice-versa? Similarly in Mexico, why did the governing party, the Partido Revolucionario Institutional (PRI), sack its old policies of government control and come out for free trade? These are truly monumental historical and partisan shifts that have no slight significance for the final outcome of North American trade regionalism.

Finally, why did President Clinton choose to back the Bush proposal at all, much less so vigorously? The short answer is that Clinton came to believe that regional free trade was in his nation's broad interest and was best for his presidency. Indeed, regional free trade become a test of Clinton's capacity to lead in foreign policy. This more than anything else determined the strategy of the president.

A large structural reason existed in favor of NAFTA. In contrast to prior periods of history, trade today is investment-driven. That is why every country in the world seeks foreign investment. Moreover, most foreign trade is intra-industry and intra-firm. Low-end jobs can be retained in the rich countries only as a part of a globalized network of production. This creates new high-end jobs where the skills, technology, and capital permit. Hence, only by using the external market forces outside North America, not by trying to exclude them, could the U.S. economy break out of its somnolence. Restructuring is painful. The only way it is likely to happen in a fashion that will keep the North American region competitive with Asia is for the United States and Canada to feel the brunt of low-wage pressure from Mexico in a kind of controlled experiment, preparing North America for the world in the next stage.

A tactical reason for NAFTA bolstered the structural argument. Without NAFTA, North America confronted the possibility of a long slide into protectionism. With NAFTA, Clinton could go to the Asia Pacific Economic Council meetings later that month, hopefully with the support of Canada, and obtain at least a symbolic show of support for additional global trade liberalization. He could then go back to Europe and the Uruguay Round of tariff talks with a balance of power composed of North America and Asia at his back, urging the Europeans to make some of the needed concessions on agriculture in order to consummate a global trade agreement.

But broader economic regionalism was quite unpopular with the American electorate, reflected in the voting behavior of both parties, but especially the Democratic Party. Only 102 Democratic members of Congress voted for NAFTA while 156 voted against it. Those voting for it often did so under intense duress, or extraordinary incentive, thus indicating the distaste for the agreement in home districts. On the Republican side, 134 members voted for NAFTA, but interestingly, despite the fact that this was a Bush proposal, combined with arm-twisting by the Republican leadership and a letter from Clinton indicating that he would not make trade a partisan issue in the next campaign, some 43 Republican members of Congress voted against NAFTA as well.

What a contrast to Canadian parliamentary behavior with its extreme party discipline! In the U.S. case, the members of the governing party, the majority party in Congress, did not accept the lead of their president, yet the measure passed because of the favorable votes of the opposition party. In the United States, partisanship is supposed to stop at the "water's edge." Here partisanship seemed to so disappear that opposition party votes were far more numerous on behalf of NAFTA than those of the governing Democratic Party. Is this the end of political party in the United States? Certainly the 1993 Canadian federal election, where the Conservative, pro-trade liberalization governing party went from 169 to 2 seats in Parliament, seems to give "party elimination" concrete meaning.

But the answer is no, party is not collapsing in either Canada or the United States. The Liberal Party after all won an astounding majority in that Canadian election. Nor were U.S. voters or Democratic members of Congress very troubled in procedural terms by the NAFTA outcome, in spite of some disclaimers regarding the "buying of a victory." As noted above, what was at stake were the prestige of the presidency in foreign policy conduct and over-whelming issues in international political economy. The NAFTA would determine whether momentum would continue in terms of trade liberalization on the part of the United States, and by extension to some degree throughout the international system. A lot was riding on this vote. No member of the Democratic Congressional majority misunderstood these facts.

Ironically, perhaps the only way the trade initiative would have passed in a period when North America was still slowly climbing out of a recession, and when all trade initiatives were looked upon by voters with suspicion, was for a Democratic president to back it vigorously while Congressional Democrats opposed it. Many Democratic members of Congress quietly voted against NAFTA, knowing that in the last analysis the agreement would pass with the polite help from the apparently very loyal Republican opposition. In Congress, a vote is not always just a vote. In assessing policy-making in the U.S. House of Representatives, the analyst must look behind the vote to comprehend its meaning.

One conclusion of this book is that governments cannot make trade policy without taking political party into account. Detailed historical chapters demonstrate the important link between party and trade policy for the United States, Canada, Mexico, and Quebec during the past century. They also document the hypothesized flip-flop and reversal in party position on trade liberalization for the principal parties in the United States and Canada. As the information on party platforms in the Uslaner chapter shows for the U.S. case, the flip-flop in party position on trade was a long-term, gradual, one-time exchange. In Canada, the Conservatives were more doctrinaire, perhaps, in their posture of protectionism for most of the twentieth century, except for hesitant apostasy under Bennett. But, superficially more prone to experimentation, as McDowall makes clear, the Liberals were true to freer trade ideas through the King governments until the middle of the post-1945 interval. That this same political phenomenon occurred in both countries suggests that the flip-flop was a mechanism of political change which had at least a region-wide origin. It certainly highlights the role of party in issues of trade liberalization.

A skeptic might argue, on the contrary, that party flip-flops and roll-call defections indicate that party is largely irrelevant in the formulation and implementation of trade policy. If party flip-flop on trade orientation has indeed taken place, certainly political party could not possibly be considered a meaningful explanatory variable. The very fact that the same political party at opposite ends of a century could hold contrasting positions on trade liberalization implies that something else, not party, is responsible for the contrary views. Add to this the reality that a Buchanan (Republican) and a Gephardt (Democrat) could both oppose NAFTA, while a Gingrich (Republican) and a Foley (Democrat) could favor NAFTA, and the immateriality of political party certainly seems unambiguous.

But the role of party is not so easily dismissed by these realities. As argued theoretically in Chapter 10, party is an intermediate variable between the voter and interest group on the one hand, and trade policy on the other. And, notwithstanding its intermediate role, political party is a crucial variable to that outcome. Moreover, insofar as party hangs together as a concept and a political force in decisive votes on trade liberalization within Congress or Parliament, roll call defections do not automatically cancel the relevance of party. Defections notwithstanding, the political party possesses an identifiable outlook on free trade that goes with the party label and is understood by press and citizen.

A multi-causal model of the trade-party relation fully acknowledges the multiple, simultaneous, and interwoven operation of several variables in explaining the party flip-flop regarding trade liberalization. Hence, different explanations can account for the mechanism and level of causation of the party flip-flop at different times, and one explanation does not operate to the total exclusion of all others. The underlying constituency or interest group base of the party could flip-flop, taking party position with it. Or, once a party comes to power, incumbency could force it into a flip-flop against the wishes of the elected party officials and/or the constituency it represents. Or, the ideology of the party itself could change. Although the level of explanation and to some extent the timing and mechanism may differ with each explanation, it is important to note that in no case is the flip-flop explained absent political party.

Moreover, as demonstrated empirically in Chapter 11, the NAFTA vote itself shows that the link between political party and trade liberalization is quite alive, strong, and enduring. Based on party unity scores, roll call on NAFTA reveals above-average party cohesion. The party split on the vote regarding NAFTA proves very little since party discipline in most democracies (with the exception of Canada) is far from perfect. Party voting on NAFTA thus is more identifiable than on many other issues.

An even more telling argument is that if Clinton had not worked so hard to change the trade vote of his own party, partisan division on NAFTA would have been even more stark. The Republicans would have voted for NAFTA, more Democrats would have voted against it, and the agreement would have failed in Congress. The general conclusion stands. Political party continues to be a strong factor in trade liberalization policy-making, even though the major parties over time have flip-flopped on this issue. Flip-flop is possible in party orientation without destroying either party unity or party identification on the trade issue.

Thus, while the main contribution of this book is its analysis of the trade-party relationship in North American polities over the past century, and its assessment of an apparent flip-flop in historic party positions across these countries, the book also challenges the notion that political parties could not possibly contribute to the formulation of trade policy. Political party may furnish a bellwether of change regarding trade matters inside the democratic polity. A kind of early warning mechanism concerning willingness to support additional liberalization in the future, political party may reveal the limits of the possible in regional bloc formation and the expansion of the global trade order. For the likely future, if governmental trade policy is the horse, political party will continue to be its essential harness.

2

Trade and Political Party Orientation in North America

Gregory P. Marchildon

This volume investigates some of the major questions on the relation between political parties and trade in North America. Seven historical chapters test the validity of the apparent flip-flop of political parties in North America on the issue of free trade introduced in Chapter 1. This chapter assumes that validity for the moment and asks why the stands taken towards trade by the various political parties in North America have changed over time. In the United States, why have the Democrats, the party of free trade since the mid-nineteenth century, increasingly trespassed on the Republican turf of economic isolationism and protectionism in the post-war era? Why has the Canadian Liberal Party, the traditional champions of free trade, recently fought tooth and nail against the Canada-U.S. Free Trade Agreement (FTA) proposed by the Conservative Party, the originators and historical guardians of Canada's protectionist policy? And in Mexico, why has the governing Institutional Revolutionary Party (the Partido Revolucionario Institutional or PRI) revoked its historic policy of high industrial tariff protection and restrictive import licensing in favor of a neoliberal strategy of free trade? These changes culminated in the implementation of the FTA in 1989 by the governing Republican and Conservative parties in the United States and Canada. In 1991, the governing party of Mexico began negotiations with the United States and Canada to extend the FTA to a North American Free Trade Agreement (NAFTA), which since January 1994 has become the framework for the economic architecture of North America.

To what extent have these changes in political party orientation towards free trade been induced by ideology, interest groups, the governing party's perception of the national interest, domestic economic constraints and external shocks? Before examining the varied answers to these questions, I will first address some of the basic economic questions which surround the notion of a trading area such as the NAFTA. I then establish some yardsticks for determining whether political party stands on trade policy have fundamentally shifted over time. These yardsticks are then used to summarize the findings of the historical chapters on political parties in the United States, Mexico, Canada, and Quebec. Finally, I explore the question whether theoretical generalization about the link between political party and trade liberalization in North America is possible.

North American Integration and Regional Blocs

The proposed NAFTA differs substantially from its logical point of comparison, the European Community (EC), in two ways: the asymmetry of its trading structure and the uncertainty over whether it is, in fact, an economic bloc. These two issues will play a significant role in understanding the different policy visions which shape party trade policy. The purpose of this section is to try to understand the basic economic story, using a few numbers, before going on to describe how various policy visions have stressed or interpreted it differently.

Table 2.1 suggests that continental integration, to the extent that it exists, is asymmetrical. Canada and Mexico are closely linked with the U.S. economy in terms of both exports and imports but have a modest (some would say minuscule) trading relationship with each other. In terms of trade, therefore, the United States is the hub while Canada and Mexico are the spokes. And while the U.S. trading relationship with Canada is the largest bilateral relationship in the world and its association with Mexico important by any standard, the United States remains highly reliant on the rest of the world for its exports and imports. In other words, there are some very significant spokes attached to the U.S. hub aside from Canada and Mexico. At the same time, more than 70 percent of all Mexican and Canadian trade is with the United States; it is little wonder that governing party elites of both countries have concentrated on a regional rather than the multilateral framework and that opposition parties in both countries have mobilized against freer regional trade on the argument that it poses a threat to national sovereignty.

This analysis must now be put into the global context of regional blocs. As can be seen from Table 2.2, North America is far less regionally integrated in terms of trade than the European Community and only at the same approximate level of integration as the East Asian economies,

TABLE 2.1 North American Trade Flows, 1992 (in percentages)

	US	Can.	Mex.	ROWᵃ	N.A. Tradeᵇ
United States					
exports to	—	17.0	7.7	75.3	130.8
imports from	—	21.5	7.6	70.9	132.2
Canada					
exports to	82.5	—	0.5	17.0	104.5
imports from	58.7	—	1.6	39.7	82.5
Mexico					
exports to	55.8	3.8	—	40.4	34.8
imports from	86.9	1.3	—	11.8	41.2

ᵃROW is trade with the rest of the world.
ᵇTrade within North America in $ billion U.S.

Source: Derived from International Monetary Fund, *Direction of Trade Statistics Yearbook* (Washington, D.C.: IMF, 1993), pp. 2, 6, 123-4, 272, 403-4.

TABLE 2.2 Total Exports and Imports Within Regions (in percentages)

Trade Region	1980	1986	1989
EC12	51	57	59
North America	32	35	36
East Asia	33	32	37

Source: Derived from Jeffrey J. Schott, "Trading Blocs and the World Trading System," *World Economy,* Vol. 14, March 1991, p. 9.

a diverse group of countries that has hardly achieved the stature of a trading bloc.[1] While regionalization of trade in North America (as in East Asia) has grown steadily during the decade, it has grown more slowly than in the European Community, especially in the early part of the decade. North America and East Asia's trading links with the rest of the world remain strong. Nonetheless, those who believe that the EC has diverted a substantial amount of European trade with the rest of the world to intra-European trade during the 1970s and 1980s would argue that regional trade agreements such as the FTA and the NAFTA will do the same for North America during the 1990s.

Three Major Policy Orientations
Towards Freer Trade

Against this backdrop of increasing regionalization of trade, three competing policy visions, based on conflicting assumptions, have generated disagreement concerning the desirability of freer trade, either on a multilateral or a regional basis. In any given historical era, one of these orientations has tended to influence a political party's stand on trade more than the others. Thus, although no political party is ideologically "pure," its stand on trade will fall at any given time into one of three camps: neoliberal, neomercantilist, or social democratic. By understanding the assumptions that underlie these policy visions, it will be easier to identify whether a political party has changed its position.

The Neoliberal View of Freer Trade

The neoliberal paradigm assumes that individuals and firms are rational calculators and aim to maximize their own welfare and profits. Freer trade enhances individual, national and global welfare by promoting a more efficient allocation of resources; in effect, delivering more goods or services than possible before trade, thereby "creating" new wealth. This "positive-sum" reasoning has a long pedigree that extends from the classical economists Adam Smith and David Ricardo to modern neoclassical trade theory represented by the Heckscher-Ohlin and Stolper-Samuelson theorems that stress differing factor endowments.[2]

By extension, the goal of governments (and governing parties) is to maximize the wealth of their respective nations. This is believed to be most effectively accomplished through policies of limited government intervention and free trade. Neoliberals also assume that increasing economic interdependence among nations is the most effective means of maintaining and enhancing world peace and stability, and thus national security. The link between a policy of freer trade and the decreased possibility of war has been deeply imbedded in the thought of liberal politicians and statesmen through the nineteenth and twentieth centuries.[3]

In the postwar era, economists have played an ever expanding role advising governments and political parties on economic policy. Almost all economists in advanced industrial countries as well as an increasing number in the developing world have adopted most of the assumptions of neoclassical trade theory. This puts them firmly within the neoliberal camp. Some neoclassical trade theorists, however, admit that in the presence of certain conditions (for example, monopoly control over production and oligopolistic international market conditions caused by increasing returns to scale), governments may be able to use protectionist trade policy to shift monopoly profits from foreign to domestic firms thus benefitting their own companies at the expense of foreign enterprises.[4] These "strategic" trade theorists nonetheless conclude that "as a rule of thumb" free trade remains the best policy in most circumstances.[5] Paul Krugman, for example, cautions "about the difficulty of formulating useful interventions" and the danger of such policy interventions going "astray." Indeed, for Krugman, such problems "combine into a new case for free trade."[6]

Although not as dominant within their own academic discipline, neoliberal political scientists, particularly in the United States, are among the most prominent commentators on issues involving political party alignment and commercial trade policy. Richard Rosecrance, Robert Keohane, Joseph Nye and Robert Reich regard open economic relations between nations as a positive-sum arrangement potentially benefitting government, business and workers in the countries concerned. All argue that whatever short-term advantages a protectionist government policy may achieve, by shielding a country against its most vigorous foreign competitors, the policy will only compromise national competitive abilities in the long-term.[7]

Beyond these general principles, however, the neoliberal consensus begins to break down. Neoclassical economists in particular have been divided over the benefits and implications of global or multilateral free trade versus regional or bilateral free trade. Uncompromising global free traders assert that regional trade agreements divert trade away from the lowest cost producer who may lie outside the trading bloc and thus reduce the inherent efficiency benefits derived from free trade. They believe that the recent shift from multilateralism as represented by the General Agreement on Tariffs and Trade (GATT) to regional agreements bodes ill for the world trading system and the future prosperity of individual countries. Jagdish Bhagwati argues that regional trade agreements seriously threaten multilateral trade by encouraging trade diversion, managed trade and the aggressive use of trade remedy laws.[8]

Pragmatic free traders admit that while some trade diversion will no doubt occur, regional agreements are really a "security blanket" for an international system which is weakening for reasons that have little or nothing to do with regional trade agreements. They argue that the increasing use of national trade remedy laws is a product of the pressures leading up to the Uruguay Round of the GATT, of the global recession of the late 1980s and early 1990s, and of the rise of nontariff barriers often introduced by the more interventionist industrial policies of countries like

Japan. For all of these reasons, regional trade arrangements may have become a more viable policy option, but pragmatic free traders nonetheless regret this tendency since regional trade agreements involve some degree of trade diversion. Moreover, they recognize that the attractiveness of bilateral and regional agreements may act as a disincentive for nations to move back into the more ideal track of multilateral trade liberalization.[9]

In contrast, regional free traders argue that the frameworks provided by the European Community (EC) and the NAFTA are significant steps towards freeing trade and investment in Europe and North America and, in some very important respects, go further than the multilateral (GATT) framework presently permits. Part of their argument is based on the perceived shortcomings of the multilateral system. Rudiger Dornbusch, for example, has argued that the GATT, because it obliges member states to initiate trade reforms only when the terms are unanimously agreed upon, impedes liberalization while encouraging free-rider behavior. The U.S. government, he believes, is justified in pursuing an aggressive unilateral (trade remedy law), bilateral (FTA), and regional (NAFTA) strategy to force open foreign markets which remain highly protected under the GATT system.[10] Regional free traders compare the more efficient dispute resolution mechanisms of the FTA and the NAFTA as well as their provisions concerning investment and intellectual property against their counterparts in the GATT. They conclude that, in these areas, the member countries of the GATT would do well to learn from the North American experience. In addition, regional agreements such as the NAFTA, with accession clauses facilitating new entrants, will expand free trade areas and thereby foster a future regime of global free trade. For regional free traders, therefore, "free trade" is not only consistent with, but best achieved through, bilateral and regional agreements.[11]

Neoliberals also disagree on the nature and the details of the North American trade agreements. John Whalley, for example, suggests that the NAFTA will have little impact on the world economic order. Based in part on his assessment of the impact of the FTA, he argues that the NAFTA is not designed to bring about, nor will it produce, the degree of regional integration experienced by the EC since the 1960s. The FTA and NAFTA are more accurately seen as "safe-haven oriented arrangements" intended to give Canadian and Mexican business limited protection from U.S. fair trade laws and give American business protection from nationalistic direct investment rules and "inadequate" intellectual property rules. These regional trade agreements are not an "effort to build wider economic and political continental integration," nor do they create the institutions that are capable of producing this type of integration.[12]

Regional free traders recognize the modest nature of the institutions and rules created under the FTA and the NAFTA, but they argue that these are dynamic arrangements that will grow and improve with time in the same way that the EC institutions and rules have evolved from a rather limited regional agreement on coal and steel to an integrated economic community.

The Neomercantilist View of Freer Trade

When it comes to trade, the neomercantilist policy vision differs from the neoliberal because it views trade relations through a "zero-sum" prism. The zero-sum notion is directly based upon assumptions concerning the nature of power. Neomercantilists emphasize the asymmetric distribution of power in the world system and the manner in which power is used by more strategically-oriented and powerful nations to structure trading relationships to benefit themselves at the expense of less focused or weaker nations. The sovereignty as well as the security of any given state may very well decrease through freer trade with other states depending on the power (including the level of industrial development) and the intentions of the other states in question. Thus neomercantilists believe that freer trade does not necessarily reduce the likelihood of armed conflict; in fact, given the way in which some nations use their power to obtain advantages over their commercial rivals, it is even possible that multilateral and bilateral agreements "loaded" in favor of the skilled and powerful can produce frustration among the less focused and the weak thereby sowing the seeds of future military conflict.[13]

In past centuries, mercantilists assumed that there existed a given volume of trade. This meant than any country increasing its level of trade could do so only by reducing the level of trade of other nations. The modern neomercantilist stand differs in that free trade benefits some nations, the more skilled or powerful, much more than others; therefore, even if freer trade increases global welfare, the lion's share of the benefits will flow to those nations most capable of manipulating the institutions and rules of the trading regime. Like their intellectual forbearers, however, neomercantilists assume that national wealth is best preserved and enhanced by policies encouraging a persistently positive balance of trade. Modern justification for this policy draws on the Keynesian argument in which trade surpluses stimulate investment and thus employment and growth. This occurs through the inflow of liquidity which produces a decline in interest rates.[14]

Perhaps neomercantilists differ from neoliberals most in their emphasis on state action. This does not mean that neomercantilists are by definition statists. As Jacob Viner pointed out, it simply means that neomercantilists "stress the duty of intervention unless, by exception, good reason existed for leaving things alone," while neoliberals "insist that the government should leave things alone unless by exception special reasons existed why it should intervene."[15] Neomercantilists are not innately opposed to free trade; but if free trade does not bring their country the benefits anticipated, or if it is causing harm to the industrial infrastructure, then they would urge policy intervention to manage trade so as to better serve the national interest.

Because of its emphasis on the integrity and sovereignty of the nation-state and domestic policy-making, neomercantilism is influential among nationalists of all stripes. Center-left parties in Canada and Mexico appear to have been greatly influenced by neomercantilism. Recently, the New Democratic Party (NDP), the Liberal Party in Canada (while in opposition) and the Party of the Democratic Revolution (PRD) in Mexico fought against regional trade agreements such as the FTA and the NAFTA because of the perceived threat these trade agreements pose to national sovereignty.

In the United States, the argument over whether freer trade remains consistent with the national interest pivots on questions concerning the nature, impact and even the existence of American industrial decline, and the extent to which countries with different approaches to trade and industrial policy are responsible for losses in America's international market position. For example, Lester Thurow and Laura D'Andrea Tyson, economists with one foot still in the neoliberal camp, have been urging for some time that the United States drop its laissez-faire policy approach in favor of an industrial policy that would provide American firms in strategic export industries with certain competitive advantages. They decry America's persistently negative trade balance, particularly for industrial goods, and urge increased public spending on research and development as well as tax credits for U.S. "high-tech" industry.[16] They are joined to some extent by an increasing number of political scientists, particularly those concerned with what they perceive as the Japanese "cause" of this trade imbalance and the decline of American global competitiveness.[17] Some, such as Clyde Prestowitz, see the formation of NAFTA as a positive force in that the United States within a larger North American economic bloc will have the power to offset Japanese and European influence.[18]

Until recently, the postwar Republican and Democratic parties have been little influenced by the neomercantilist policy vision. Both have previously rejected comprehensive industrial policies in favor of a neoliberal agenda backed by a forceful neoliberal policy view of the world. The Clinton administration may mark a turning point for the Democratic Party and the United States in this respect. Tyson's appointment to chair the Council of Economic Advisors may be the first step away from postwar neoliberal policies and towards a more neomercantilist policy that attempts to reverse America's deteriorating trade deficit through more managed trade and through an industrial policy that attempts to improve the international competitive position of American business.

The Social Democratic View of Freer Trade

From the social democratic perspective, freer trade increases the mobility of commodities and capital thereby augmenting business profitability. Since business, particularly the large multinationals, can move their operations to "exploit" labor in lower-wage jurisdictions, workers as well as the communities abandoned by the multinationals bear the burden of adjustment.[19] In addition, business can lower costs by moving to host countries with less costly social welfare infrastructures (and correspondingly lower taxes) and less stringent labor and environmental standards. This encourages corporations remaining in the home country to demand that domestic taxation and standards be reduced so that they can be competitive with the firms that have left. Thus, according to social democrats, neoliberal trade policies result in the further exploitation of unprotected workers, particularly in the Third World, the destruction of communities in both the Third World and the First World, and the erosion of organized workers' gains in the advanced industrial world. To avoid the negative fallout, free trade must be regulated so that the multinationals taking advantage of commodity and capital mobility are required to protect or compensate the communities that they are considering leaving while continuing to comply with suitable labor and environmental standards in their new locations.[20]

The social democratic policy view of freer trade is the dominant perspective within the NDP in Canada and within the PRD in Mexico. Moreover, its assumptions are held in part by grassroots anti-free trade coalitions such as the Pro-Canada Network in Canada that had some influence over Liberal and NDP opposition party platforms during the 1988 FTA election campaign, and the Citizens Trade Coalition in the United States which, although gaining many supporters within the Democratic Party, found itself in bitter opposition to the Clinton administration's pro-NAFTA policy.[21] Such coalitions, perhaps because they embrace such diverse interests and ideologies, have been defensive rather than proactive in the sense that they oppose the FTA and the NAFTA without offering clearly-defined alternatives. However, individual social democratic intellectuals, often in the course of advising parties such as the NDP and the PRD, do suggest concrete policy alternatives. One group of Canadian academics, for example, has recently argued that the Progressive Conservative government's neoliberal trade policy, permitting increased capital and commodity mobility without responsibility for the larger community, be replaced by a high-consumption model of internal development that responds to globalization by encouraging productivity gains through greater investment in research, development and labor retraining rather than through low wages.[22]

North American social democrats have been particularly critical of multinational exploitation of cheaper Mexican labor. All, particularly the Mexican social democrats, question the "maquiladora" model of development, a reference to the thousands of foreign-owned plants located primarily in the northern Mexican border region that assemble final products from imported components and then export those goods to the United States under special tariff exemptions. The maquiladoras are creatures of both Mexican and American commercial policy in the sense that they are expressly exempt from the normal Mexican investment and U.S. tariff requirements. With these exemptions and the attraction of inexpensive labor, American, Canadian and Japanese multinationals have flooded into Mexico in recent years.[23] They pay their Mexican workers a fraction of what workers in their home countries receive and are subject to less enforceable labor and environmental standards.[24]

Social democrats suggest that the NAFTA, which would prevent future Mexican restrictions on foreign direct investment and would eliminate tariffs, might make the maquiladoras the dominant mode of economic development in North America. Neoliberals respond that the maquiladoras are an artifact of the border and would be replaced by more-highly integrated enterprises paying higher wages through free trade. Social democrats insist, however, that neoliberal trade policy encourages a levelling-down of wages, working conditions and environmental standards, and they urge parties of the center-left such as the NDP, the Liberal Party, the PRD and the Democratic Party to replace regional trade agreements such as the NAFTA with a North American order that brings Mexico's workers, social infrastructure and environment up to Canadian and American levels rather than the opposite. Indeed, the PRD in Mexico has urged the adoption of a North American social charter that embraces the "levelling-up" alternative.

All of the policy visions discussed embrace assumptions concerning the existing trade and investment order in North America. Neoliberals would, for example, emphasize the extent to which markets have shaped this order while neomercantilists and social democrats would tend to stress the role of institutions and the state. This means that neoliberals will often see regional trade agreements such as the FTA and the NAFTA as perhaps reinforcing but nonetheless following a trend already established by the market while neomercantilists and social democrats see regional free trade as an attempt not merely to reinforce but to spearhead a certain type of freer trade. These differences are then reflected in North American political parties.

Individual Country Studies

Six scholars were invited to write essays on the relationship between trade and political parties in Canada, Mexico and the United States. Because of the unique attributes of one sub-state unit within North America, a further essay was elicited on the relationship between trade and political parties within Quebec. All are individual assessments in the sense that the authors analyzed domestic political parties and their respective trade doctrines and policies in isolation from the attitudes and actions of political parties in the other North American polities. Together, these essays provide a rich empirical source concerning the shifts of political parties on the issue of trade since the nineteenth century. The purpose of this section is briefly to summarize party positions on trade since the nineteenth century and the main arguments of the contributors to this volume.

The United States

From the Civil War until the election of President Woodrow Wilson in 1912, the Republican Party dominated the American executive and a policy of protectionism reigned supreme. After the First World War, a protectionist coalition under the Republicans again took control. The Smoot-Hawley Tariff of 1930 represented the zenith of the Republicans' high-tariff politics. With the coming to power of Franklin D. Roosevelt's Democrats in 1933, however, the policy of protectionism was slowly reversed. Facilitated by the passage of the Reciprocal Trade Act of 1934, tariffs were reduced or held steady through limited bilateral agreements that included Canada in 1935 and 1938 and Mexico in 1942. The U.S. liberal position was consolidated internationally through the creation of the GATT in the early postwar years, a period when most of America's competitors were just emerging from the rubble of the Second World War.[25] To be sure, this shift was never complete. Agriculture and certain sectors such as textiles were subject to separate rules. In addition, postwar U.S. governments occasionally resorted to nontariff barriers such as import quotas and voluntary export restraints to protect certain industries.[26] Nonetheless, the Democratic Party continued to espouse the politics of free trade during the 1950s and 1960s as the Republican Party loosened its ties to its protectionist past. By the 1980s, the Republicans had moved firmly into the free trade camp while the Democratic Party found itself backing into a more protectionist stance.

In his essay, Eric Uslaner argues that since Smoot-Hawley and the Great Depression, the political party most capable of electing Presidents and thereby controlling commercial relations with other countries is the party that best convinces the electorate that it is the party of prosperity. Uslaner illustrates his argument with a table amassing historical data on party electoral platforms since 1884. The party with the clearest message of prosperity and economic growth has also been the party most actively espousing the benefits of free trade. This was the message of the New Deal and later the Kennedy and Johnson administrations. It was also the message of Republic administrations from the late 1960s, and reached a crescendo during President Reagan's two terms in office. With the exception of the Carter administration, Democratic presidential hopefuls during the 1970s and 1980s began to break away from their free trade position and were not as successful in selling their message of prosperity. During the 1992 presidential campaign, however, Bill Clinton successfully projected his message of growth while emphasizing his support of free trade in general, and the proposed NAFTA in particular. He did this despite intense pressure by labor and environmental groups on the Democrats to attack the accord and to advocate policies that would shield American industry and workers. Clinton's refusal during the 1992 election campaign to adopt an antagonistic stance on NAFTA, and his powerful resolve to get the agreement through Congress in November 1993, seem to support Uslaner's hypothesis.

While Uslaner stresses shifts in party stands with interests following in their wake, other scholars believe that ideology and interests play a causal and interactive part in precipitating shifts in party orientations toward trade. As Timothy McKeown points out, the Democrats were pulled into a protectionist direction because of organized labor's increasing mistrust of trade liberalization during the 1970s and 1980s. This skepticism was directly related to the competitive decline of basic

"American" industries such as automobiles, electronics and steel in the face of European and, most importantly, Japanese imports. As downward wage pressures exerted themselves, as workers were laid off, and as union membership began to fall, organized labor increasingly urged the Democrats to support an "America-first" policy restricting the inflow of foreign imports that were devastating American industry and high-wage jobs. At the same time, the decline in the economic importance of these same industries meant that their major shareholders lost some of their traditional economic clout within the Republican Party relative to other owners of capital, including the financial interests that were servicing the expansion of foreign direct investment in the United States. And most recently, as a result of deindustrialization and falling union membership, organized labor has lost some of its former power within the Democratic Party thus giving Clinton greater flexibility than past Democratic presidential hopefuls.

McKeown questions whether anything more than a superficial shift on the issue of trade took place within the Republican and Democratic parties. He points out that both parties rejected the old form of wholesale tariff protection, what he calls "categorical protection," after the Second World War. Neither adopted a policy of what economists would call "free trade" but variations on free trade mixed with protection. For example, the Democratic Party adopted a sectoral policy best represented by Kennedy's protection of the domestic textile industry at the same time that he promoted multilateral tariff reductions. The Republican Party used American trade remedy law to punish foreign competitors when their actions harmed American industry, a policy that reached its high-water mark during the Reagan-Bush administrations, at the very time that the United States was urging that agriculture and services be brought into the GATT. The Clinton administration's trade policy may yet turn out to be an even more complex and subtle mix of free trade and protection. McKeown's essay is a useful reminder of the difficulty of characterizing any administration as free trade or protectionist and the necessity to look beyond the rhetoric of the president and his advisors to the many, often conflicting, actions of the administration.

Canada

The Republican Party's decision to adopt a protectionist stance in the wake of the Civil War directly affected Canadian policy. To retaliate against Britain's alleged support of the Confederacy during the Civil War and to protect its infant industries from British import competition, the

United States abrogated its trade reciprocity agreement with the British North American colonies in 1864. The Canadian confederation under the political stewardship of the Conservative Party soon adopted a highly protectionist tariff to create its own manufacturing industry capable of servicing its geographically dispersed market.   Under the Liberal government elected in 1896, the tariff was reduced for Britain but would remain raised against American goods for decades to come despite an attempt by the Liberals to ratify a free trade agreement with the United States.   Canadian and Empire retaliation to Smoot-Hawley brought even higher tariffs against American goods, but the Canadian-American Tariff Agreement of 1935, negotiated by a Conservative government and implemented by a Liberal government, marked the beginning of the reversal of this policy.   In the aftermath of World War II, Canada joined the GATT (along with the United States) and pursued a gradual process of multilateral liberalization, led by successive postwar Liberal governments.[27] Like the Republican Party in the United States, the Conservative Party gradually dropped its protectionist stance in the postwar decades.   Meanwhile, during the 1970s and early 1980s, the Liberal Party began to experiment with controlling the flow of U.S. investment into Canada.   Shortly after the election of 1984, the Conservative government began to make overtures for a bilateral free trade agreement with the United States. As the 1988 election approached, the Liberal and Conservative parties had swapped positions, compared to the 1911 election, on the issue of free trade with the United States.[28]

Duncan McDowall's essay on why the two leading Canadian political parties "traded" positions on the issue of free trade reflects the fragile nature of Canada's nationality and the profound divisions that exist within that society. Any political party that wants to gain and keep power within such a society must be able to balance effectively the regions and constituencies, and only those parties that develop what McDowall calls an "instinct for pliable politics" can govern the country for any length of time.[29] Although in ideological terms the Liberal Party has traditionally favored free trade and the Conservative Party protectionism, the policies of both have indeed been remarkably flexible. There is some evidence that Sir John A. Macdonald's Conservative Party, which ingeniously marketed tariff protectionism as the National Policy in the election of 1878, would have preferred a free trade agreement with the United States at the time if the Republicans had not been so wedded to a protectionist policy. When Liberal Prime Minister Laurier continued the policy of protectionism (with, however, reciprocity extended to Britain) after his election in 1896, he demonstrated the strength of the new protectionist lobby in Canada and his own ability in pliable trade politics. Laurier's political judgment only came into questions in 1910-11 when he underestimated the strength of this industrial lobby and overestimated the strength of the agrarian free trade element.

This party flexibility on trade has continued throughout twentieth century Canada. During the Great Depression, the Conservative Party swung back into power on the slogan that they would raise tariffs to blast Canada's way into protected foreign markets. This strategy was entirely ineffective and, by 1935, the Conservatives were negotiating a tariff-reduction agreement with the United States. Similarly, the Liberal Party under Prime Minister Mackenzie King, although eventually supporting postwar multilateral liberalization under the GATT framework, could not bring itself to close a free trade agreement with the United States in 1948. After its election in 1984, the Progressive Conservative Party under Brian Mulroney was able to initiate and consummate the FTA by 1988. Although the Liberal Party fought very hard against free trade, it might have supported the FTA itself if it had been the governing rather than the opposition party at the time.

This policy pragmatism on trade has not, however, been the trademark of the NDP. As Douglas Owram points out in his essay, ideology plays a much larger role in the formulation of the NDP's policies, and the party has, in recent decades, been ideologically opposed to closer integration, economically and politically, with the United States. In this sense, the NDP sees the FTA as a threat to Canadian independence and sovereignty and opposes the NAFTA for exactly the same reason.

It is important to emphasize that the NDP's contemporary opposition to greater North American economic integration is not based primarily in terms of its opposition to trade liberalization *per se*. In fact, the early history of the NDP or the Cooperative Commonwealth Federation (CCF) as it was known until 1961, reveals that the party supported both free trade and closer ties with the United States. Of the two main influences within the early CCF, the Western-Canadian farmers' movements strongly supported free trade policies, while the party's central Canadian intelligentsia favored Canada tilting its policies away from the British Empire and towards the United States. As Owram points out, the CCF supported the GATT, NATO and IMF frameworks consistently and most apparently during the federal elections of 1945, 1949 and 1953. As the Cold War developed, however, party intellectuals and politicians felt that the United States posed a much graver threat to Canada's sovereignty than Great Britain. Rearmament by the United States, the McCarthy witch hunt and the Korean war convinced some members of the CCF/NDP that the United States was not to be trusted. The real watershed was the Vietnam War when the majority of the rank and file membership joined the NDP's intelligentsia in criticizing American ownership and control of the Canadian economy and society in the late

1960s and the 1970s. By the 1980s, the agrarian wing of the national NDP had declined in importance and free trade had become a non-issue. The NDP opposed the FTA because of the extent to which it would put Canadian health, labor and social policy under pressure.[30]

Prime Minister Mulroney was able to win the 1988 "free trade" election in part because he was able to enlist the support of the Liberal Party of Quebec and the Parti Quebecois (PQ). This fact alone illustrates why party politics in Quebec must be treated as separate from the Canadian case. First, the Liberal Party of Quebec is functionally autonomous from the Liberal Party of Canada and has therefore been able to adopt different positions on trade. In fact, it supported the federal Conservative Party during the 1988 election. Second, the PQ, which is currently in opposition to the governing Liberal Party of Quebec, is dedicated to taking Quebec out of Canada, and the party's stand of freer trade is directly shaped by this main objective. Thus, the PQ supports free trade with the United States on the basis that this would further weaken Quebec's economic links with the rest of Canada thereby making separation a more viable option for the future.

According to Pierre Martin, the two main Quebec parties have recently reached a bipartisan consensus on the issue of freer trade with the United States. At the elite level, both parties have leaderships ideologically committed to free trade with the United States. At a broader level, the consensus on freer trade with the United States stems from the open nature of the Quebec economy and, in particular, with the importance to the Quebec economy of trade with the United States. Finally, unlike many English-speaking Canadians whose identity is closely tied to differentiating themselves from Americans, French-speaking Quebecers do not fear cultural assimilation as a consequence of closer economic ties with the United States.

Mexico

Unlike the United States and Canada, Mexico under Porfirio Díaz (1876-1910) eschewed an import-substituting industrialization (ISI) strategy in favor of a policy encouraging resource exports and industrial imports. This policy continued despite the Mexican Revolution and not until the creation of the PRI in 1929 did an industrial strategy begin to be forged in the form of loans and credits to infant industry. Nonetheless, it took until 1947 before a fully-fledged ISI strategy of protectionist tariffs, import licenses and foreign-exchange regulations was implemented.[31] This apparatus remained largely in place until the reforms of the De la

Madrid and Salinas administrations from 1982 until 1994. During the 1980s, the PRI has slashed tariff levels, removed import licensing requirements for a majority of imports and brought Mexico into the GATT. Then, in 1990, the Salinas government approached the U.S. about the possibility of a free trade agreement which subsequently resulted in the NAFTA negotiations joined by Canada. In the span of less than a decade, the PRI has shed its neomercantilist stand on trade in favor of a neoliberal view of the world.[32]

According to Gustavo Vega-Canovas, the commitment of Presidents De la Madrid and Salinas, in combination with their closest advisors, were the key elements in Mexico's abandonment of a nationalist ISI policy in favor of a neoliberal economic development strategy. As Dale Story points out, this neoliberal approach soon became identified with regional free trade, an understandable trajectory given Mexico's reliance on the U.S. market. Moreover, like Canada, Mexico had also felt the sting of U.S. contingent protectionism and looked for more trouble-free access to the U.S. market. Though Mexico joined the GATT in 1986, the FTA implemented three years later meant that Mexico would need a regional agreement to gain an access to the United States equal to Canada's access under the new bilateral agreement. This pushed the regional option according to Vega because Mexican and Canadian automotive, petro-chemical, steel, paper, textile and machinery industries were competing with Canada for export markets in the United States.[33]

Vega and Story both point out that by the 1980s ISI had run its course in Mexico and could no longer produce, much less guarantee, a high rate of economic growth. The PRI, historically dedicated to the principle of nationalist industrial self-determination, now wanted to shed its ideological baggage. This precipitated a power struggle within the PRI which is not yet over. By virtue of its monopoly power, however, the PRI has been able to make the shift thus far without worrying (overly) about constituency support. This control, effected through various forms of political suppression, is slowly beginning to loosen, too slowly for opposition parties who still suffer significant disadvantages at the hands of the PRI monopoly.

The National Action Party (Partido Acción Nacional or PAN), first created in 1939, gained new prominence in state and federal elections during the last decade. A party of the right, the PAN gains most of its support in the industrialized north. Despite this fact, the PAN has been opposed to the NAFTA on the basis that the agreement would place limits on Mexican sovereignty by forcing Mexican business, for example, to comply with "foreign" labor and environmental standards. As the president of the PAN recently explained, the Mexican nation is a "living reality superior to its individual components" in which the "national interest is preeminent." In fact, the PAN expressly opposes the "neoliberal economic approach" of the PRI precisely because it "produces greater concentration of power" and because it does not embrace political liberalization at the same time; instead, it further centralizes decisionmaking to a technocratic and unelected elite within the party.[34]

The PRD, a left-wing coalition party formed after the 1988 elections holding a social democratic view of free trade with some neomercantilist elements, supports, for example, a strategy of selective protection, subsidies and support to increase the competitiveness of existing and new industries. At the same time, the PRD is opposed to the maquiladoras because of their low labor and environmental standards, a direct result of Mexico's inadequate regulation of the multinationals and the governing party's unwillingness to force compliance with existing standards. According to party leader Cuauhtémoc Cárdenas Solórzano, "the NAFTA in its present form will consolidate the imbalances existing between Mexico and the United States. It is the means by which Mexico is being inserted into the world economy through a path of subordination."[35] Nonetheless, unlike the NDP in Canada, the PRD sees advantages in a North American agreement for trade and development that produces a levelling up rather than down for labor and the environment in all three countries. This proposed regional agreement would be a social charger guaranteeing free mobility of labor, more effective dispute resolution mechanisms and income transfers to Mexico to help it through the transitional stages. Such a North American charter would, the PRD contends, ensure that the maquiladoras do not become the model of development for North America.

Is Theoretical Generalization Possible?

Moving from historical detail to theoretical generalization is invariably arduous. Perhaps the most one can expect at this stage of our understanding is a few well-selected hypotheses. Yet both the policy-maker and the scholar are impatient. They demand more, and they are right to do so. However preliminary, a causal model of the party-trade relationship could move empirical testing forward. This Charles Doran attempts in Chapters 10 and 11.

Political party is clearly a variable located somewhere mid-way between the trade policies governments effect and the interest group pressures that tug party and government in various directions. Doran suggests that trade policy outcomes can originate from any one of three levels: (1) from the party itself in terms of *ideology* and party platform, (2) from the *constituency* of the party, that is, those for whom the party acts and by whom its representatives are elected, or (3) from *incumbency*, namely, the governing party which actually takes the lead in formulating and implementing most trade policy. But which of these levels of explanations is most compelling, for most states, most of the time? The country essays do not resolve this matter. Indeed some of the authors reject the possibility of such generalization, although most suggest that the answer is specific to time period, issue and place. This much more difficult question challenges further theoretical development.

In the Doran model, each of these three sources of trade policy outcomes is allowed to vary, freeing us of mono-causal preconceptions. In fact the model incorporates other variables that are also likely to affect the party-trade linkage. In particular, the impact of exogenous variables (external shocks) that catalyze trade liberalization are included as "conditioning" variables. These include the impact of the Great Depression or the consequence of major war on the structure of the world market relationship.

The model helps address Doran's original question at the outset of the study, namely, why and how principal parties flip-flopped on trade liberalization in North America. While both ideology and constituency play some role in explaining why the Republican Party and the Progressive-Conservative Party became, by the last decade of the twentieth century, the standard-bearers for free trade, incumbency is the most convincing overall explanation for trade outcomes in the contemporary setting. The incumbent political party attempts to act in a way that expresses its interpretation of the national interest. Because of increasing external competition as well as receptivity to the neoliberal policy vision and strong international business community pressure, the incumbent political party moves forward with the free trade agenda. Opposition parties tend to express the alternative position which often appears more nationalistic and protectionist.

The multi-causal model highlights how dynamic the party-trade linkage has been over time. There is therefore no guarantee that trade liberalization (or protection for that matter) will proceed continuously. Backsliding can occur. Indeed, regional free trade was in part a bluff used by the United States to catalyze the Uruguay Round of multilateral tariff talks. But a regional orientation soon became an end in itself. Will regional free trade itself be translated into multilateral free trade as a global strategy? An important part of the answer to this question is determined by which parties are elected in North America, what the nature of their policy visions towards trade will be, and the extent to which constituencies support free trade at the time of trade strategy formulation. Ultimately what this study reflects is an awareness that trade liberalization is itself multi-faceted and can change in terms of its composition and strategic emphasis and that the role of the political party is a vital element of any causal explanation of trade policy outcomes.

Notes

I would like to thank Charles Doran, Pierre Martin, and James Robinson for their constructive criticism. I am particularly indebted to Nicolas Crowley for carefully reviewing and critiquing successive drafts of this chapter.

1. In fact, the proposed East Asian Economic Area embracing Japan and parts of South East Asia is unlikely to succeed given the diverse countries involved and the historic fear of Japanese hegemony.
2. See Richard Pomfret, *International Trade: An Introduction to Theory and Policy* (Oxford: Blackwell, 1991) for an accessible review of neoclassical trade theory and policy and its assumptions.
3. See David A. Baldwin, *Economic Statecraft* (Princeton: Princeton University Press, 1985), pp. 76-80, Robert O. Keohane, "International Liberalism Reconsidered," in John Dunn, ed., *The Economic Limits to Modern Politics* (Cambridge: Cambridge University Press, 1990), and Robert Gilpin, "Economic Interdependence and National Security in Historical Perspective," in Klaus Knorr and Frank N. Trager, eds., *Economic Issues and National Security* (New York: National Security Education Program, 1977).
4. See J. David Richardson, "The Political Economy of Strategic Trade Policy," *International Organization*, Vol. 44, Winter 1990.
5. Robert E. Baldwin, "Are Economists' Traditional Trade Policy Views Still Valid?" *Journal of Economic Literature*, Vol. 30, June 1992, p. 826.
6. Paul Krugman, "Is Free Trade Passé," *Journal of Economic Perspectives*, Vol. 1, Fall 1987, p. 143. On strategic trade theory see Krugman's *Rethinking International Trade* (Cambridge, MA: MIT Press, 1990).
7. Richard Rosecrance, *The Rise of the Trading State: Commerce and Conquest in the Modern World* (New York: Basic Books, 1985) and *America's Economic Resurgence: A Bold New Strategy* (New York: Harper & Row, 1990). Robert O. Keohane, *After Hegemony: Cooperation and Discord in the World Political Economy* (Princeton, NJ: Princeton University Press, 1984). Robert O.Keohane and Joseph S. Nye, *Power and Interdependence: World Politics in Transition* (Boston: Little, Brown and Company, 1977). Joseph S. Nye, *Bound to Lead: The Changing Nature of American Power* (New York: Basic Books, 1990). Robert B. Reich, *The Work of Nations* (New York: Knopf, 1991).
8. See Jagdish Bhagwati, "The Threats to the World Trading System," *World Economy*, Vol. 15, July 1992, "Regionalism versus Multilateralism," *World Economy*, Vol. 15, September 1992, and *The World Trading System at Risk* (Princeton: Princeton University Press, 1990).

9. Jeffrey J. Schott, "Trading Blocs and the World Trading System," *World Economy*, Vol. 14, March 1991. For a brief discussion of the rise of the "New Protectionism", see Robert Gilpin, *The Political Economy of International Relations* (Princeton: Princeton University Press, 1987), pp. 204-30, and Richard Pomfret, *Unequal Trade: The Economics of Discriminatory International Trade Practices (Oxford*: Basil Blackwell, 1988). The Third World customs unions and free trade areas have been less than successful in part because of the lack of economic complementarity among the participating countries.

10. See Rudiger Dornbusch, "The Case for Bilateralism," in Robert Lawrence and Charles Schultze, eds., *An American Trade Strategy* (Washington, D.C.: The Brookings Institution, 1990).

11. Peter Morici is perhaps the most vocal exponent of NAFTA as promoting free trade. See "The Canada-U.S. Free Trade Agreement: A Laboratory for the World Trading System," *American Review of Canadian Studies*, Vol. 21, Summer-Autumn 1991; *Trade Talks with Mexico: A Time for Realism* (Washington, D.C.: National Planning Association, 1991), and "Free Trade with Mexico," *Foreign Policy*, No. 87, Summer 1992.

12. John Whalley, "CUSTA and NAFTA: Can WHFTA Be Far Behind?" *Journal of Common Market Studies*, Vol. 30, June 1992, p. 126. Certainly, NAFTA has no common external tariff like a customs union and has no community-wide decision-making organizations like a common market establishing basic rules capable of eliminating nontariff barriers.

13. See Albert Hirschman, *National Power and the Structure of Foreign Trade* (Berkeley: University of California Press, 1945) and Kenneth Waltz, "The Myth of National Interdependence," in Charles P. Kindleberger, ed., *The International Corporation* (Cambridge, Mass.: MIT Press, 1970).

14. H. Schmitt, "Mercantilism: A Modern Argument," *Manchester School*, Vol. 47, June 1979. Paolo Guerrieri and Pier Carlo Padoan, "Neomercantilism and International Economic Stability." *International Organization*, Vol. 40, Winter 1986.

15. Jacob Viner quoted in Baldwin, *Economic Statecraft*, p. 85.

16. Lester C. Thurow, *The Zero-Sum Society* (New York: Basic Books, 1971), *The Zero-Sum Solution* (New York: Simon & Schuster, 1985) and *Head to Head* (New York: William Morrow, 1992). Laura D'Andrea Tyson, William T. Dickens and John Zysman, eds., *The Dynamics of Trade and Employment* (Cambridge, Mass.: Ballinger 1988). Laura D'Andrea Tyson, *Who's Bashing Whom? Trade Conflict in High-Technology Industries* (Washington, D.C.: The Institute for International Economics, 1992).

17. Chalmers Johnson, *MITI and the Japanese Miracle: The Growth of Industrial Policy, 1925-1975* (Stanford: Stanford University Press, 1982). Chalmers Johnson, Laura D'Andrea Tyson and John Zysman, eds., *Politics and Productivity: The Real Story of Why Japan Works* (Cambridge, Mass.: Ballinger, 1989). Clyde V. Prestowitz, Jr., *Trading Places: How We Allowed Japan to Take the Lead* (New York: Basic Books, 1988).

18. Clyde V. Prestowitz, Jr., et al., *The New North American Order: A Win-Win Strategy for U.S.-Mexico Trade* (Lanham, MD: University Press of America, 1991).

19. Some empirical support for this argument can be found in Jeffrey A. Frieden's "Invested Interests: The Politics of National Economic Policies in a World of Global Finance," *International Organization*, Vol. 45, Autumn 1991.

20. See Robert W. Cox, *Production, Power, and World Order: Social Forces in the Making of History* (New York: Columbia University Press, 1987), J. Grahl and P. Teague, "The Cost of Neo-Liberal Europe," *New Left Review*, No. 174, March-April 1989, Sadequl Islam, "Free Trade and Protection: The U.S.-Canada Case," *Monthly Review*, Vol. 39, November 1987.

21. See Peter Bleyer, "Coalitions of Social Movements as Agencies for Social Change: The Action Canada Network" in William Carroll, ed., *Organizing Dissent: Contemporary Social Movements in Theory and Practice* (Toronto: Garamond Press, 1992). See also Bob Davis, "U.S. Grassroots Coalition Unites Against NAFTA," Toronto *Globe and Mail*, 26 December 1992, pp. B1-B2.

22. See the various essays in Daniel Drache and Meric S. Gertler, eds., *The New Era of Global Competition: State Policy and Market Power* (Montreal: McGill-Queen's University Press, 1991).

23. See the various essays in Khosrow Fatemi (ed.), *The Maquiladora Industry: Economic Solution or Problem?* (New York: Praeger, 1990) for an introduction to this debate. For sectoral studies, see Sidney Weintraub et al., eds., *U.S. Mexican Industrial Integration: The Road to Free Trade* (Boulder: Westview, 1991).

24. David Barkin, *Distorted Development: Mexico in the World Economy* (Boulder: Westview Press, 1990), and James M. Cypher, *State and Capital in Mexico: Development Policy Since 1940* (Boulder: Westview Press, 1990). According to U.S. Department of Labor statistics, the 1990 average wage for maquiladora workers (including fringe benefits) was $1.26 per hour, about one-eleventh the U.S. level. Moreover, from 1980 to 1989, average hourly compensation in maquiladora industries was approximately one-half the hourly compensation in non-maquiladora industries. Gary Clyde Hufbauer and Jeffrey J. Schott, *North American Free Trade: Issues and Recommendations* (Washington, D.C.: Institute for International Economics, 1992), chapter 6. See Roberto A. Sánchez, "Health and Environmental Risks of the Maquiladora in Mexicali," *National Resources Journal*, Vol. 30, Winter 1990, where he discusses American companies affected by stricter environmental regulations in California relocating part or all of their operations to Mexico and documents the lack of environmental enforcement in one maquiladora region.

25. F. W. Taussig, *The Tariff History of the United States* (New York: Augustus M. Kelley, 1967). John Mark Hansen, "Taxation and the Political Economy of the Tariff," *International Organization*, Vol. 44, Autumn 1990. G. John Ikenberry, David A. Lake and Michael Mastanduno, eds., *The State and American Foreign Economic Policy* (Ithaca: Cornell University Press, 1988). David A. Lake, *Power, Protection and Free Trade: International Sources of U.S. Commercial Strategy, 1887-1939* (Ithaca: Cornell University Press, 1988).

26. Judith Goldstein, "The Impact of Ideas on Trade Policy: The Origins of U.S. Agricultural and Manufacturing Policies," *International Organization*, Vol. 43, Winter 1989. Timothy J. McKeown, "A Liberal Trade Order? The Long-Run Patterns of Imports to the Advanced Capitalist States," *International Studies*

Quarterly, Vol. 35, June 1991. Alan M. Rugman and M.V. Gestrin, "U.S. Trade Laws as Barriers to Globalization," *World Economy*, Vol. 14, September 1991.

27. R. N. Kottman, *Reciprocity and the North Atlantic Triangle, 1932-1939* (Ithaca: Cornell University Press, 1968). Ian M. Drummond and Norman Hillmer, *Negotiating Freer Trade* (Waterloo: Wilfrid Laurier University Press, 1989). Bruce Muirhead, "Perception and Reality: The GATT's Contribution to the Development of a Bilateral North American Relationship, 1947-1951," *American Review of Canadian Studies*, Vol. 20, Autumn 1990.

28. G. Bruce Doern and Brian W. Tomlin, *Faith and Fear: The Free Trade Story* (Toronto: Stoddart, 1991).

29. For an illustration of the non-ideological nature of Canadian party position on trade matters, see Robert Bothwell and John English, "Canadian Trade Policy in the Age of American Dominance and British Decline, 1943-1957," *Canadian Review of American Studies*, Vol. 8, Spring 1977.

30. For the NDP's formulation of its anti-free trade policy during the 1988 election, see Alan Whitehorn, *Canadian Socialism: Essays on the CCF-NDP* (Toronto: Oxford University Press, 1992), pp. 220-2.

31. On early tariff and industrialization policies, see Roger D. Hansen, *The Politics of Mexican Development* (Baltimore: Johns Hopkins University Press, 1971), and Timothy King, *Mexico: Industrialization and Trade Policies since 1940* (London: Oxford University Press, 1970).

32. See Nora Lustig, *Mexico: The Remaking of an Economy* (Washington, D.C.: The Brookings Institution, 1992) for an analysis of the changes in Mexican economic policy since the 1970s.

33. Also see Vega's "El Acuerdo de Libre Comercio entre Canadá y Estados Unidos: Implicaciones para México y los Países en Desarrollo," *Commercio Exterior*, Vol. 38, March 1988; and Gerardo Bueno, "A Mexican View," in William Diebold, Jr., ed., *Bilateralism, Multilateralism and Canada in U.S. Trade Policy* (New York: Council on Foreign Relations, 1988).

34. Luis H. Alvarez, "Political and Economic Reform in Mexico: The PAN Perspective," in Riordan Roett, ed., *Political and Economic Liberalization in Mexico: At a Critical Juncture?* (Boulder: Lynne Rienner, 1992), pp. 144, 146.

35. Cuauhtémoc Cárdenas Solórzano, "The False Hopes of Economic Reform," in Roett, ed., *Political and Economic Liberalization in Mexico*, p. 152.

3

Political Parties and Free Trade in the United States

Eric M. Uslaner

"Protectionism isn't a prescription for prosperity." On the contrary, "protectionism amounts to a smokescreen for a country that is running scared."[1] President George Bush, announcing the official beginning of his reelection campaign in February 1992, spoke the words that for most of the nineteenth and twentieth centuries would have more typically been uttered by Democratic aspirants for the White House. The most dramatic reductions in tariff rates in the twentieth century occurred during Franklin D. Roosevelt's New Deal and the [John F.] Kennedy Round in the 1960s. The Democrats charged that tariffs imposed costs against the lower and middle classes that long formed the bulk of the party's electoral base while they gave benefits to monopoly capital. The Republicans consistently defended the tariff as essential to economic development.[2]

Bush's defense of free trade was aimed primarily at Republican challenger Pat Buchanan, but it just as easily could be targeted at most Democratic challengers for the White House in the 1980s. Representative Richard Gephardt (D, MO) in 1988 and Senators Bob Kerry (D, NB) and Tom Harkin (D, IA) in 1992 strongly emphasized "fair" trade. While all three candidates fared poorly, their protectionist stands[3] were as representative of their party stands as Bush's attack on trade barriers had become of Republicans. Had the Democrats become the party of the trusts and the Republicans the defenders of the less fortunate in America? Mostly, but not entirely, no.

Why the parties traded places on protectionism is a different question from what drives tariff policy. The extensive literature on outcomes provides more than just a useful starting point; it raises the central issues behind party positions. The decision-making accounts largely divide into two opposing camps, one focusing on societal accounts (electoral coalitions and interest groups), the other on institutions (autonomous political actors such as the President and the independent power of ideas). Party positions, as outcomes, reflect the electoral coalitions and interest groups that congregate in each party's camp. The stands also correspond to more general ideologies that each party espouses. Yet both societal and institutional accounts must confront anomalies that challenge each of their positions.

The story of party switching on trade policy is ultimately an amalgam of interests and ideas, but not according to the terms of either societal advocates or institutionalists. Nor is it some halfway point that "takes the best of both worlds." The conflict between free trade and protectionism mirrors tensions over more fundamental values and the relative positions of groups and ideas in those battles. The idea of free trade has been associated with the politics of great expectations for the future, at least since the New Deal. Protectionists have been more pessimistic. Americans have long expressed confidence that the future will be better than either the past or the present. Political leaders who adhere to this line regularly establish electoral hegemony. From the New Deal to the late 1960s, the Democrats were the party of prosperity. Since then, the Republicans have seized that mantle and the corresponding belief that free trade will make the United States even wealthier.

As ideas follow values, interests often lead them. The Democrats waded into protectionism, but were pushed by organized labor into the deeper waters. The Republicans had begun their long trek toward free trade in the 1950s, having long been stung as the party of the Depression and the protectionist Smoot-Hawley Tariff of 1930. As party positions clarified in the 1970s, the Democrats found their core electorate, union members and blacks, less responsive to the thesis that the American economy was destined to grow without bounds. The message of growth, and the linking of free trade and free markets, played well where Republican strength was blossoming, the Sunbelt.

Before laying out my argument in detail, I must first put the party history on the tariff in context and then consider the contending societal and institutional explanations. I come to the conclusion that each of those explanations is incomplete. My own characterization of party positions seeks to overcome those shortcomings. Admittedly, it necessarily simplifies what is a highly complex process. For instance, I focus mostly on tariff barriers, although this is but one aspect of trade. I also assume that party positions reflect actors' sincere preferences, although there is plenty of room for strategic behavior. To cover over a century of party positions on trade, some simplifications are necessary, but I doubt that they distort the overall record.

Parties and the Tariff

The tariff was the United State's principal source of revenue for most of the nineteenth century. For much of the pre-Civil War period customs duties accounted for more than 90 percent of all federal receipts; after the war, the figure dropped to about 50 percent. Not until the adoption of the income tax, however, did the tariff's share fall to less than a quarter of all revenues.[4] Both Democrats and Republicans accepted the tariff as an important source of revenue throughout the nineteenth century. They differed over how much money should be raised and what else customs duties should do.

From the early days of the new republic, first Whigs and then Republicans favored high tariffs to protect fledgling domestic industries from foreign competition.[5] The Whigs and Republicans favored a relatively more activist government. Before the Civil War, they used the revenues for extensive public works programs; after the war, the Republicans financed a generous pension program for veterans through customs duties.[6] The Democrats saw tariffs as rents accruing to monopolies at the expense of average citizens.[7] The parties were badly split over the issue.[8] For most of the past century, party positions on trade have been highly polarized. It mattered a great deal which party controlled the government. From 1840 to 1932, there were eight such shifts in the party controlling the government: in 1840, 1844, 1860, 1892, 1896, 1912, 1920, and 1932.[9] At each shift, the party gaining power adjusted tariff rates, the Whigs and Republicans upward and the Democrats downward.[10]

Let us trace party positions on the tariff from 1884 to 1992.[11] Table 3.1 presents data derived from party platforms. Stands on the tariff are presented in bold and will be discussed here. Related issues of foreign policy and economics are in regular typescript and will be discussed below. Entries marked by an asterisk represent at least a partial shift in policy on trade.

From 1884 to 1904, the Republicans are "uncompromisingly" in favor of the tariff to protect American industries and labor. The Democrats stood just as firmly on the other side, arguing in 1892 that there was no constitutional basis for duties and calling the tariff a "monstrous perversion" in 1904. The Democrats linked tariffs with trusts. The Republicans believed that duties created markets for American products, higher wages for workers, and equity between business and agriculture.[12] The tariff divided Congressional parties as strongly as any other issue for most of this period.[13]

TABLE 3.1 Positions of Parties on the Tariff 1884-1992

Year	Democrats	Republicans
1884	**Promises reductions in tariffs** Tax reductions Isolationist Prevention of monopolies	**Favors tariffs to protect industries** Protection of labor Moderate isolationist
1888	**Promises reductions in tariffs** Tax reductions Government spending reductions	**"Uncompromisingly" favors protection** Opposes eliminating tariffs on wool Opposed to trusts Greater U.S. role in foreign affairs
1892	**Protection a "fraud" & "robbery"** **No constitutional basis for tariff** **Trusts natural result of tariffs** Moderate isolationism Federal role in public works	**For "American doctrine of protection"** **Foreign goods admitted free** **Tariffs protect labor and agriculture** Active role in world No statement on government activism
1896	**Tariffs for revenue only** **Tariff changes depend upon** **money standard** **Tariffs lead to trusts** Favors Monroe Doctrine For federal role in public works	**"Protection for what we produce"** **More equitable tariff to protect labor** Restrictions on immigration Non-interference in hemisphere
1900	**Tariffs breed trusts** **Products of trusts: no tariffs** "Unceasing warfare" against trusts Opposes foreign affairs militarism Restrictions on immigration Spending reductions	**Protection secures high wages** **Tariff revenue funded war** Restrictions on immigration Activist role in world
1904	**Tariff "monstrous perversion"** **Tariffs breed trusts** **Liberal trade with Canada, others** Fight against trusts Reductions in spending Supports public works Supports Monroe Doctrine	**Protection secures high wages** **Shipping industry needs protection** Proud of budgetary surplus For activist role in world
1908	**Favors tariff reductions** **Paper tariffs tax on "knowledge"** Reductions in spending and taxes Supports income tax Supports public works Activist world role, no militarism	**Revise tariff, rates equal difference** **between production costs*** **Tariffs protect high wages** **Promotes foreign commerce** Supports public works Government regulation of business Activist role in world
1912	**Tariff only justified for revenue** **Immediate lowering of tariffs** **Tariffs benefit trusts** Favors income tax Reductions in spending and taxes For public works and regulation Activist, non-militarist, world role	**Reaffirms "belief in protection tariff"** **Tariffs keep wages high** Restrictions on immigration Supports public works

1916	Tariffs only justified for revenue War demands non-partisan tariff commission U.S. take active world role Gov. role in working conditions Supports public works	Supports "reasonable" tariff protection Favors tariff commission More economy in government Peaceful resolution of world conflicts Favors regulation of business
1920	Tariffs only justified for revenue Activist role in world affairs Gov. role in aiding farmer Gov. role in working conditions Widespread support of public works Gov. role in education	Supports protective tariff Non-interventionist foreign policy Reduction in taxes and spending Restrictions on immigration Modest regulation of workplace

1924	Tariffs only justified for revenue
	Tariffs make difficult foreign
	    purchase of U.S. farm and
	    manufactured goods
	Activist, but pacific, world role
	Widespread support of public works
	Restrictions on immigration
	Gov. role in working conditions
		Tariff protects "high American economic
		    level of life"
		Non-interventionist foreign policy
		Supports public works
		Reduction in taxes and spending
		Modest regulation of workplace
		Restrictions on immigration

1928	Reduction of "monopolistic and
	    extortionate" tariff rates
	Protectionism leads to monopoly
	Activist role in world
	Gov. aid to farmers and miners
	Gov. role in working conditions
	Widespread support of public works
	Liberalization of immigration
	More vigorous anti-trust laws
		Tariff essential for "continued prosperity"
		Tariffs support farmers, manufacturers,
		    lead to higher levels of imports
		Non-interventionist foreign policy
		Reduction in taxes and spending
		Supports aid to farmers and miners
		Supports public works
		Restrictions on immigration

1932	Competitive tariff for revenue International conference to facilitate trade Non-interventionist role in world Economy in gov., balanced budget Gov. role in working conditions Gov. aid to farmers and miners Support for public works	Reduced tariff lowers living standards Supports tariff commission Tariffs provide support for farm prices Non-interventionist role in world Supports public works Restrictions on immigration Gov. role in working conditions

1936	Favors international accords to
	    lower taxes
	Non-interventionist role in world
	Gov. role in working conditions
	Gov. intervention in economy
	Gov. aid to farmers, unemployed
		Reimpose tariffs on goods made
		    in U.S.
		Isolationist role in the world
		Reductions in taxes and spending
		Gov. aid to farmers
		Limited support for public works
		Limited regulation of business

1940	Favors "cultivation of foreign trade through desirable...agreements" Activist role in world Activist role throughout economy	Support for protective tariffs Moderate non-interventionism in world Reductions in taxes and spending Criticizes regulation of business

(continues)

TABLE 3.1 *(continued)*

1944	Extend present trade policies Activist role in world Activist role throughout economy	Fair protective tariff means prosperity Post-war world requires "Great extension of trade" * Activist role in world Reduce taxes/spending after war Favors some regulation of business Gov. aid to farmers
1948	Restore trade accords limited by Republican Congress Activist role in world Activist role throughout economy	Supports reciprocal trade accords while protecting industry, agriculture* Activist role in world Reduce taxes and spending Gov. aid to farmers Regulation of monopolies Limited gov. role in economy

1952	"Expansion and liberalization
	    of world trade" which would
	    spread prosperity in world
	Activist role in world
	Activist role throughout economy
		Favors reciprocal trade accords which
		    would safeguard domestic
		    industries/payrolls*
		Activist role in world
		Reduce taxes and spending
		Gov. aid to farmers
		Limited gov. role in economy

1956	Change "flagrant disregard" for
	    free trade
	Activist role in world
	Activist role throughout economy
		Favors reciprocal trade with safeguards
		    against unfair competition
		Activist role in world
		Liberalized immigration policy
		Reduce taxes and spending
		Gov. aid to farmers
		Limited gov. role in economy

1960	"World trade raises living standards"
	Help affected industries adjust by
	    gov. assistance/contracts
	Activist role in world
	Activist role throughout economy
		Favors reciprocal trade with safeguards
		    against unfair competition
		Activist role in world
		Reduce national debt, balance budget
		Gov. aid to farmers
		Limited gov. role in economy
		Strongly liberalized immigration policy

1964	Expansion of trade accords
	Help affected industries adjust by
	    gov. assistance/contracts
	Break down barriers against
	    unfair competition*
	Activist role in world
	Activist role throughout economy
	Liberalized immigration policy
		Will "remove...discriminatory and
		    restrictive trade practices" of nations
		Protection against imports for meat,
		    textiles, oil, glass, coal, lumber, steel
		Activist role in world
		Reduce debt and taxes, balance budget
		Limited gov. role in economy
		Emphasis on free market system

1968	Expand trade accords, especially
	    for Third World
	Remedy "unfair and destructive
	    competition"
	Activist role throughout economy
		Expand trade accords through
		    "hard-headed bargaining"
		Protect against "sudden influx of imports
		Restrict market share of imported goods*
		Protect farming from "unfair competition"

	Activist role in world without being "international policeman"	Activist role in world Moderate gov. role in economy (more active than in 1964) Reduce debt and taxes, balance budget
1972	"In a weak economy...foreign imports bring hardships"* "Commitment to liberal trade...takes its toll when times are bad"* Seek reciprocal trade accords that limit exploitation of labor* Farmers need to be "free of unfair competition"* More restrained role in world Activist role throughout economy	Create more open world market* Protect workers from sudden dislocations from trade, esp. in steel, beef, textiles, wool Gov. assistance in adjustment* Activist role in world (Nixon Doctrine) Moderate gov. role in economy Cap gov. spending, pursue tax reform
1976	Favors "orderly reduction in trade barriers" on reciprocal basis Limit exploitation of foreign labor Gov. role in managing trade* Restrict activities of multinationals* Moderately activist role in world Activist role throughout economy	Oppose "new restrictions on trade," "guard against protectionism"* Oppose "replacement of free market...by cartels...or commodity agreements"* Expand trade with Third World* Protect farmers from unfair competition Moderate gov. role in economy Cap spending, balance budget, cut taxes
1980	Free and fair trade "enhancing exports while safeguarding domestic industry"* Enforce anti-dumping actions* Regulate imports of textiles, color televisions, footwear* Enforce customs laws with penalties Take swift anti-dumping actions Gov. role in managing trade Moderately activist role in world guided by "principle and strength" Activist role throughout economy	Favors free trade based on reciprocity "Increased exports...result in jobs and a rising standard of living"* Gov. incentives for exports* Protect autos, steel, textiles, electronics Encourage foreign markets for agric.* Activist role in world Emphasizes market rather than gov. role in economy Reduce spending/taxes, balance budget
1984	Supports free and fair trade Bring agriculture, high technology into GATT* Subsidize exports on European and Japanese models* Require foreign auto makers to invest in United States* Assist workers and companies hurt by trade Develop industrial policy* Moderately activist role in world Activist role throughout economy	"Tremendous expansion of...trade has increased...standard of living" "All Americans benefit from free flow of goods" "Will not tolerate"loss of jobs in protected industries abroad Activist role in world Limited role for gov. in economy Reduce spending/taxes, balance budget Limit immigration
1988	Supports fair and managed trade Enforce workers' rights abroad	Favors "more open trading system" Extols free trade accord with Canada *(continues)*

TABLE 3.1 *(continued)*

	Moderately activist role in world	**Use GATT to resolve multilat. problems***
	Activist role throughout economy	Activist role in world
		Limited role for gov. in economy
		Reduce spending/taxes, balance budget
1992	**Work to expand trade through multinational agreements***	**"Tough free traders" fighting to reduce farm subsidies and gov.-industry collusion in Europe and Japan***
	Trade accords must balance free trade and fair trade	**Seek multilateral accords, especially in Asia and with Canada/Mexico**
	Trade accords must give weight to environment, health and safety, and labor standards*	**Fight trade restrictions, taxes, quotas, but back Super 301***
	Activist role in world*	Activist role in world
	Activist role throughout economy	Limited role for gov. in economy

Stands on tariffs are in bold typescript.
Related issues of foreign policy and economics are in regular typescript.
*Represents partial change in policy

Sources: Compiled by the author from party platforms in Donald Bruce Johnson and Kirk H. Porter, comps., *National Party Platforms, 1840-1972* (Urbana,IL: University of Illinois Press, 1973); *Congressional Quarterly* (1977, 1981, 1985, 1988); and Ronald D. Elving, "Comity on Platform Collapses as Angry Jackson Forces Dig In," *Congressional Quarterly Weekly Report*, July 16, 1988, pp. 1967-70.

The Republicans briefly and partially shifted direction in 1908 under Theodore Roosevelt. The platform restated the traditional protectionist position, but also called for downward revision in rates. The Progressive wing of the party echoed the anti-monopoly sentiments of the Democrats. Its tariff policies reflected the Progressive skepticism toward big business. Roosevelt again emphasized tariff reform as the Progressive candidate in 1912,[14] when the GOP had shifted back to its traditional protectionism. The Democrats reiterated their opposition to high rates and pledged immediate reductions. Woodrow Wilson was the first President to make the linkage between free trade and an expanding international economy.[15]

The Democrats continued their opposition to high tariffs in 1916; the GOP policy remained largely intact, although the platform expressed support for a bipartisan tariff commission. For the next several elections, party positions remained constant except for 1928, when party positions were temporarily reversed by stands taken by the nominees. Democrat Al Smith took protectionist positions; Republican Herbert Hoover rejected a proposed platform plank that would have condemned capital exports.[16] Both parties equivocated on trade in 1928.[17] The vote on the protectionist Smoot-Hawley tariff in 1930 was highly partisan.[18]

Smoot-Hawley and the Depression (Democrats liked to argue that the first caused the second) led to plummeting trade. World exports fell by 50 percent from 1928 to 1932, U.S. exports by 66 percent.[19] Voters tossed out the Republicans, and high tariffs fell into disrepute. Yet Franklin D. Roosevelt was reluctant to implement the strong free trade position in the Democratic platform.[20] Democrats pushed through the Reciprocal Trade Act of 1934, which marked the beginning of the free trade era in contemporary American politics.[21] Throughout Roosevelt's first three terms, the parties stood fast. House Democrats appointed only free traders to the coveted Ways and Means Committee.[22] Party cleavages in the House were greater on trade than on any other issue from 1921 to 1944.[23]

The fault lines began to break in 1940. Even as the Republican platform continued to endorse tariffs, its presidential nominee, Wendell Wilkie, was a confirmed internationalist. The GOP was torn in the 1940s. Republican legislators, including some of the party's protectionist gatekeepers on Ways and Means, backed an extension of the 1934 trade act in 1943, arguing that the war required a bipartisan foreign policy.[24] In 1944, the GOP platform acknowledged that the post-war world would require a "great extension of trade." Republicans battled Harry S Truman from 1945-1953, especially in 1947-48 when they controlled Congress.[25] But the party's platform moved toward a less protectionist stance.

The clean Republican break with the past came with the election of Dwight D. Eisenhower in 1952. The party platform on trade did not shift from four years before, but its leader was now a war hero who had both an internationalist viewpoint and little concern for the routines of politics that create protectionist coalitions.[26] Eisenhower called for an extension of the Reciprocal Trade Act and pulled many Republican legislators in both the House and the Senate with him.[27] Republicans remained more protectionist than Democrats, but only half as likely to oppose reciprocal trade legislation in the 1950s than they had been a decade earlier.[28] Democrats were tugged in the opposite direction. By 1955 over a third of House and Senate Democrats defected from party positions on trade.[29]

When John F. Kennedy became President in 1960, Congress granted him the greatest authority to reduce tariffs in American history.[30] Legislators of both parties banded together to enact it. Party cohesion did not disintegrate on trade. From 1948 through 1964 trade was still the sixth (out of 29) most partisan issues facing the Congress, but the level of conflict was "nowhere near what it was" before the 1940s.[31] In the post-World War II era, "neither party used trade policy as a major means of defining its differences with the other."[32] By 1964 both party platforms gave moderate commitments to free trade. Republicans presented an extensive list of industries they would protect; Democrats initiated a commitment to "break down barriers against unfair competition."

Both parties pledged in 1968 to expand trade accords and to protect American firms against "unfair competition," but the GOP now pledged to restrict the market share of imported goods. Yet four years later the Republicans, in addition to listing their familiar litany of industries worthy of protection, pledged to create a more open world market, while the Democrats shifted toward an explicitly protectionist platform. Democrats argued there that "in a weak economy. . . foreign imports bring hardships" and that "commitment to liberal trade...takes its toll when times are bad." Thus while the Democrats adopted a protectionist platform in 1972, the GOP plank that year moved sharply in the direction of free trade, a journey that was essentially complete by 1976. In 1976, Democratic nominee Jimmy Carter, who broke eight years of GOP dominance, espoused free trade," and the Democratic platform edged toward an industrial policy of "managed trade" to accommodate Carter's views.[33] Business, labor, and government were to work together to decide which industries would be subsidized in the race to produce goods competitive on the world market.

Although the Democrats accommodated Carter in 1976, the shift to protectionism was complete by 1980. While the Republican platform of 1980 promised protection for some key industries, it contained a ringing endorsement of free trade: "Increased exports. . . result in a rising standard of living." Democrats, on the other hand, focused on anti-dumping provisions and advancing an industrial policy. By 1984 the Republican platform sang the praises of free trade in several choruses, while Democrats continued to promise an industrial policy. By 1988 the Democrats explicitly endorsed "managed trade," while the Republicans promised a "more open trading system."

During the 1970s and 1980s, partisanship fluctuated. On Ways and Means, trade was the least partisan of five major issues from 1975-86.[34] Yet the International Trade Commission responded to demands for protection in partisan terms. Districts represented by Republican members of the Ways and Means trade subcommittee were significantly *less* likely than other legislators to get trade protection.[35] The parties became more sharply polarized on trade then they had been in the 1950s and 1960s.[36] In 1970, over 60 percent of Democrats took a protectionist position on a trade bill while the Republicans were evenly divided.[37] By the 1980s there was far greater polarization. Democrats shepherded "domestic content" legislation through the House in 1982 and 1983. The restrictive Gephardt amendment enacted in 1987 drew support from three-quarters of all Democrats but just 20 percent of Republicans in the House.[38] While Congressional Democrats had been significantly more likely to support free trade before 1970, afterwards they were prone to back protectionist measures.[39]

Congress, the Tariff, and Society

Societal explanations focus on how public opinion and interest groups shape policy. Democratic governance is distinctive because it responds to public preferences, and generally does so consistently.[40] When mass preferences don't shape policy outcomes, organized interests do. In either case, we should see a relationship between shifts in party positions and the supporting coalitions in the electorate or the interest group universe.

Since survey research is a relatively new phenomenon, we cannot trace public opinion on trade before or during the New Deal. There are data for the more recent party shift, but they tell us little about shifts in trade outcomes or party positions. Schneider reports little variation in public support for protectionism from 1976 to 1990, even as policies have wandered all over the place.[41] Public opinion on the tariff may appear stable over time, but over a series of questions at the same time it has the texture of jello. Politicians can claim support for almost any trade policy depending upon the wording of questions in national surveys. It is difficult to trace shifts in public support for trade policy, and thus for changes in party positions, simply because we just don't know what people want.[42]

If public opinion does not drive trade policy shifts, might interest groups? From Schattschneider's (1935) classic discussion of the forces that led to the adoption of Smoot-Hawley to contemporary formal models,[43] students of the tariff have pictured interest groups as demanding protection while the less organized "public" favors free trade. A logrolling coalition among interest groups often overwhelms the "public interest" to enact protectionist legislation. This view of the world is not limited to academics: When Democrats denounced tariffs as tools of trusts in the late nineteenth and early twentieth centuries, and when contemporary Republicans attack customs barriers, they employ similar language.

How do parties matter in a policy world driven by interest groups? Interest groups and parties are not adversaries; they complement each other. Groups have historically been linked to parties.[44] Party positions on the tariff should follow the stands of their affiliated groups, or groups' partisan loyalties should track the parties' positions on trade.

The partisan-group linkage was very clear in the late nineteenth century. The protectionist GOP reflected business interests in the Northeast and Midwest. Manufacturers and financiers sought tariffs to protect their economic stakes. Steel, textiles, coal, and (to a lesser extent) shoes, all labor-intensive industries that were strong opponents of unions, joined with bankers to support the tariff and the Republican party. The Democrats were divided between their "gold" (Grover Cleveland) and "silver" (William Jennings Bryan) factions. "Gold" Democrats were tied to Northeastern banking interests that favored the tariff, "silverites" to Westerners who opposed the duties. In 1896 the "Free Silver" movement, focused in the Populist party, captured the Democratic party and tipped the balance toward free trade.[45]

The ties began to wane early in the twentieth century. Small business was no longer a protectionist monolith. By 1908, 40 percent of the National Association of Manufacturers favored free trade.[46] Business unity was further disrupted by World War I. The United States emerged as a net creditor in the world economy and the international economy became more integrated. Manufacturers traditionally linked to the GOP became even more protectionist as they feared greater competition from imports. These labor-intensive industries made their peace with unions and they lived together in relative harmony under the Republican tent.[47] Bankers and some manufacturers, seeking investment and export opportunities overseas, tilted toward free trade and even began to flirt with the Democratic party.[48]

The conflict over Smoot-Hawley split manufacturers and importers.[49] Many agriculture interests supported protection, but those heavily involved in exporting (rice, tobacco, and cotton) did not. The economic dislocations of the Depression increased pressures for protection from industries that feared obliteration by foreign competition.[50] The Republicans were discredited and so was protectionism. The era of good feelings between protectionist business and labor ended as the working class shifted its allegiance to the Democrats.[51] At first, most business executives saw Roosevelt as a "class enemy" because of his vast expansion of the role of the federal government.[52] By the mid-1930s, however, the labor-business alliance had been reconstituted in the Democratic party on the trade issue. Export-oriented firms such Coca-Cola, General Electric, Sears, and United Fruit, together with tobacco, oil, and banking interests supported Roosevelt, who had by then committed his administration to free trade. The businesses that sought accords with labor and agriculture were firms that depended heavily on foreign trade. They were also more capital-intensive and were able to bear higher labor costs.[53] Most business executives remained in the GOP, but a substantial share, by one estimate about 30 percent, aligned themselves with the Democrats.[54]

North America's share of world imports doubled to 36 percent after World War II. In this environment, most of business and labor favored free trade.[55] The AFL-CIO worked with the Chamber of Commerce in 1962 to back Kennedy's extensive tariff reduction plan.[56] With both parties backing tariff reductions, the protectionist coalitions in the postwar period had no clear partisan slant. From 1945 to 1955 the bloc consisted of some large firms, including previous backers of the New Deal (General Electric), and a wide range of less prominent interests: glassware, pottery, handicraft, watchmaking, coal, lumber, lead, zinc, textile, livestock, railroads, and independent oil. Agricultural interests were divided, while unions in industries that were adversely affected stood apart from most others.[57]

The labor-business bipartisan coalition stood intact throughout the 1950s and 1960s. Groups seeking protection conformed to a pure logrolling model. They formed an unusual coalition, were willing to trade support for each other's demands, and were not bound to either party. Yet they were not numerous enough to prevail within either the legislative or executive branches. Coalitions became more fluid in the 1970s. The United States registered a trade deficit in 1971 for the first time since the end of World War II.[58]

Textiles, footwear, steel, automobiles, fertilizers, semiconductors, telecommunications, machine tools, lumber, sugar, cotton, and copper formed the business protectionist coalition in the next two decades, while oil, real estate, aerospace, defense interests, farm machinery, coal, sugar users, many agricultural interests, the Chamber of Commerce, and the National Association of Manufacturers backed free trade.[59] Organized labor retreated from its free trade position in 1973, although the United Auto Workers did not join the protectionist coalition until 1979. Only the textile unions, among the big organizations, broke ranks earlier.[60]

The various interests in the free trade bloc began to lean toward the GOP, especially bigger business, oil, and defense. Labor has been a central element in the Democratic coalition since the New Deal, while the textile industry work force draws heavily from minorities and women.[61] Yet other protectionist forces such as machine tools, sugar, cotton, and lumber defy ready partisan classification. Steel and automobiles divide along management-labor lines in party affiliation. Many sectors remained split on trade, with the fault lines falling along importing-exporting dimensions. Such divisions contravened normal political cleavages.

Unions pressured the Democrats into greater protectionism. Yet they jostled an actor with one foot already over the precipice. The Democratic platform of 1968 warned against "unfair trade" (see Table 3.1). Congressional Democrats had moved in a protectionist direction in 1970,[62] before the major unions jettisoned free trade. The Democratic Presidential vote declined in the 1970s and 1980s. The union contribution to this smaller base fell from almost 40 percent in the 1950s to about 30 percent in the 1980s.[63] Some Democrats felt pressured to secure union support. Walter Mondale endorsed domestic content legislation in 1982 to get UAW endorsement for his 1984 Presidential bid.[64] There were countervailing pressures to secure backers who favored free trade. In 1976 the Democrats won with a free trade candidate (Carter) through the added votes of the South, which otherwise asserted its loyalty to the free trade GOP in the 1970s and 1980s. In the 1970s and 1980s, the Democrats also became closely allied with the consumer movement which largely opposed protectionist legislation[65] but which could not rival labor's electoral mobilization efforts; yet, their stands could not be ignored. The South was hardly uniform in its anti-protectionism. It proved elusive to most Democratic candidates, and its moderate-to-conservative Democrats were a distinct minority in the nominating process.

The Democrats shifted toward protectionism before labor, but were pushed toward a consistent stance by the unions. While union members' contribution to the Democrats declined beginning in 1968, their increased loyalty in 1976, when they voted Democratic almost as strongly as in 1960,[66] proved how critical they were to a victory for the White House. Even as worker fidelity to Democratic Presidential candidates waned, labor's clout remained strong. Unions kept up pressure on the Democratic-controlled Congress by their unwavering loyalty in campaign contributions to the party's Congressional candidates. Corporate political action committees were more likely to be fair weather friends, shifting loyalties to Republicans when national tides favored the GOP.[67]

Union members and Southerners were the two core elements of the New Deal electoral coalition that had become substantially less loyal to Democratic Presidential candidates.[68] While the South returned to a native son nominee in 1976, the region's fealty to the Republicans since 1968 offered little hope of a revival of a Democratic South. Without the South, recapturing labor became an even higher priority for the Democrats. Southern Democrats, those representing agricultural districts especially, had traditionally been among the strongest advocates of free trade in the party.[69] The migration of Southerners to the GOP bolstered free trade advocates in that party and protectionists among Democrats.

The Republicans played a game of catch-up with much of their interest group coalition. Major industries had backed free trade long before the party put itself on record as opposed to protectionism. The high technology industries in the emerging GOP bastion of the Sunbelt might have tilted the Republicans against free trade, but they did not. Group positions track party stands on trade imperfectly, and perform less well in explaining why parties switched stands at particular times. In the 1930s business leaders joined a majority electoral coalition that had already formed. The business-labor-agricultural coalition that sustained the New Deal provided benefits for each actor that could not be obtained in isolation.[70] Yet the Democratic majority did not *depend* upon business support. Without business, the New Deal might have looked rather different, but it is not likely that it would have collapsed. The Democrats had advocated free trade for most of the past century. Business did not change Democratic policy; it padded support for the dominant coalition.

Public opinion offers few clues to party shifts on trade. The parties, especially the Democrats, did respond to interest group demands. Yet, the big impact of organized interests came *after* the parties had changed positions. Groups solidified the new positions on trade. Why the parties shifted stands remains elusive.

Institutions, Ideas, and Trade

If societal factors provide only a partial explanation of the shift in party positions on trade, can an institutional account do better? Institutionalists (or "statists") stress the autonomous power of institutions and ideas.[71] Political leaders are not simply mirrors of societal forces. They have their own ideologies, which can often overwhelm particularistic demands. Some leaders are privileged because of their institutional positions. In the United States the President is uniquely favored as the central figure in international politics, as the leader of a political party, and as the only official with veto power in national politics. Goldstein argues of the post-Smoot-Hawley era:

> A free trade bias seems to exist among central decision-makers and is part of an explanation for policy. . . . The Office of the President has been active in protecting America's liberal position. Although the Congressional position on trade has varied, the position of the executive has been unambiguous.[72]

When tariff policy shifted from a purely domestic concern of raising and distributing revenue to a foreign policy issue in the 1930s, Presidents came to dominate the Congress.[73]

Institutionalists highlight the role of the executive in trade policy. It is one thing to argue that Presidents favor free trade but another to trace shifts in party positions to executive leadership. Keech and Pak contend that Presidents who depart from their party protectionist orthodoxy can pull their party's legislators with them; their conclusions rest on just two Presidents (Eisenhower for the Republicans, Carter for the Democrats). Such an account does not explain why either party shifted positions in the first place. Magee and Young don't see much of a shift at the executive level, with Democratic Presidents more consistent supporters of free trade than GOP chief executives through Ronald Reagan. Yet,

Democratic and Republican Presidents have espoused both free trade and protectionist positions. Nixon sent a protectionist bill to Congress in 1971 and a free trade bill two years later.[74] Even Presidents who mouth free trade positions, most notably Reagan and Bush, have backed protectionist measures.[75] Partisan control of the Presidency has not affected tariff rates from 1950 to 1988.[76] Presidents are not uniformly favorable to free trade; they do not always follow the party positions they are supposed to lead.

If the linkage between the executive and free trade is weak, is there a more direct connection between ideas and party positions? Institutionalists argue that the Reciprocal Trade Act of 1934 marked a turning point in trade policy-making. Prior to 1934 trade was a domestic issue, but "Smoot-Hawley taught Congress and the president that trade policy was not like distributing water projects to different states."[77] The Reciprocal Trade Act marked the beginning of a long-term decline in customs duties and the development of a new consensus that free trade brought prosperity.[78] Leaders such as Secretary of State Cordell Hull saw free trade as part of an overall vision of an economic strategy that would promote international cooperation.[79]

The vision was called "liberalism." It stressed reliance on market forces to promote prosperity and abjured the logrolling arrangements that led to Smoot-Hawley. Protectionism was "delegitimized." Industries seeking duties were claimants against the larger public interest and were to be ignored.[80] Liberal values permitted protection only for brief periods of time for industries in distress or facing "unfair" competition from abroad.[81] Tariffs distorted markets and inhibited growth, so they would only be tolerated for brief periods under exceptional circumstances. The argument for free trade did not arise from public demands, but from the intellectual community, especially academic economists.[82]

Institutionalists admit that economic liberalism did not emerge from the Smoot-Hawley debacle. The economic growth argument was long part of anti-protectionist rhetoric, especially prominent in Woodrow Wilson's free trade positions. In the 1930s, however, liberalism achieved hegemony.[83] Liberalism did bring wealth. From 1960 to 1980 the value of merchandise exports and imports tripled in proportion to goods production in the United States.[84] The economic downturn of the 1970s and the roller coaster years of the 1980s were rough on U.S. exports. The American share of world manufactures was cut in half from 1950 to 1980, while the percentage of world exports dropped almost as much. A trade surplus in 1981 became a massive ($141 billion) deficit by 1986. Many economists began to rethink liberal theory. A new set of ideas, "strategic trade theory," emerged to challenge the free trade orthodoxy.[85]

Ideas matter, and clearly liberalism gained hegemony in the 1930s and lost its privileged place in the 1970s and 1980s. Yet, ideas are not autonomous. Nor do they necessarily lead, much less push, political leaders. Liberalism on trade was part of a broader package of ideas called Keynesianism, which advocated governmental stimulation of the economy.[86] The ideas behind Keynesianism came to be central to the New Deal and to the strong governmental role in the economy that has been part of Democratic party policy ever since. Yet, Keynesian doctrine was not fully accepted by the Democratic party until the first Roosevelt administration was largely over.[87] The overall game plan that was to become economic liberalism came *after* the older-line ideas of free trade had already been accepted as Democratic party ideology. Similarly, if "strategic trade theory" developed in the mid-1970s through the 1980s, it too was playing catch-up with Democratic party policies that had shifted as early as 1968. Ideas justified interests. This does not mean that ideas are unimportant; far from it. They are just not autonomous.[88]

If ideas are determinative in party positions on trade, stands on protection should fit into a larger ideology. Let us delve a bit deeper into Table 3.1. The entries in regular type refer to economic and foreign policy issues that relate to the tariff. I have no rough and ready test to determine ideological coherence, but an examination of the entries should give us at least a rough idea of how ideas hang together.

From 1884 to 1908 Democrats stood firmly against the tariff and an activist government role in the economy. When the Populists joined the Democrats in 1896, the party toned down its rhetoric on reducing spending. It backed spending on public works, but still promised tax cuts. The party was all over the map on foreign policy during this period, from isolationism to advocating an activist role in the world. Trade and foreign policies were not yet aligned. The GOP was consistently pro-protection and generally in favor of an activist role in world affairs. It also emphasized defense of American labor and a restrictive immigration. Throughout these seven platforms, the parties were largely consistent over time and across issues.

Beginning in 1912 the Democrats took a moderately activist role in the domestic economy that lasted until 1936, when they accepted the ideas of Keynesianism. Their advocacy of tariff reductions continued apace, while the party became somewhat more activist (even if not uniformly so) in world affairs. The Republicans beat a retreat on world affairs and moved away from governmental intervention in the economy. Ideological coherence grew among Democrats and weakened among Republicans, who had previously linked protectionism with a more general role for government in managing economic growth.

The New Deal continued Democratic support for free trade, which lasted through 1964. By 1936 the party was committed to an expanded government role in the economy, which it still advocates. The link of trade with an activist role in the world did not come until 1940. In 1936 Democrats were still non-interventionist as the world prepared to go to war. The Republicans began to support freer trade in 1944, after the United States had entered World War II (which the party supported). By the time of U.S. entry into the war, both parties advocated at least a modicum of free trade and an activist role in the world. The GOP backed reductions in government spending and taxes and a modest degree of economic interventionism.

The parties' trade positions remained consistent from the years of Republican dominance to the cementing of the New Deal realignment in 1936. The Democrats' rhetoric did change. They de-emphasized the linkage between protectionism and trusts in 1916. Ironically, when the connection reappeared for a last hurrah in 1928, it came when the party nominated the protectionist Al Smith. As important as the idea of liberalism was to the trade debate, the Democrats did not stress how free trade brings about prosperity until their 1952 platform, when the GOP had already moved to a less protectionist stance. If the two parties had coherent ideologies from 1936 to 1964, they did not center around trade. Reciprocal trade had not become quite the consensus issue that institutionalists suggest. The parties were badly divided on trade through 1944, over 10 years after the "consensus" supposedly had formed. Thereafter, the Republican platform was rather muted in its praise of free trade through 1964, even in the year the party nominated free-marketeer Barry Goldwater. Throughout the entire period, the Republicans promised an activist role in the world. Yet they never fully bought into the trade consensus, perhaps because they rejected so much else of Keynesian economics.

The Democrats tilted toward protectionism in 1968 and moved forthwith into that corner four years later. Their foreign policy stands, reflective of the Vietnam experience, became less interventionist, while they continued to advocate a strong government role in the economy. The party's trade positions emphasized the exploitation of foreign labor. Beginning in 1976, Democrats advocated a strong role for government in managing trade, eight years after shifting ground on protection. Not until 1984 did the magic words "industrial policy" appear in the Democratic platform, and, like a jack-in-the-box, they disappeared four years later.

The Democratic platforms were coherent from 1968 to 1988, but the ideas on trade were at the periphery of the ideology. When the nominee was a free-trader (Carter in 1976) or a reluctant protectionist (Mondale in 1984), the party back-pedaled on tariffs and gave at least passing mentions to expanding trade accords. The wounded Carter, buffeted by a challenge from his left in party primaries in 1980, ran on a plank that was a laundry list of specific retaliatory actions rather than an overall trade strategy.

The Republicans moved decisively toward free trade in 1972. As late as 1980 their platform called for some tariff barriers. The party moved from support for a moderate role for government in the economy to a critique of governmental intervention and praise of the market. They linked opposition to protectionism with support for markets. Yet, the party's support for free trade predated the victory of the right in presidential nominating politics. In 1984 the party departed from a pure free-market ideology to endorse limits on immigration. Throughout the entire period the GOP backed an activist role in the world.

Trade sometimes reflects a coherent ideology and often does not. Free trade has been a Democratic position through calls for budgetary restraint and demands for large-scale government programs, through support for an activist role in the world and a prescriptions that the United States not police the world. The party shifted to protectionism while changing few of its other stands and without a grander theory of the United States economic role in the world. The Republicans were protectionist when they believed the government should be active in the economy, when they hailed the free market, when they were isolationists, and when they were interventionists. They shifted to free trade *after* the 1964 flirtation with a free-market economy but *before* the 1980 conservative renaissance. If ideas had independent power, there should be greater evidence of a coherent ideology.

Ideas, Interests, and Policies

If politics only depended upon ideas, all parties would support tariff reductions in the post-Smoot-Hawley era. Politicians are constrained, however, by economic circumstances and the ideologies of their parties and associated groups. When the economy is performing well there are fewer demands for protection. Tariff barriers go down in prosperous times and up when things turn sour. However, when the economy is performing poorly, both Democrats and Republicans, both the President and Congress, respond to demands for protection.[89]

The recession of 1958 led free trade Democrats in Congress to enact protectionist legislation.[90] There was a sharp increase in the number of protectionist bills submitted to Congress and petitions for relief to the International Trade Commission in the late 1970s and the 1980s; even the free-trader Ronald Reagan was far more willing than his predecessors to grant protection.[91] George Bush, who has denounced protectionism and called for expanding the free trade accord with Canada to include Mexico, imposed additional barriers on lumber and Japanese cars from Canada during the 1992 recession.[92]

The business cycle thesis brings us part of the way to an explanation. Both parties and their Presidents can deviate from their trade orthodoxy when economic circumstances dictate closer attention to their most vociferous constituents. Such short-term forces ultimately run up against the parties' ideological tenets over the longer term. The Democrats kept to a consistent free trade position from the 19th century to 1968. The Republicans maintained strong support for protectionism until the 1940s and did not fully shift to free trade until 1972. What finally moved the parties? To a considerable extent, the positions of key actors in their electoral coalitions pushed the two parties apart: Labor moved the Democrats toward protectionism, Sunbelt firms the GOP toward free trade. Yet, these accounts are incomplete.

Are both ideas and interests wrong? No. They are both right, but in a slightly different way.

Let us go back to the beginning and reconsider Bush's statement that protectionism is "a smokescreen for a country that is running scared." The President was reiterating the liberal idea of trade. Few Americans know anything about economic theory. Not many have coherent views of world trade either. Yet, virtually all citizens have clear ideas of what they expect from government, particularly from the President: prosperity. American elections are largely referenda on the state of the economy, and the President's handling of it.[93]

Trade comes in indirectly. Ideas have trickled down to citizens from elites such that free trade has been associated with prosperity since the New Deal. People don't need economic theories to make this link. All they need to do is to look at the products they use every day. People buy more goods of all kinds, including imports, in good times. Demands for protection means increasing the price of, if not taking away altogether, imported consumer goods. People working in export-oriented industries also fear for their jobs if tariffs are raised.

One need not be an economist to know which way the economy blows. Ever-increasing prosperity is a cardinal feature of American values. Americans are a "people of plenty" with "an unparalleled bonanza of natural resources" that "made America wealthy."[94] Henry Steele Commager stated, "Nothing in all history had succeeded like America, and every American knew it."[95] A guiding aspect of American political culture is that the future will be even better than the past.[96] American political leaders are expected to give citizens the boom times people feel they deserve.

In the post-Smoot-Hawley era, American elites have largely accepted the idea that free trade brings prosperity. In 1954-55 two thirds of business leaders held that the best arguments for free trade are that low tariffs benefit either the world in general or American consumers.[97] Experience bore them out. Open markets lead to greater economic growth and an expansion of the public economy.[98] Government spending, at least according to liberal thought, will further stimulate economic growth. Free trade, then, is part of a set of economic ideas that will make never-ending growth possible. The beliefs that matter most are not those of academics, but the values of the citizenry.

Free trade, I suggest, is the policy prescription of a party that is, or is becoming, dominant in Presidential politics. From the 1930s to the 1970s the Democrats had an overwhelming advantage in party identification in all years but 1944; afterwards the Republican strength grew.[99] Even more critically, the Republicans began a streak of winning the Presidency in 1968 that had been broken only once (1976). The party of prosperity, which usually wins the Presidency, is typically less protectionist.

The Democratic reversal on trade in 1968 is part of the partisan de-alignment that began about that time.[100] The de-alignment marked the deterioration of traditional party coalitions with no clear ideologies or electoral blocs emerging. The waning of the old order reflected a loss of faith in core values, ranging from enlightened individualism (trust in other people) to faith in science and religion. Most critically for trade was the fading belief in American exceptionalism and its promise that the future would be better than the past.[101]

The Democratic message, beginning in the late 1960s, reflected this pessimism. The party was pulled by labor, which faced declining membership and weakening of traditionally accommodationist policies by employers,[102] and by environmentalists, who offered a limits to growth message. The Republicans, on the other hand, fared increasingly well in parts of the country where economic growth was strong from the 1970s onward. The Democrats became the minority party in races for the Presidency because they were associated with a message of bad news when voters wanted reassurance that the future would be better than the past. Ronald Reagan's strength was precisely his message of renewed growth. Yet, the public remained skeptical, so it kept the Democrats in power in the Congress. Americans expect the President to manage the economy, the Congress to distribute benefits to protect people from harm.[103] The division of power among a fearful electorate that nevertheless sought an upbeat message makes a lot of sense.

While neither party was able to establish electoral hegemony, the Republicans have dominated Presidential contests since 1968. Presidential elections are far more likely to be referenda on the state of the economy than are Congressional contests.[104]   Free trade offers a message of economic hope not only because of the linkage to growth, which is likely to be obscure to most voters. It is an attractive policy to winners in the marketplace, just as demands from protectionism come from losers. Ordinary citizens don't need to understand economic theories. They can identify winners (growth industries in the Sunbelt) and losers (unions and minorities) in the current climate rather easily.   After all, public opinion plays a central role in determining who wins and loses. The party associated with winners will dominate in presidential contests, while the party of losers will fall behind, picking up the pieces only in exceptional circumstances such as 1976.

Losing parties don't adopt protectionism in a lemming-like attempt to seal their fate. Nor do winning parties rationally select free trade to secure domination over presidential elections. Changing policies takes time as the slow GOP progression from protectionism to free trade shows. Winning parties must project a message of economic optimism for some time before they become dominant.   Hence the free trade consensus in the late 1950s and early 1960s. They must wait for some trauma to upset the dominant party and be ready to pounce on the opportunity. The losing party retreats into protectionism. The economic troubles that rousted it from its perch lead it to abandon free trade as its constituencies demand relief. Such movement provides the opposition with its opening for a message of optimism, and ultimately leads the losing party further into the abyss of pessimism and minority status. This is the scenario of the Democrats in the 1970s through the 1990s.

Politicians rationally attempt to tinker with the economy to bolster their popularity. They owe their greatest obligation to their core supporters, who hold parties to their long-standing macroeconomic priorities.[105] Democrats in the late 1960s had to meet their commitment to reducing unemployment. Protecting key industries and their workers appeared to be a short-term solution to economic problems, much as Nixon in 1973 would resort to wage and price controls to limit inflation. The specific policies adopted mattered less than the party's macroeconomic objectives. The Democrats were thus willing to jettison their long-standing support for free trade.

Once they took the first step of offering labor the tempting apple of protectionism, Democrats began the slide away from a message of economic growth and toward redistribution. In the 1950s and especially the early 1960s the two goals seemed compatible. By later in the decade, they had been decoupled. Democratic constituencies placed a higher priority on redistribution, as "losing" groups must. The party found itself in quicksand. It took the first step and was pulled in by its followers, ceding the message of growth to the Republicans.

The weakening economy, the War in Vietnam, the rise of the counterculture and emerging interests such as blacks, women, gays, and environmentalists led to the challenge to core American values. Each of these forces pushed the Democrats away from free trade and toward redistribution. So did the changing face of the international economy. Trade exploded in the 1970s, raising the stakes for all key actors. Protection was no longer just a short-term adjustment to unbalanced markets. It became a central feature of the message of redistribution.

Realignments and less consequential party shifts such as that on trade begin with seemingly rational calculations by the "losing" party, but lead to a dialectic that locks the party into an unpopular position. At the outset the party's stand may have seemed as popular as the alternative. This was clearly the case in the realignment of the 1920s. Free trade had *not* been the message of prosperity. Only two Democrats, the "Gold Democrat" Cleveland and Wilson, held the White House between Abraham Lincoln and Franklin D. Roosevelt.[106] Yet, economic liberalism had not been lying low. There was no consensus on the highly salient trade issue. Party competition for House seats was very strong prior to the 1896 realignment, but declined dramatically thereafter. Both parties had pockets of strength so the partisan division was rather close.[107]

The realignment that followed the 1932 election led to the hegemony of the free trade era. The Democratic victory was as deep as it was wide,[108] sending the GOP into minority status for all but four of the next 60 years in House contests. The decision of the internationalist business sector to cast its lot with the emerging dominant coalition may have been more central to the hegemony of free trade than was the consensus among economists.[109] Protectionism and free trade had jousted for preeminence throughout the nineteenth century and into the twentieth century. The 1896 realignment was simply not broad enough to declare a victor once and for all; the 1930s realignment was. Protectionism and the Republican party that advocated it both went into retreat as the bearers of economic bad news.

How realistic is this account? I perform a very rough test of the explanation by classifying the platforms of the parties in Table 3.1 from 1952 to 1988. I assigned a score of +2 if the Democrats were more pro-free trade, +1 if they were slightly more favorable to free trade, -1 if they were slightly more protectionist and -2 if strongly more protectionist. I adjusted the score by subtracting one if a Republican candidate (Eisenhower) or adding one if a Democratic candidate (Carter) was a free trader when his party platform indicated otherwise.[110] If positions on trade are associated with the party of prosperity, then this rough indicator should correlate with the share of the electorate that sees the Democratic party as better able to keep the country prosperous.[111]

The sample is small (ten cases), but the results are impressive. A generalized least squares regression indicates that the party seen as much more supportive of free trade will have a 20.25 percent advantage as being seen as the harbinger of prosperity (R^2 = .743). Yet, these results are distorted by one election, 1976. The Democrats had a 28 percent advantage as the party of prosperity, despite a neutral value on the trade index. Clearly, factors other than trade, especially a sluggish economy, affect people's evaluations of the party best equipped to run the economy. When we eliminate 1976, the results are even stronger. The party that more emphatically advocates free trade is 21.34 percent more likely to be seen as best able to lead the country to good times (R^2 = .927). When Democrats are strongly pro-free trade, they have an advantage over the Republicans on keeping the country well off, averaging 29 percent. When the Republicans are much more free trade oriented than the Democrats, they average 16 percent higher ratings on the economy.[112]

These results support my general thesis that ideas and interests both matter, but within the context of the larger macropolitical environment. They also account for the presumed trade liberalism of the executive. Institutionalists argue that Presidents are more liberal on trade policy because they represent some broader "national interest."   Instead, I suggest that the party of prosperity, that is the free trade party, is more likely to succeed in electing Presidents. When a party is down and out, the Republicans following World War II and the Democrats following 1968, it can regain the White House, if only temporarily, by mimicking the other party's message of economic growth. No wonder Keech and Pak had only two exceptions to explain. Republicans in the 1940s and 1960s and the Democrats in the Democrats in the early 1970s and the 1980s did not elect chief executives because they were not seen as the party of growth and prosperity.

There is a message for the parties in these results. Protectionism may have sold to the electorate in the nineteenth and early twentieth centuries, but it has become associated with a message of pessimism that the electorate has rejected in contemporary American politics. Americans may be skeptical that the future will be better than the past, but they want a President who will reassure them that it isn't necessarily so. The Democrats seemed to learn this message at an opportune time.   Bill Clinton, the first Democratic President in 16 years, rejects protectionism. He waged a strong and successful campaign to get NAFTA approved by Congress.

The NAFTA victory in the House of Representatives was a close call. The accord prevailed by just 34 votes, with Republicans strongly united in support and Democrats divided but largely against. Sixty percent of House Democrats and more than two-thirds of party members whose districts Clinton carried voted "no." Among the leaders of the opposition were the second- and third-ranking Democrats in the House.[113] Trade pacts generally pass by much larger margins, especially under single-party control of the two branches. NAFTA was unpopular with the electorate. Most surveys found that opponents outnumbered supporters by about 10 percent. Until shortly before the November 1993 roll call in the House, opponents seemed to have the upper hand. The adversaries were led by former independent candidate H. Ross Perot, unions, and environmentalists. The latter ultimately had little impact on the vote, but Perot and unions scared many members, especially marginal Democrats, into opposition.

The NAFTA fight marked the weakening of the nexus between free trade and economic growth. The two core ideas that affected public support for the accord were tied to growth, namely, the belief that all countries would benefit because trade would make their economies grow, and the expectation that free trade would lead to long-term economic growth.[114] Yet, in both cases, almost 60 percent rejected the linkage throughout most of the debate. Unions and Perot both emphasized how NAFTA would cause loss of jobs. Popular accounts attribute the administration's victory to the debate between Perot and Vice President Gore. The debate had a minimal impact on public attitudes in November, which had turned toward a pro-NAFTA position by a 10 percent margin. The linkage between free trade and economic growth was reestablished, even if politicians could not be sure the nexus would last. Americans not only supported NAFTA but also now believed that trade would lead to more jobs and that the United States would *not* lose jobs to Mexico. These changes in public attitude occurred in October, at least two weeks before the debates.

The linkage collapsed early in the debate because Americans fear the future. This "people of plenty," reared on the ideas that resources are unlimited and the future will be better than the past,[115] now hold by 68 to 25 percent that life for the next generation will be worse than it is now. The fight over trade is now one over who will control a shrinking rather than expanding pie. As Senator Bill Bradley (D, NJ) stated, "NAFTA has become a symbol for other things, a lightning rod for people's anxieties about changes in their lives they have no control over."[116]

The worry is that future trade accords may face a skeptical public unless there is a long-term shift in economic prospects, or, as appears to be the case for the General Agreement on Tariffs and Trade accord, they shift most of the economic costs onto other nations. The hope is that, as in 1993, people do listen to dialogues among elites. They are persuadable. Politicians need to ensure that there is substance behind the linkages on trade and growth.

Notes

The research assistance of Jennifer Moyer is greatly appreciated, as is the support of the General Research Board of the University of Maryland College Park, the College of Behavioral and Social Sciences, and the Everett McKinley Dirksen Center for Congressional Research. The comments of Charles Lipson, Timothy McKeown, I. M. Destler, Gregory Marchildon, Alvin Drischler, Robert Pines, and Edith Wilson made this a much better paper. Mary Klette of NBC News and Eric Wolf of Peter Hart Associates graciously provided the survey data on NAFTA.

1. Quoted in Andrew Rosenthal, "Bush Announces Candidacy, Claiming Reagan Mantle," *New York Times*, February 13, 1992, p. A24.

2. See Robert E. Baldwin, "The Changing Nature of U.S. Trade Policy since World War" in Robert E. Baldwin and Anne O. Krueger, eds., *The Structure and Evolution of Recent U.S. Trade Policy* (Chicago: University of Chicago Press, 1984), pp. 7-9.

3. Harkin proudly proclaimed himself a protectionist.

4. John Mark Hansen,"Taxation and the Political Economy of the Tariff," *International Organization*,Vol. 44, 1990, p. 530.

5. David W. Brady, *Critical Elections and Congressional Policy Making* (Stanford: Stanford University Press, 1988), p. 20; Robert E. Baldwin, "The Changing Nature of U.S. Trade Policy since World War" in Robert E. Baldwin and Anne O. Krueger, eds., *The Structure of Evolution of Recent U.S. Trade Policy* (Chicago: University of Chicago Press, 1984), p. 9.

6. Brady, *Critical Elections*, p. 45. Richard Franklin Bensel, *Sectionalism and American Political Development: 1880-1980* (Madison: University of Wisconsin Press, 1984), p. 68.

7. Baldwin, "The Changing Nature of U.S. Trade," p. 7.

8. Brady, *Critical Elections*, p. 45.

9. Charles Stewart III and Barry R. Weingast, "Stacking the Senate, Changing the Nation," paper presented at the Annual Meeting of the American Political Science Association, August-September 1991, Washington, D.C., p. 43.

10. Ibid., p. 43.

11. The sources of the platforms are Donald Bruce Johnson and Kirk H. Porter, comps., *National Party Platforms, 1840-1972* (Urbana, IL: University of Illinois Press, 1973); *Congressional Quarterly* (1977, 1981, 1985, 1988); and Ronald D. Elving, "Comity on Platform Collapses as Angry Jackson Forces Dig In," *Congressional Quarterly Weekly Report*, July 16, pp. 1967-70.

12. Brady, *Critical Elections*, p. 54.

13. Bensel, *Sectionalism*, p. 70; Brady, *Critical Elections*, p. 77.

14. Ronald Rogowski, *Commerce and Coalitions: How Trade Affects Domestic Political Alignments* (Princeton: Princeton University Press, 1989), p. 48.

15. David A. Lake, "The State and American Trade Strategy in the Pre-Hegemonic Era" in G. John Ikenberry, David A. Lake and Michael Mastanduno, eds., *The State and American Foreign Economic Policy* (Ithaca: Cornell University Press, 1988), p. 51.

16. Thomas Ferguson, "From Normalcy to New Deal: Industrial Structure, Party Competition, and American Public Policy in the Great Depression," *International Organization*, Vol. 38, 1984, p. 78.

17. E. E. Schattschneider, *Politics, Pressures, and the Tariff* (New York: Prentice-Hall, 1935), p. 7.

18. Stephan Haggard, "The Institutional Foundations of Hegemony: Explaining the Reciprocal Trade Agreements of 1983" in Ikenberry, Lake and Mastanduno, eds., *The State and American Foreign Economic Policy*, p. 96.

19. David B. Yoffie, "American Trade Policy: An Obsolete Bargain?" in John E. Chubb and Paul E. Peterson (eds.), *Can the Government Govern?* (Washington, D.C.: The Brookings Institution, 1985), p. 106.

20. Peter Gourevitch, *Politics in Hard Times: Comparative Responses to Economic Crises* (Ithaca: Cornell University Press, 1986), p. 150.

21. Robert Pastor, "The Cry and Sigh Syndrome: Congress and Trade Policy" in Allen Schick, ed., *Making Economic Policy in Congress* (Washington, D.C.: American Enterprise Institute, 1983), p. 163.

22. John F. Manley, *The Politics of Finance: The House Committee on Ways and Means* (Boston: Little, Brown, 1970), p. 45.

23. Julius Turner with Edward V. Schneier, *Party and Constituency: Pressures on Congress rev. ed.* (Baltimore: Johns Hopkins University Press, 1970), p. 45.

24. Holbert N. Carroll, *The House of Representatives and Foreign Affairs* (Pittsburgh: University of Pittsburgh Press, 1958), p. 42; Manley, *The Politics of Finance*, p. 181.

25. Manley, *The Politics of Finance*, p. 188; Pastor, "The Cry and Sigh Syndrome," p. 100.

26. See M. Stephen Weatherford, "The President and the Political Business Cycle" in James P. Pfiffner, ed., *The President and Economic Policy* (Philadelphia: Institute for the Study of Human Issues, 1986).

27. Raymond A. Bauer, Ithiel de Sola Pool and Lewis Anthony Dexter, *American Business and Public Policy: The Politics of Foreign Trade*, 2nd. ed. (Chicago: Aldine-Atherton, 1972), p. 26; Richard A. Watson, "The Tariff Revolution: A Study of Shifting Party Attitudes," *Journal of Politics*, Vol. 18, 1956, pp. 685-687; see also Turner with Schneier, *Party and Constituency*, p. 71.

28. Leroy N. Rieselbach, *The Roots of Isolationism* (Indianapolis: Bobbs-Merrill, 1966), p. 50.

29. Watson, "The Tariff Revolution," p. 687.

30. Manley, *The Politics of Finance*, p. 291.

31. Turner with Schneier, *Party and Constituency*, p. 71.

32. I. M. Destler, *American Trade Politics: System Under Stress* (Washington, D.C.: Institute for International Economics, 1986), p. 143.

33. Pastor, "The Cry and Sigh Syndrome," p. 177.

34. The stage was set in 1970 when the panel's noted chair, Wilbur Mills (D, AK) abandoned his long-standing support for free trade and sponsored a bill establishing import quotas on textiles and footwear. Stephen P. Magee and Leslie Young, "Endogenous Protection in the United States, 1900-1984" in Robert M. Stern, ed., *U.S. Trade Policies in a Changing World Economy* (Cambridge, MA: Massachusetts Institute of Technology Press, 1987), p. 148. Also see Randall Strahan, *New Ways and Means: Reform and Change in a Congressional Committee* (Chapel Hill, N.C.: University of North Carolina Press, 1990), pp. 168-169.

35. Wendy L. Hansen, "The International Trade Commission and the Politics of Protectionism," *American Political Science Review*, Vol. 84, 1990, p. 33.

36. Destler, *American Trade Politics*, p. 143.

37. Magee and Young, "Endogenous Protection," p. 148.

38. Larry L. Wade and John B. Gates, "A New Tariff Map of the United States House of Representatives," *Political Geography Quarterly*, Vol. 9, 1990, p. 288.

39. William R. Keech and Kyoungsan Pak, "Partisanship, Institutions, and Change in Contemporary American Trade Politics," unpublished mimeo, University of North Carolina at Chapel Hill (1992). Susanne Lohmann and Sharyn O'Halloran, "Delegation and Accommodation in U.S. Trade Policy," unpublished manuscript, Stanford University, 1991, p. 29, present a model of tariff rates 1950-88 in which "Republican controlled Congresses. . . implement more liberal trade policies than when the Democrats or neither party controls both Houses of Congress." But this is a null finding (something the authors don't stress) since the GOP held both chambers only in 1953-54 of their sample years. The recent Democratic Congresses (including 1969-80 and 1987-88) and the only years of split control (1981-86) came after the shift in partisan roles on the tariff.

40. Benjamin I. Page and Robert Y. Shapiro, *The Rational Public* (Chicago: University of Chicago Press, 1992).

41. William Schneider, "The Old Politics and the New World Order" in Kenneth A. Oye, Robert J. Lieber and Donald Rothchild, eds., *Eagle in a New World: American Grand Strategy in the Post-Cold War Era* (New York: Harper Collins, 1992), p. 59.

42. Destler, *American Trade Politics*, pp. 5, 150-151.

43. See Magee and Young, "Endogenous Protection."

44. Robert H. Salisbury, "Political Parties and Pluralism," Eric M. Uslaner, ed., *American Political Parties* (Itasca, Ill: F.E. Peacock, 1993).

45. Robert Pastor, *Congress and the Politics of U.S. Foreign Economic Policy* (Berkeley: University of California Press, 1980), p. 75; Thomas Ferguson, "Party Realignment and American Industrial Structure: The Investment Theory of Political Parties in Historical Perspective" in Paul Zarembka, ed., *Research in Political Economy*, Vol. 6, 1983, p. 54; Ferguson, "From Normalcy to New Deal," p. 63; and James L. Sundquist, *Dynamics of the Party System*, rev. ed. (Washington, D.C.: The Brookings Institution, 1983), p. 151.

46. Ronald Rogowski, *Commerce and Coalitions: How Trade Affects Domestic Political Alignments* (Princeton: Princeton University Press, 1989), p. 48.

47. Ferguson, "From Normalcy to New Deal," p. 63; Gourevitch, *Politics in Hard Times*, p. 148.

48. Jeff Frieden, "Sectoral Conflict and U.S. Foreign Economic Policy, 1914-1940" in Ikenberry, Lake, and Mastanduno, eds., *The State and American Foreign Economic Policy*, p. 73.

49. Schattschneider, *Politics, Pressures, and the Tariff*, p. 121.

50. Ibid., p. 149; Haggard, "The Institutional Foundations of Hegemony," p. 98.

51. Sundquist, *Dynamics of the Party System*, p. 215.

52. Gourevitch, *Politics in Hard Times*, p. 148.

53. See Ferguson, "Party Realignment," p. 59; Ferguson, "From Normalcy to New Deal," p. 91; and Gourevitch, *Politics in Hard Times*, pp. 151-2.

54. Sundquist, *Dynamics of the Party System*, p. 215.

55. Rogowski, *Commerce and Coalitions*, p. 119.

56. See Pastor, *Congress*, p. 111.

57. Bauer, de Sola Pool, and Dexter, *American Business*, p. 358; Carroll, *The House of Representatives*, p. 41; and Watson, "The Tariff Revolution," pp. 691, 694.

58. See Destler, *American Trade Politics*, p. 37.

59. Vinod K. Aggarwal, Robert O. Keohane and David B. Yoffie, "The Dynamics of Negotiated Protectionism," *American Political Science Review*, Vol. 81, 1987; Destler, *American Trade Politics*, p. 118; I.M. Destler, John S. Odell with Kimberly Ann Alliot, *Anti-Protection: Changing Forces in United States Trade Politics* (Washington, D.C.: Institute for International Economics, 1987), chs. 2-3; Gourevitch, *Politics in Hard Times*, p. 209; Pietro S. Nivola, "Trade Policy: Refereeing the Playing Field" in Thomas E. Mann, ed., *A Question of Balance* (Washington, D.C.: The Brookings Institution, 1990), p. 221.

60. Pastor, *Congress*, p. 156; Destler, *American Trade Politics*, p. 72.

61. See Aggarwal, Keohane, and Yoffie, "The Dynamics of Negotiated Protectionism," p. 355.

62. Magee and Young, "Endogenous Protection," p. 148.

63. Robert Axelrod, "Presidential Election Coalitions in 1984," *American Political Science Review*, Vol. 80, 1986, p. 282.

64. Pastor, *Congress*, p. 147.

65. See Destler and Odell, *Anti-Protection*, ch. 3.

66. Axelrod, "Presidential Election Coalitions," p. 282.

67. Gary G. Jacobson, *The Politics of Congressional Elections*, 3rd ed. (New York: Harper Collins, 1992), p. 66.

68. Axelrod, "Presidential Election Coalitions."

69. Watson, "The Tariff Revolution."

70. Gourevitch, *Politics in Hard Times*, p. 209.

71. Peter A. Hall, *Governing the Economy* (New York: Oxford University Press, 1986); Stephen D. Krasner, *Defending the National Interest* (Princeton: Princeton University Press, 1978). Statists are not all cut of the same cloth. Krasner is much closer to a societal view than is Hall.

72. See Judith Goldstein, "The Political Economy of Trade: Institutions of Protection," *American Political Science Review*, Vol. 80, 1986, p. 215.

73. Manley, *The Politics of Finance*, p. 331.

74. Pastor, *Congress*, pp. 123-136.

75. Magee and Young, "Endogenous Protection," on Reagan.

76. Lohmann and O'Halloran, "Delegation and Accommodation."

77. See Pastor, "The Cry and Sigh Syndrome," p. 163.

78. Pastor, *Congress*, pp. 196-7.

79. See Krasner, *Defending the National Interest*, p. 87.

80. Judith Goldstein, "Ideas, Institutions, and American Trade Policy," p. 187.

81. See Aggarwal, Keohane, and Yoffie, "The Dynamics of Negotiated Protectionism," p. 348.

82. See Goldstein, "The Political Economy of Trade," p. 165.

83. See Destler, *American Trade Politics*, p. 4.

84. Destler and Odell, *Anti-Protection*, p. 27.

85. David B. Yoffie, "American Trade Policy," pp. 101-2.

86. Peter Gourevitch, *Politics in Hard Times*, p. 99.

87. Walter S. Salant, "The Spread of Keynesian Doctrines and Practices in the United States" in Peter A. Hall, ed., *The Political Power of Economic Ideas* (Princeton: Princeton University Press, 1989), p. 35.

88. John W. Kingdon, "Ideas, Policies, and Public Policies," paper presented at the Annual Meeting of the American Political Science Association, Washington, D.C., September 1988.

89. James Cassing, Timothy J. McKeown and Jack Ochs, "The Political Economy of the Tariff Cycle," *American Political Science Review*, Vol. 80, 1986, p. 843. See also John Mark Hansen, "Taxation and the Political Economy of the Tariff," p. 539.

90. Manley, *The Politics of Finance*, p. 286.

91. Yoffie, "American Trade Policy," pp. 113-116.

92. Rowen writes of "George Bush's lamentable election-year descent into protectionism." See Hobart Rowen, "Now It's Canada-Bashing," *Washington Post*, March 12, 1992, p. A-27.

93. Edward R. Tufte, *Political Control of the Economy* (Princeton: Princeton University Press, 1978).

94. David Potter, *People of Plenty* (Chicago: University of Chicago Press, 1954), p. 80.

95. Henry Steele Commager, *The American Mind* (New Haven: Yale University Press, 1950), p. 5.

96. Eric M. Uslaner, *The Decline of Comity in Congress*, unpublished manuscript, 1992.

97. Bauer, de Sola Pool, Dexter, *American Business and the Public Policy*, p. 146.

98. Mancur Olson, *The Rise and Decline of Nations* (New Haven: Yale University Press, 1982), ch. 5; David R. Cameron, "The Expansion of the Public Economy: A Comparative Analysis," *American Political Science Review*, Vol. 72, 1978, p. 1255.

99. Harold W. Stanley and Richard G. Niemi, comps., *Vital Statistics on American Politics*, 3rd ed. (Washington: CQ Press, 1992), p. 160.

100. Walter Dean Burnham, *Critical Elections and the Mainsprings of American Politics* (New York: W.W. Norton, 1970).

101. See Uslaner, *The Decline of Comity in Congress*, ch. 5.

102. Table 1 in Michael Goldfield, "Labor in American Politics—Its Current Weakness," *Journal of Politics*, Vol. 48, 1986, p. 10 has data on employer opposition to unions.

103. Gary C. Jacobson, *The Electoral Origins of Divided Government* (Boulder, CO: Westview Press, 1990).

104. Morris P. Fiorina, *Retrospective Voting in American National Elections* (New Haven: Yale University Press, 1981).

105. Edward T. Tufte, *Political Control of the Economy* (Princeton: Princeton University Press, 1978).

106. Gourevitch, *Politics in Hard Times*, p. 148.

107. Brady, *Critical Elections*, pp. 143-7.

108. Ibid., p. 154.

109. Gourevitch, "Keynesian Politics," p. 99.

110. There were two +2 values (1960, 1964), one +1 value (1968), three zeros (1952, 1956, 1976), two -1 values (1972, 1980), and two -2 scores (1984, 1988).

111. These data were extrapolated from Figure 5-8 in Stanley and Niemi, p. 168. The measure employed is the percentage saying Democrats to percentage saying Republicans in Gallup surveys.

112. The t-value for the 10 cases is 5.278, which is significant at p < .001. 1976 was identified as having a very high studentized residual; the t-value for the 9 cases is 13.516, which is significant way beyond p < .0005.

113. This section follows John J. Audley and Eric M. Uslaner, "NAFTA, The Environment, and American Domestic Politics," *North American Outlook,* 1994, in press.

114. This result comes from probit analysis of public support for NAFTA using data from NBC News/*Wall Street Journal* surveys in September and November, 1993.

115. Potter, *People of Plenty.*

116. David Rosenbaum, "Good Economics Meet Protective Practices," *New York Times,* Sept. 19, 1993, p. E5.

4

What Forces Shape American Trade Policy?

Timothy J. McKeown

Although foreign trade, historically, has represented a smaller proportion of national income in the United States than in many other advanced capitalist states, American trade politics has been the subject of some of the most influential works in American political science. These studies have been motivated partly by the historical importance of trade issues in American politics, and partly by the fact that in dealing with foreign trade, economic theory has developed to the point where the distributional consequences of various policies are understood with unusual clarity. The latter condition seems to have made trade politics the social scientific equivalent of the biologists' fruit fly, that is, a naturally occurring "test bed" on which one can try out all sorts of theories about why a given policy measure might prevail. As a result, we have studies of trade policy that attribute central importance to everything from the alignment and relative strength of the great powers to the role of ideas in policy-making, from brutally simple interest group calculations of pecuniary gain to the role of the design of government institutions in favoring one type of interest at the expense of another.

In this chapter, I assess previous studies of trade politics in the United States and elsewhere in order to identify some general features of the making of trade policy that could be relevant to the consideration of NAFTA. The first section covers the most common explanation for trade politics, theories based on the actions of private interest groups, and discusses some special features of interest group politics surrounding NAFTA. Addressing the role of political parties in trade politics, in particular how shifts in comparative advantage affect parties's positions on trade issues, the second section shows that conclusions depend on assumptions about both the relative political strength of old and new industries, and the degree of "stickiness" in the redeployment of economic resources. Next I ask how macroeconomic conditions and governments' macroeconomic policies affect the making of trade policy, concluding that the macroeconomic environment of the 1980s partly explains recent American trade policy. Finally, I assess the thesis that the ideologies of relatively unconstrained public officials are central to understanding trade policy, and critique the most widely cited empirical evidence for it.

In what follows I do not pretend to have ransacked the scholarly literature.[1] The theory which we take up is empirically oriented, and it has been applied to and is based on the history of developed liberal democracies. As such, its value as an explanation for trade policy-making in a modified one-party state such as Mexico is open to question.[2]

Interest Group Politics

From the standpoint of an interest group theory, the distribution of protection[3] is a function of the political strength of the various interests mobilized on the issue.[4] Because final consumers are usually not well organized, they are generally viewed as having only a limited impact on trade policy. Similarly, members of Congress play a largely passive role in these accounts, serving mainly as targets for interest group influence attempts. Because the heart of the matter is taken to be interest group activity, distinguishing between the behavior of the President and Congress is not very important, since the President is, by implication, just another passive target of interest group demands. The theory is thus all about demand, saying very little about forces that might independently shape the supply of policy.

Interest group theories treat productive resources as tied to particular industries because in the short run it is often costly to re-deploy them. Thus, labor and capital in the same industry are treated as having an incentive to take common positions and to lobby as a team.[5] In the short run, such a theory says nothing about capital or labor in general. But it implies that the resources devoted to trade politics by peak associations of labor and capital (the U.S. Chamber of Commerce or the AFL-CIO are two examples) ought to be modest, because the heterogeneity of interests on both sides would make it difficult for either type of peak association to have very wide or deep support for any given trade policy position.

Such a theory deliberately sacrifices richness and complexity in favor of a simple and clear-cut argument: industries that are well organized, employ large numbers and command considerable wealth will achieve their political objectives; those that are not, will not. Such a theory can in principle explain inter-industry differences in protection, but it does not pretend to explain the average level of protection over time or changes in that level; nor does it address cross-national differences in protection. It can explain differences in the way that various foreign countries are treated in trade negotiations, but only by treating these differences as arising from different countries' profiles of production and consumption, and how they create conflicts or natural areas of harmony with domestic producers in the United States.

The least painful and most valuable agreement is one between two countries whose production is complementary, and whose consumption patterns create a large demand for the products of the other country. Increased competitive pressure on import-competing industries, such as that faced by American lumber from Canadian imports or by American low wage manufacturing faces from Mexican imports, creates economic adjustment costs and political opposition to agreements. This opposition may lead officials to consider side payments to such industries if they calculate that the opposition is too strong to ignore.

Systematic studies motivated by this approach reveal that industries that are low wage, labor-intensive, have low ratios of value-added to output, are declining in output or employment, and face strong or growing import competition are the ones that are likely to receive protection.[6] These results generally accord with what one would intuitively expect. However, the variation in these industry characteristics typically accounts for only 20 to 50 percent of the inter-industry variation in levels of protection in the OECD countries, and it clearly cannot account at all for inter-temporal variation in the average level of protection. Even as a theory of inter-industry differences in protection, the existing theory is obviously incomplete.

The stances of various domestic producer groups on a North American Free Trade Agreement are sometimes motivated by factors that have not been included in previous attempts to model the demands of these groups for protection.[7] The degree to which firms can take advantage of opportunities for direct investment in Mexico, the extent of firms' existing production and sourcing arrangements in the country, and their production and sourcing arrangements in third countries, all seem to be related to their reaction to the proposed agreement. Within the universe of import-competing firms, those with a lack of existing connections to Mexico and reliant on relatively immobile assets resist liberalization more energetically.

Firms that are outward oriented, of course, have a strong motive for seeking greater access to foreign markets, and are generally willing to trade away protection of the domestic market for access to foreign ones, particularly when it is other commodities in the domestic market that are being affected by liberalization, not their own. Firms whose profitability depends heavily on international protection of their intellectual property rights likewise tend to favor the trade agreement because it ties trade liberalization to enhanced protection for these rights in Mexico. U.S. banks which are creditors to Mexico favor the agreement because it will enable the Mexicans to service their debts more readily. Some firms which supply services and which are currently not large participants in international markets favor the agreement because they anticipate that access to the Mexican market will materially improve their profitability.

Party Politics

Studies of Congressional voting on trade policy measures commonly find that party identification affects votes, independent of the effect of constituency interests.[8] Why exactly do the parties often have identifiable party positions on trade issues?

The simplest answer to this question is that the positions of parties reflect the interests of their supporters, and that these interests are sufficiently homogenous (or susceptible to a log-roll) that a coherent party position is possible. From this standpoint, a party is simply a container for a set of interests that have enough in common to permit working together on a number of issues, one of which might be trade. One would then expect parties to shift their positions on trade when economic interests move into or out of them, or when economic interests within a party experience a shift in their international comparative advantage. A party or a government need not do anything for this to happen: events in a foreign country such as the rise of new industries or changes in exchange rates, or domestic market processes leading to shifts in relative prices, are redistributing comparative advantage all the time.

This view of parties would explain recent shifts in Democratic and Republican Congressional voting on trade issues in terms of the shifting comparative advantage of party supporters. In the case of the Democrats, the declining comparative advantage in carbon steel and autos has affected the positions of unions in these industries and thus pulled the entire AFL-CIO in the direction of greater skepticism towards open trade. In the case of the Republicans, the decline in the relative economic importance of import-competing manufacturing implies a weaker role for these interests in Republican trade policy formation.

These observations may account for shifts in trade politics in some important industries, but they do not adequately explain shifts in relative party positions on trade policy. Let us postulate that labor unions support the Democrats, capital and management support the Republicans, and economic returns on assets are tied to their use in specific industries. Any loss of comparative advantage in an industry ought to shift the position of management in that industry towards protectionism. They would have the same effect on overall Republican trade policy preferences as the unions in those industries would have on Democratic preferences. Thus, under these assumptions, a shift in comparative advantage might find parties' stances on trade issues converging.

For a given comparative advantage shift to move parties in opposite directions on trade policy, it is necessary to introduce some additional factors. One way to do this is to note that every time an industry loses comparative advantage, some other industry is gaining it. If the rising industries have less importance in the Democratic party than in the Republican party (perhaps because labor there is unorganized), then they would tend to offset the new protectionist pressures in the Republican party more completely than they would in the Democratic party. Thus, the Democratic party would become relatively more protectionist. However, the Republican party would become absolutely more liberal only if the new industries had more political weight than the old ones.

Although in general there are reasons to suspect that old industries are more politically influential than new ones,[9] a new industry in which barriers to entry allow the temporary accumulation of abnormally high profits may possess the wealth necessary to outweigh the political influence of older industries that are having difficulties remaining profitable. Under these conditions, capital and management in the new industries could conceivably have a net liberalizing effect on the Republican party.

Another way to generate opposing party movements would be to drop the assumption that connects parties to factors. Some unions support Republicans. The Democrats have always been successful in attracting support from important segments of capital. (Indeed, whatever the situation in the 1930s and 1940s, by the time of the 1980 election, the shift in Presidential control from Democrat to Republican had no overall effect on stock prices.)[10] If parties are coalitions of sectoral interests, then labor and management may be in the same party rather than opposing ones. Then the decline of one sector would cause an increase in the strength of protectionist sentiment in the party containing that sector. If a corresponding rising sector is found in the same party, it will tend to offset the protectionist pressures from the declining sector. If it is in the opposing party, then that opposing party will move in a more liberal direction.

If political parties do not converge on common positions on trade issues, then variations in party control of the executive and legislative branches would be associated with shifts in trade policy. Evaluations of U.S. tariff history suggest the conclusion that the Democrats have been less protectionist than the Republicans, at least until the last two decades.[11] Evaluations of the recent party positions are considerably more mixed. There seems to have been some shifts in the language of the two parties' platforms on trade issues that leave the Republicans looking less protectionist and the Democrats somewhat more so.[12] One can also readily observe that Congressional voting patterns now more often find Democrats on the side labelled "protectionist," while the Republicans are less likely to take such positions.

On the other side of the ledger is the fact that the Reciprocal Trade Agreements Act, the Trade Expansion Act of 1962, and the successful completion of the Dillon, Kennedy and Tokyo Rounds of multilateral trade negotiations have all taken place under Democratic administrations. Despite Republican dominance of the White House since 1968, since then only Democrat Jimmy Carter managed to bring a negotiated multilateral agreement to Congress and get it passed. (Republican negotiating successes in the 1980s were in bilateral or "mini-lateral" realms). More evidence suggesting continuing ties between the Republican party and protectionism has been the pattern of executive branch protective measures in the last two decades. David Richardson summarizes this succinctly: "Before the 1980s, the United States' own recourse to quantitative and managed-trade policies was small compared to its trading partners. During the 1980s, the United States ceased to be an outlier."[13] "Voluntary" export restraint agreements covering autos, carbon steel, and machine tools, and an unprecedented agreement with Japan on semiconductors were produced by the executive branch, not by Congress. Studies of party positions that rely on analyzing party platform language or Congressional voting patterns of course do not pick up any of this.

Macroeconomic Policies
and Macroeconomic Conditions

While the possibility of Congressional action no doubt played a role in Executive branch calculations, in other postwar situations where a Republican President faced a Congress partially or completely controlled by the opposition, these sorts of policy initiatives from the executive branch were not forthcoming. Why are the 1980s different in this regard?

One obvious source of variation is the macroeconomic context within which trade policy is made. Evidence is accumulating that for firms, nations, or the international system as a whole, growth creates the political conditions for trade openness, while the lack of growth does the opposite.[14] There is more limited evidence that governments may use trade liberalization as a weapon against inflation and that inflation creates (or is at least associated with) conditions in which openness is more easily pursued.[15] Monetary policies which are designed to dampen inflation also tend to raise the relative value of a nation's currency, which cheapens imports and exposes import-competing industries to import surges. Thus, low growth periods (a reasonable characterization of the 1980s compared to the two previous decades) would not be propitious times for trade liberalization. Both parties therefore may have become more protectionist as a reaction to these conditions. The fact that the trade openness of the American economy (measured as (exports + imports)/GNP) actually declined from 1980 to 1988 is consistent with this line of argument.[16]

At least some of the time macroeconomic conditions may render incompatible a party's preferences in trade, monetary and fiscal policy.[17] To the extent that they can shape macroeconomic outcomes in the short run, governments which emphasize price stability at the expense of reductions in unemployment will find that this policy mix leads to idle people and equipment, and hence to political pressures for protection.[18] Thus, even if there were no other differences between the parties, differences between the Democrats and Republicans in their degree of interest in these two policy objectives would tend to lead to differing levels of pressure for protection.

The Design of Legislatures and Inter-branch Relations

Changes in the majority party in a legislature will likely shift the position of the median legislator on trade issues. More importantly, a shift in party control usually shifts the control of the legislative agenda from one party to another through the shift in control of the "gate-keeper" functions of committees and sub-committees. Thus, a small shift in voting patterns which is enough to "tip" control from one party to another could have large consequences for legislation. Whatever means exist for enforcing party discipline can be applied to those legislators whose voting record on trade otherwise might be markedly different from the position of the median party member. Although the United States is often viewed as having relatively weak mechanisms for enforcing party discipline, recent work suggests that pressures for discipline are not trivial even in the American congress.[19]

Finally, a more mundane reason for the continued (statistical) importance of party affiliation in previous studies of legislative voting is that most attempts to measure the constituency economic interests of individual members of Congress rely on measures of these interests that are so coarse and so tenuously related to some underlying theory that it is a wonder they are statistically significant as often as they are. A better measurement of economic activities within a legislator's district would help matters, but it is also necessary to measure the various interests of a legislator's supporting coalition that are not necessarily tied to the geographic district of the legislator. One attempt to utilize improved measures of constituency economic interests resulted in a finding of significantly stronger constituency effects than were obtained with the more limited measurement of constituency.[20]

The fact that the presidency and Congress can be held by different parties can lead to a more protectionist trade policy. If, as some argue, representatives of smaller districts have a greater tendency to support policies that create costly spill-overs for other districts (such as Federal construction projects), then the Senate ought to be on average less protectionist than the House, and the President less protectionist on average than either chamber.[21] If the presidency and the Congress are held by the same party, then Congress is more willing to delegate trade policy authority to the president.

Delegation avoids the "pork barrel" problem associated with the log-rolling of particularistic demands for protection, and it is a way for members of Congress to avoid partaking in such an inefficient process without leaving their own districts (and hence their re-election chances) at a competitive disadvantage to those who do. However, when the presidency is controlled by an opposing party, delegation is less likely, since the preferences of the president on trade are more likely to be different than those of the party which controls Congress. Because delegation is less likely, there is more scope for particularistic interests to affect trade policy; if one argues (as most do) that protection is a less public good than liberalization, this implies that most particularistic demands will be for protection and that trade policy itself will become more protectionist. In addition, the majority party in Congress is far more willing to let a president of its own party claim credit for an international negotiating success than they would be for a president of an opposing party. The available empirical evidence tends to support this general line of analysis.[22]

Arguments about inter-branch relations shed light on the changing patterns of party support for liberalizing and protectionist measures. If a member of Congress is more willing to vote for a measure proposed by a president of her own party, then if the party occupying the White House changes, Congressional voting patterns will change even if the issues and the members of Congress do not. In the context of Republican presidents and Democratic congresses, the Democrats in Congress seem less willing to support internationalist positions than they did under Democratic presidents, while the Republicans in Congress are more willing. This phenomenon first attracted scholarly attention in studies conducted in the early 1960s of the transition from the Truman to the Eisenhower years, but there is no reason to believe that the process is not stable through the current era.[23]

Strategic Calculations

Of course, the parties-as-containers view is a caricature, and not just because of party discipline or the role of party control in setting the legislative agenda. Parties might well set their position on policy strategically, in anticipation of or in response to the positions of other domestic actors, foreign governments and foreign private interests. Trade policy choices by a country as large as the United States are bound to have an effect on the rest of the world, and the rest of the world is bound to react. It is in this context that the relation between parties and the trade policy "strategy" of the United States merits attention. The difference between the Republicans and Hawley-Smoot and the Democrats and the Reciprocal Trade Agreements Act is not that one was protectionist and the other was not. Rather, the first was categorical protection, whereas the second was contingent. (The fact that, at the time of Hawley-Smoot, some legislators saw the Europeans as the first to defect or about to defect anyway does not explain why they would adopt a non-contingent form of protection that offered little incentive for foreigners to bargain over liberalization).[24]

It is not liberalism *per se* but rather reciprocity that is the dominant American trade policy strategy in the post-1934 world. If American policy were not founded on reciprocity, it would be a simple matter to repeal the Hawley-Smoot tariff and have a unified tariff schedule. The fact that no President since Hoover has done so (in the absence of most-favored-nation status, Hawley-Smoot is still the governing tariff of the United States) is ample testimony to the potency of reciprocity.

The more recent interest in "fair" trade is but another manifestation of a policy option that has been persistently attractive to policy-makers in the United States since the 1890s. Given the size of the American internal market, it would be surprising indeed if nobody thought about using access to that market as a bargaining chip to open foreign markets. A party in which import competing interests dominated the formation of party positions would be much less likely to pursue this strategy; conversely, a party that appealed particularly to large, oligopolistic and at least potentially outward looking industries would be most likely to favor policies that embodied the insights of "strategic" trade theory.[25] Regardless of the domestic interests that are politically ascendant, the fact that all countries tend to view the lowering of trade barriers as a "concession" rather than as something that is in their own interests means that the United States must either hope to take a free ride on the tariff negotiations of others via most-favored-nation treatment extended to it, or else it must "play the game" by offering reciprocal reductions in exchange for those extended to it.[26] Given the size and importance of the United States, it is not likely that it could free ride for long, so reciprocity is the only reliable way for the United States to improve its access to foreign markets.

Another dimension of American trade strategy has been its degree of commitment to multilateralism. Preferential trade agreements are a way of exploiting trade bargaining power without permitting the benefits given to foreigners to "leak" through most-favored-nation clauses to those who did not themselves make any concessions. In the 1980s American trade policy for the first time in the post-1934 era turned away from a single-minded commitment to multilateralism and towards a more mixed strategy, relying more on "mini-lateral" preferential trading arrangements such as the Caribbean Basin Initiative, the free trade agreement with Israel, the free trade agreement with Canada, and now the proposed agreement with Mexico and Canada. To some extent this change can be attributed to increasing American pessimism about the prospects for continued progress on trade issues within the multilateral GATT framework.[27]

Seen in this light, "mini-lateral" initiatives accomplish two tasks. First, they provide immediate and specific market openings without depending on the successful completion of the Uruguay Round. Thus they offer stable or improved market access to internationally oriented US producers as a sort of "insurance" against lack of progress within GATT or even the disintegration of the GATT system. Second, the demonstrated willingness of the US to negotiate such agreements demonstrates that the US is not willing to take the "sucker's payoff" that would result if it were the last nation to cling to a multilateral framework while other important actors defected to preferential trading arrangements. This demonstration, however, is double-edged, because it could just as plausibly promote more boldness in other nations' efforts to create preferential arrangements and dishearten those whose interest in making the multilateral system work is contingent on their perception of the degree of American commitment to the cause. When the nation that for decades has championed multilateral trade arrangements begins to adopt numerous preferential arrangements, others may well conclude that only a *pro forma* commitment to multilateralism is sufficient.

The shift towards preferential agreements may also be partly due to firms' changing strategic calculus. Although the issue is usually neglected in discussions of their political preferences for trade legislation, it requires no great leap of the imagination to argue that firms react to the political risks posed by potential or actual changes in foreign and domestic openness. A slightly more specific point is that firms can evaluate markets in the same way that investors evaluate possible changes in their portfolios, in terms of both expected rates of return and the variability of that return. Both moments are affected by market-driven phenomena in addition to political risk. From both a political and a purely economic point of view, "global" strategies may now be riskier or promise relatively less attractive returns than "mini-lateral" trade strategies that guarantee market access on a privileged basis. Scholarly investigations of firms' current strategizing on trade politics are scarce, but enough is known to substantiate the claim that they can change their positions on domestic legislation depending on their reading of the political environment for trade in foreign countries.[28]

A third strategic issue in trade policy has to do with the decisions about what to liberalize, and what to leave alone or even to protect further. There is no reason why tariff or non-tariff barriers all must move in the same direction at the same time.

The selective granting of protection to some large import-competing industries can remove any incentive they might have to organize a larger, more encompassing protectionist coalition that would launch a large-scale attack on open trade. The side payments given by the Kennedy administration to textiles and apparel, oil and a few other industries in order to secure the smooth passage of the Trade Expansion Act of 1962 are a classic example of this. The use of voluntary export restraints could have the same effect, as long as they are limited in number, confined to the most politically sensitive industries and do not stimulate even more demands for non-tariff protection. Judging whether selective protection is in fact "protectionist" in overall effects requires an analysis of the political consequences of such protection in addition to the analysis of the economic consequences.

A fourth dimension of trade policy strategy arises from the fact that there are different audiences for trade policy, and that their degree of sophistication varies greatly. A theory of "optimal obfuscation" in the making of trade policy is appropriate for understanding a world in which there are large pockets of (rationally?) ignorant voters.[29] The phenomenon of members of Congress voting one way in committee and another way on the floor is a well known example of this kind of obfuscating behavior. Voting for and even passing protectionist legislation in full knowledge that it will be successfully vetoed, or taking a hard line in multilateral negotiations over agricultural protection in full knowledge that one is proposing a position that will result in deadlock are examples of obfuscation that could never occur if all participants in the political system were fully informed.

The Role of Ideas and the Possibility of a "Statist" Policy Process

Within economic theory very little attention is given to the question of how agents form perceptions of their world, and whether these perceptions are accurate. Economists have generally argued that market forces are sufficiently strong that they either furnish prompt feedback to the agents that their views are incorrect, or else they simply lead to extinction of the agents with incorrect views. However accurate this may be as a characterization of purely economic events, it is questionable as a characterization of political systems.

The limited number of political parties, the relative infrequency of elections compared to the number of decisions that a government makes, the "principal-agent" problems involving voters (they "hire" the politicians, but they generally do not have access to accurate and inexpensive information about the performance of those they hire or the hypothetical performance of alternative hires) all work to reduce the promptness and certainty of political feedback mechanisms. (Of course, if we no longer assume that people know what they want, then feedback as a corrective to bad policy becomes even more problematic.) Because of this, some have concluded that the study of policy formation ought to focus more on the sources of decision-makers' beliefs about the effects of policies.[30] A claim sometimes made about the decision-makers' beliefs is that government officials pursue a conception of the national interest that is at least partially informed by an ideology, a view of how the world works and how it should be organized that is independent of the personal desires of the officials or the specific demands made on them by private interests.[31]

In principle, this contention is highly plausible. It might well be true that in the short run government officials are essentially unconstrained by societal pressures. Then the logic of "public choice" models, which generally treat political processes as having feedback mechanisms comparable to those of idealized markets, would not hold. However, whether this view is accurate is an empirical matter. Let us consider one well known case that is often taken to be a classic example of the role of ideas in the formation of trade policy, the Trade Expansion Act of 1962.

The Trade Expansion Act of 1962 was the subject of one of the most ambitious and most influential research projects in political science. The project findings, published in 1963 as *American Business and Public Policy: The Politics of Foreign Trade*, essentially stood the argument of Schattschneider on its head: regardless of what happened in 1930, by the 1950s and early 1960s interest groups were led by rather than leading the government; they were weak and ignorant, rather than strong and sophisticated; and government decision-makers held all the high cards.[32] Thus, Schattschneider is made to appear to be offering at most a description of policy making in a world where Congress still makes tariffs directly, rather than delegating this authority to the President.[33] However, just why this act of delegation would serve to weaken interest groups is never made clear.

If *American Business and Public Policy* is correct in its contention that private interests had relatively little influence over this legislation, it should be a simple matter to identify those members of the new Kennedy administration who were ideologically committed to more open trade and follow the process by which these officials fashioned this legislation and secured its passage. I began to do just this using published and unpublished material and quickly noticed some startling anomalies.

First, the new president was not a free-trader, even in a loose sense of that term. John Kennedy has been described by Seymour Harris, the Harvard economist who had worked with him since 1952, as "what you might call a structuralist." Partly because of his New England background, he tended to support protection for textiles, and he was hardly a doctrinaire free trader.[34] His interest and involvement in the content of the Trade Expansion Act was minimal until the fall of 1961, after most of the major decisions about the content had already been made.[35]

Kennedy's major concerns seem to have been tactical: a bill in 1962 or 1963? an ambitious bill or a narrowly inscribed one?[36] George Ball, Kennedy's Under Secretary of State for Economic Affairs, initiated work on what became the Trade Expansion Act during the presidential

transition period. Ball, who has been described as "working largely
outside the State Department bureaucracy,"[37] eventually turned over day
to day management of the legislative effort to Howard Petersen.
Petersen, a Republican banker, and a member of the Committee for
Economic Development, had been an active spokesman for CED views on
trade and aid beginning in the mid-1950s.

The Committee for Economic Development took a position favoring
foreign aid, multilateral tariff reductions and direct foreign investment to
integrate both western Europe and the less developed world into a global
economy.[38] After the 1960 election, Petersen was appointed by Kennedy
to the National Security Council staff. (This was at a time when the staff
was small enough that the opportunity cost of a specialized position was
much larger than later). Petersen's assistant, Myer Rashish, describes
their work on the bill as being conducted with little involvement by even
the White House staff. After senior officials, including Kennedy,
approved the legislation and authorized the effort to achieve its passage,
Petersen enlisted a corps of what used to be called "dollar a year men" to
manage the lobbying effort:

> But we had people on our staff, some of them, in fact most of them, sort
> of casual people who were there on a non-payment basis, they were there
> for free, who got assignments. There was one fellow who got sort of the
> international business community, and another guy drew labor, and so on.
> But it was awfully mixed up and, as I say, haphazard. We also made sure
> that the various agencies—State and Commerce principally, Treasury and
> Agriculture and so on, were doing their share with regard to their
> constituencies both in the public at large and on the Hill.[39]

If Rashish's account is accurate, then the involvement of elected officials
and the formal organizations of the Federal government in this legislative
effort was peripheral to the work of persons whose ties to the
administration were far more ephemeral. Indeed, in their efforts to pass
the legislation it seems that these outsiders directed the actions of the
government agencies.

And, further, if Rashish's account is correct in its depiction of a policy-
making process that runs largely outside of the White House and the
Cabinet departments, and if *American Business and Public Policy* is correct
in arguing that there was very little interest group involvement in this
legislation, then the Trade Expansion Act would seem to be a political
orphan, or an example of statutory spontaneous generation. Such an
apparently absurd conclusion only raises more questions.

For instance, why would the president and other high officials delegate
responsibility for managing this legislative effort to a group with such a

tenuous connection to the administration? If producer groups have a lot at stake in comprehensive trade legislation, why was their Congressional lobbying effort neither particularly well-funded or skillful? If their Congressional lobbying effort was so anemic, why then did Kennedy and his advisors expect "a more bitter political fight than anything they have had to face so far"?[40]

The resolution to these puzzles is to be found in an aspect of political communication neglected by *American Business and Public Policy.* That work errs decisively in focusing heavily on interest groups' lobbying of Congress at the expense of an in-depth analysis of their lobbying of the executive branch.[41] Interest groups lobby the executive branch all the time, and their lobbying extends from the various agencies and their officials through the White House to the president himself.

In the case of the Trade Expansion Act, the most important negotiations between an interest group and the executive branch involved the textile industry. The industry and the Kennedy Administration began to bargain before the 1960 election, when Senator Hollings of South Carolina approached the Kennedy campaign on behalf of the textile industry. Rashish describes what happened next:

> Mike Feldman [a Kennedy aide] asked me to draft an exchange of correspondence on this point. I drafted both ends of the exchange. The response from Kennedy to Hollings was, however, modified, contrary to what I would have liked to have seen at the time. I thought it was a premature commitment to do some things for the textile industry. And that letter served as a basis for a lot of dealings, comings and going, on textile policy which followed. That was the first commitment, so to speak, that Kennedy made in that area.[42]

Kennedy carried the textile producing states of South Carolina, North Carolina, Georgia and Alabama in 1960. In fact, they were the only Southern states east of the Mississippi that he did carry. After he took office, his administration made a series of administrative decisions and embarked on a series of policy initiatives designed to aid the industry, but the industry was not always fully satisfied with these efforts. These initiatives sparked a lot of communication between the administration on the one hand and the industry and its Congressional allies on the other. In the course of this process, the two sides seemed to converge on a solution to their bargaining problem.[43]

Most importantly for the subsequent success of a general trade bill, the administration fought hard and successfully for both a Short Term and a Long Term Agreement on international regulation of textile imports. It was widely understood at the time that success on this front was necessary if a comprehensive trade bill had any chance of passage. Some analysts even argued that the global textile trade would have become even more ridden with protectionism had not these agreements been enacted.[44]   Presidential aides meeting with officials of the American Cotton Manufacturers Institute secured their support for Kennedy's trade legislation in March, 1962.[45]   Kennedy subsequently received the Congressional votes from the textile states that he needed to pass the Trade Expansion Act.

Seen in this light, the fixation of *American Business and Public Policy* on the capacity of interest groups to lobby Congress and to mobilize grass roots sentiment on specific legislation seems at best incomplete. In the context of the relationships between the textile industry and the administration, these kinds of high visibility Congressional lobbying efforts were the icing on the cake. What seems much more central to the outcome were the high-level bargains that were worked out between the Executive branch and industry representatives. Whatever the weaknesses of the textile interest groups, they were apparently cohesive enough to deliver on their end of the bargain in the 1960 election and in the 1962 Congressional voting. They were apparently able to mobilize members of Congress and, through their contacts with notables, area voters without being very sophisticated or devoting a great amount of trade association resources to doing so.

The fact that the textile interest groups seem less aggressive and sophisticated in dealing with Congress in 1962 than in 1930 may be due, as the authors of *American Business and Public Policy* noted, to the fact that with the Reciprocal Trade Agreements Act of 1934 Congress had delegated much of its authority in making trade policy to the President.[46] Interest groups were not as good at dealing with Congress as a whole because they did not have to be. In the formulation of trade legislation, much of the game had shifted to the other end of Pennsylvania Avenue, and the kinds of broad lobbying efforts apparently envisioned by Bauer, Pool and Dexter as the hallmark of effective lobbying are only critical on close floor votes. Arguably, a good lobbyist is one who is never in the position of having to beat the bushes to win such a vote.   There is nothing in the history of the interaction between the textile industry and the Federal government in this period to suggest otherwise.

In summary, the events surrounding the passage of the Trade Expansion Act seem to support a somewhat more sophisticated interest group model of trade policy formation than the one offered by *American Business and Public Policy*. Accordingly, is difficult to see how these events would impel students of trade politics to jettison that more sophisticated model in favor of a "statist" interpretation that treats government officials as unconstrained, at least in the short run.

Conclusion

Social scientific theories are often more useful for explanation than prediction, and theories of American trade policy are no exception. This brief survey of forces impinging on trade policy has identified a lengthy list of factors that might plausibly affect the future of the North American Free Trade Agreement and overall American trade policy. Given certain assumptions about macroeconomic conditions, the electoral success of the two dominant political parties, changes in comparative advantage and in the composition of the parties' support coalitions, the course of events in multilateral trade talks, and the likely policy trajectory of other major trading nations, one could perhaps make some intelligent guesses about the trajectory of American policy. However useful that exercise may be to some, a less ambitious but less speculative application of these findings is simply as a guide to the consequences for trade policy of the specific interventions or events mentioned here. Given the limitations of existing work, particularly the limited empirical base for many conclusions, perhaps some of the "stylized facts" about trade policy presented here may eventually turn out to be not very robust.

A more general but perhaps more enduring insight that can be gained from this research is that what matters in shaping political outcomes in trade politics is much less the general equilibrium consequences of policies than the set of specific partial equilibrium effects on politically influential groups. Politicians are not philosopher kings or queens, bent on maximizing national income over some time period. They may well have their own ideas about what is the best trade policy for the nation, but in implementing those ideas, they will be heavily influenced by the contours of the political landscape that they confront. In politicians' thinking about a possible North American Free Trade Agreement, and thus in their decision-making about whether or not to vote for NAFTA, its general economic effects in the long run will be much less salient to them than the specific economic effects in the short run.

Just as in the case of the 1962 Trade Expansion Act, one can expect politicians to be prepared to accommodate those who are harmed by a new, liberalizing trade policy and have the capacity to bring pressure to bear. The accommodation of interests that do not possess politically relevant resources, particularly organization and money, is a far more uncertain matter. The political incentives for addressing long-term environmental degradation or the welfare of unorganized or weakly organized workers are hardly compelling. Because of this, it is an open question whether the redistributive effects of agreements such as this one are not so large that they swamp whatever aggregate improvement in national income may occur.

Notes

1. A recent survey of the literature on the political economy of trade is Arye L. Hillman, *The Political Economy of Protection* (New York: Harwood Academic, 1989). Hillman concentrates on formal models that for the most part are not specific to any single nation.

2. Ibid., page 4, describes these models as applying to democracies. Hillman's viewpoint is overly restrictive, since regimes that are not democracies might nonetheless have highly competitive political systems. It is competition, rather than democracy *per se*, that is required for these models to make sense.

3. Throughout this chapter the term "protection" will refer to tariff and non-tariff barriers to international trade.

4. E. E. Schattschneider, *Politics, Pressures and the Tariff* (New York: Prentice-Hall, 1935).

5. Steven Magee, "Three Simple Tests of the Stolper-Samuelson Theorem," in Peter Oppenheimer ed., *Issues in International Economics* (Stocksfield, England: Oriel Press, 1978).

6. Kym Anderson and Robert E. Baldwin, "The Political Market for Protection in Industrial Countries," in Ali M. El-Agraa, ed., *Protection, Cooperation, Integration and Development: Essays in Honour of Professor Hiroshi Kitamura* (London: Macmillan, 1987).

7. Margaret M. Commins, "From Security to Trade in U.S.-Latin American Relations: Explaining U.S. Support for a Free Trade Agreement with Mexico," paper presented at the Seventeenth International Congress of the Latin American Studies Association, Los Angeles, California, September 24- 27, 1992.

8. A recent example in this genre is William R. Keech and Kyoungsan Pak, "Partisanship, Institutions, and Change in Contemporary American Trade Politics," unpublished paper, University of North Carolina, Chapel Hill, 1992. Another is Susanne Lohmann and Sharyn O'Halloran, "Delegation and Accommodation in U.S. Trade Policy," paper presented to the National Bureau of Economic Research Conference on Political Economics, November 15-16, 1991.

9. James Cassing, Timothy J. McKeown and Jack Ochs, "The Political Economy of the Tariff Cycle," *American Political Science Review*, Vol. 80, 1986, p. 853.

10. Brian Roberts, "Political Institutions, Policy Expectation and the 1980 Election: A Financial Market Analysis," *American Journal of Political Science*, Vol. 34, 1990, pp 289-310.

11. Frank W. Taussig, *The Tariff History of the United States*, 7th edition (New York: G. P. Putnam's Sons, 1923). Stephen P. Magee, William A. Brock and Leslie Young, *Black Hole Tariffs and Endogenous Policy Theory: Political Economy in General Equilibrium* (Cambridge, U.K.: Cambridge University Press, 1989). Sidney Ratner, *The Tariff in American History* (New York: Van Nostrand, 1972).

12. In addition to Eric Uslaner's treatment of platform positions in this volume, Keech and Pak, "Partnership, Institutions, and Change," briefly surveys recent platform changes, with conclusions similar to Uslaner's.

13. J. David Richardson, "U.S. Trade Policy in the 1980s: Turns—and Roads not Taken," Working Paper #3725 (Cambridge, MA: National Bureau of Economic Research, 1991), p. 26.

14. Anderson and Baldwin, "The Political Market for Protection." Wendy Takacs, "Pressures for Protectionism: An Empirical Analysis," *Economic Inquiry*, Vol. 19, 1981, pp. 687-693. Michael Wallerstein, "Collective Bargaining and the Demand for Protection," *American Journal of Political Science*, Vol. 31, 1987, pp. 729-752. Cassing, McKeown and Ochs, "The Political Economy of the Tariff Cycle." Magee, Brock and Young, *Black Hole Tariffs*. Timothy J. McKeown, "A Liberal Trading Order? The Long-run Pattern of Imports to the Advanced Capitalist States," *International Studies Quarterly*, Vol. 35, 1991, pp. 151-172.

15. Magee, Brock, and Young, *Black Hole Tariffs*, chapter 13.

16. Data on U.S. exports, imports and GNP are taken from *Statistical Abstract of the United States, 1991* (Washington, D.C.: U.S. Government Printing Office, 1991), pp. 432, 790.

17. The possibility of incompatibility of a party's fiscal and monetary policy objectives with macroeconomic conditions is discussed by Timothy W. Amato, "Shocks to the System: A Theory of Partisan Political Economy," Ph. D. diss., University of North Carolina (Chapel Hill, 1991). However, he does not extend his analysis to cover trade policy.

18. For the theory, see Richardson, "U.S. Trade Policy in the 1980s." For some evidence on the role of the macro policy environment in the United States, see Magee, Brock and Young, *Black Hole Tariffs*, chapter 13.

19. D. Roderick Kiewiet and Matthew D. McCubbins, *The Logic of Delegation: Congressional Parties and the Appropriations Process* (Chicago: University of Chicago Press, 1991).

20. Sam Peltzman, "Constituent Interest and Congressional Voting," *Journal of Law & Economics*, Vol. 27, April 1984, 181-210.

21. Arguments supporting the contention that more efficient policy emanates from those with larger constituencies are found in Kenneth A. Shepsle and Barry R. Weingast, "Political Preferences for the Pork Barrel: A Generalization," *American Journal of Political Science*, Vol. 25, 1981, pp 96-111; Magee, Brock and Young, *Black Hole Tariffs*, pp. 98-99; and Susanne Lohmann and Sharyn O'Halloran, "Delegation and Accommodation in U.S. Trade Policy."

22. See Lohmann and O'Halloran, "Delegation and Accommodation in U.S. Trade Policy."

23. Leroy N. Rieselbach, *The Roots of Isolationism: Congressional Voting and Presidential Leadership in Foreign Policy* (Indianapolis: Bobbs-Merrill, 1966).

24. Barry Eichengreen, "The Political Economy of the Hawley-Smoot Tariff," National Bureau of Economic Research Working Paper #2001 (1986).

25. The literature on strategic trade theory has mushroomed in the last ten years. For a good introduction, see Paul Krugman, ed., *Strategic Trade Policy and the New International Economics* (Cambridge, MA: M.I.T. Press, 1986). Regardless

of its value as a normative basis for economic policy, strategic trade theory is a powerful analytical tool for understanding the political behavior of particular sectors.

26. Kenneth S. Chan, "The International Negotiation Game: Some Evidence from the Tokyo Round," *Review of Economics and Statistics*, Vol. 67, August, 1985, pp. 456-464.

27. Sidney Weintraub, "A Note on Trade Discrimination," *Rivista Internazionale di Scienze Economiche e Commerciali*, Vol. 33, 1986, pp. 353-370; Commins, "From Security to Trade."

28. See Commins, "From Security to Trade." See also Vinod K. Aggarwal, "Service Sector Negotiations in the Uruguay Round," *The Fletcher Forum of World Affairs*, Vol. 16, 1992, pp. 35-54.

29. Magee, Brock and Young, *Black Hole Tariffs*, pp. 257-263, theorize that greater sophistication does not necessarily portend lower protection if protectionist forces can create or take advantage of policy measures that result in more "net obfuscation" than occurred previously. They cite the increased fashionability of VERs as a possible example of this.

30. For a recent example, see Judith Goldstein, "Ideas, Institutions and American Trade Policy," *International Organization*, Vol. 42, 1988, pp. 179-218.

31. A clear statement of this position can be found in Stephen D. Krasner, *Defending the National Interest: Raw Materials Investments and U.S. Foreign Policy* (Princeton, NJ: Princeton University Press, 1978), especially chapter one.

32. Raymond A. Bauer, Ithiel de Sola Pool and Lewis Anthony Dexter, *American Business and Public Policy: The Politics of Foreign Trade* (New York: Atherton, 1963).

33. Ibid., p. 455.

34. Oral history interview of Seymour E. Harris, conducted by Arthur Schlesinger, Jr. for the John F. Kennedy Library Oral History Program, 24 and 31 August, 1964.

35. Oral history interview of Myer Rashish conducted by John F. Stewart, September 11, 1967, Washington, D.C., John F. Kennedy Library Oral History Program, p. 18.

36. Thomas W. Zeiler, *American Trade and Power in the 1960s* (New York: Columbia University Press, 1992), pp. 64-67.

37. Rashish oral interview, p. 7.

38. Thomas Victor DiBacco, "Return to Dollar Diplomacy? American Business Reaction to the Eisenhower Foreign Aid Program, 1953-1961," Ph. D. dissertation, The American University, 1965, pp. 114-115.

39. Rashish oral interview, p. 21.

40. On this latter point, see Wallace Carroll, "President Ready for Early Move on Freer Trade," *New York Times* November 13, 1961, p. 1.

41. This point is developed at much greater length in Jeri-Lynn Scofield, "Foreign Policy as Domestic Politics: The Political Economy of U.S. Trade Policy 1960-1975," D. Phil. dissertation, Oxford University, 1992.

42. Rashish oral interview, pp. 2-3.

43. Zeiler, *American Trade and Power*, chapter 3, describes this process in detail.

44. On the 1961 negotiations, see Vinod K. Aggarwal, *Liberal Protectionism: The International Politics of Organized Textile Trade* (Berkeley: University of California Press, 1985), pp. 85-94.

45. Bauer, Pool, and Dexter, *American Business and Public Policy*, p. 362.

46. Ibid., p. 455. It might also be due to different macroeconomic conditions in 1962 than in 1930. See Cassing, McKeown and Ochs, "The Political Economy of the Tariff Cycle," p. 860.

5

The Trade Policies of Canada's Grits and Tories, 1840-1988

Duncan McDowall

It was March 1876, and the nation, particularly its would-be manufacturers, anxiously awaited the federal budget. Depression stalked the land. The Parliamentary Committee on the Causes of the Present Depression had just provided a grim portrait of the woes of Canada's stripling manufacturers. American producers, it was alleged, were "dumping" surplus goods onto the Canadian market. Expectations ran high. Would Ottawa protect its suffering manufacturers, or would the foreign onslaught be allowed to continue?

Now nearly a decade into their nationhood, Canadians were getting their first taste of alternative government. Three years earlier, Canada's first prime minister, John A. Macdonald, had been shamed into resignation, the result of a sordid railway scandal. The next spring, the voters unceremoniously dumped his Liberal-Conservative coalition and brought in the Liberals. Earlier, Macdonald's political pragmatism had fashioned Canadian nationhood in the mid-1860s and in 1867 given it its first administration. His party was little more than a loose coalition, held together by a vaguely-defined commitment to national unity and certain inherited precepts of acceptable policy. One was the notion, dating from the late 1850s, that government might levy tariffs on imports for revenue purposes and to provide "incidental protection" for fledgling Canadian manufacturers. Such was his instinct for the fragility of Canadian polity that Macdonald knew that any precipitous departure from this minimal protection, upward or downward, would surely cause discontent on the farm or in the factory, thereby endangering his shaky coalition.

The Pacific Scandal of 1873, not trade policy, proved Macdonald's undoing. In an age that gave political corruption wide latitude, the blatant influence-seeking activities of some of Macdonald's railway supporters managed to sour public confidence in Canada's preeminent "Father of Confederation." The principal beneficiary of this revulsion was the opposition Liberal Party, a ragtag of Confederation "also-rans" led by dour and straight-spoken Alexander Mackenzie. Lacking an alternative vision of nationhood, the Liberals (or Grits, as they were known) had pecked away ineffectually at Macdonald's regime. Mackenzie lacked Macdonald's plasticity. His heart was closest to the interests of rural Canada, his mind shaped by Manchester Liberalism. Canada's farmers lived and died by foreign markets, and anything that impeded their trade smacked of inefficiency and special interest. If Canada had ever enjoyed a golden age, it was when its products enjoyed unrestricted access to the U.S. market under the Reciprocity Treaty of 1854-66. On this Mackenzie's party was united. Free trade was the loud advice the Liberal leader received from the country's ranking Liberal, Senator George Brown, the proprietor of the Toronto *Globe* and arch foe of Macdonald. For finance minister, Mackenzie selected another free-trading Grit stalwart, Richard Cartwright, who in 1869 had defected from the Tories when Macdonald passed him over for the finance portfolio; he would bear the grudge for life. Tories soon branded him the "Blue Ruin Knight."

Having exiled Macdonald, Canadians tried to discern what a Grit Canada might be. Much was unclear. For instance, the Liberals had only a tenuous presence in all-important Quebec. It was clear that Mackenzie's government would be lean and economical, little inclined to meddle in the economic life of the nation with tariffs. Almost immediately, Senator Brown was despatched to Washington to sniff out the possibilities of renewed reciprocity with the United States. Rumors indicated that the Americans might be interested in a twenty-one year pact invoking free trade in natural resources. It seemed a welcome tonic for a nation locked in an economic recession. Cartwright would provide the descant with a budget that would revise the tariff downward.

The Liberals quickly learned that Manchester Liberalism was more easily promised on the hustings than practiced in the cabinet room. The Americans proved cool to Brown's blandishments, while back home the manufacturing community found common cause in decrying any move towards a nation they claimed was "dumping" goods onto the depressed Canadian market. The depression, Cartwright learned, had cut severely into government revenues. Any tariff cut would further impoverish Ottawa. In his 1874 budget, Cartwright therefore stood pat. He would not "disturb existing interests." A mild inflation of tariffs was the result, Cartwright arguing that his party could live with a revenue tariff.

Cartwright's inability to banish protectionism in 1874 seeded an anxiety in political and economic circles that festered for the next two years. The depression persisted, and ailing manufacturers daily demonstrated new skill in bringing collective pressure on the government for continued if not heightened tariff relief. They cleverly presented themselves as acting in the 'national' interest, not as a selfish single interest. Cartwright wavered. Perhaps another 2 1/2 percent on the general tariff might ease the depression and help to replenish Ottawa's coffers. The disconcerted Tories, their leader Macdonald dispirited and often intoxicated, watched delegations of industrialists trek through Cartwright's office. Interspersed were visits of low tariff advocates, namely, importers, agriculturalists and ardent free traders. Which way would the minister turn?

These taut days preceding the 1876 budget spawned one of Canada's most durable political anecdotes. Charles Tapper, the Tories' finance critic, is said to have been so befogged by Cartwright's deliberations that he appeared in the House of Commons on budget day, March 10, with two speeches. In his right pocket, Tapper bore a stinging attack on the Liberals' decision to embrace protectionism by boosting tariffs by as much as 20 percent. In the left, he carried a defence of the tariff, readied to uphold protectionism if Cartwright failed to abandon his free trade principles. Not long after Cartwright began his budget speech, Tapper pulled the text from his left pocket. Cartwright was sticking with the revenue tariff. A new polarity in Canadian trade politics was, almost by political accident, asserting itself: the Grits were the free traders and the Tories the incipient protectionists. "I had made up my mind on the question of protection," Cartwright later recalled, "and was in no way inclined to give it any countenance. We intended to stand or fall on a revenue tariff." This was "no time for experiments." Sensing opportunity, Macdonald sprang into action. A "national policy" of tariff protection could create wealth for *all* classes and in doing so perpetuate the work of national solidification he had begun in 1867.[1]

Whether or not the contents of Tapper pockets that March day are apocryphal, the story provides a wonderful weather vane of Canadian politics and trade policy.[2] It suggests steadfastness and opportunism. Although the Tories had flirted with protectionism before 1876, Macdonald seized on Cartwright's adherence to free trade to take exclusive possession of the principle. Through that summer, he tested the idea at a series of political picnics across Ontario and Quebec. When farmers, businessmen and laborers warmed to his protectionist talk, he dubbed it the National Policy and marched with it to victory at the polls in 1878. The Grits emerged from the drama of the 1876 budget tightly bound to a rump of free trade support, largely on the farm and in the Maritimes, but unable to maintain a national platform of support.

It was twenty years before the Liberals again won national favor. Macdonald went to his grave in 1891, bequeathing to the nation a party riddled with the cancer of cultural and linguistic dissension. By the time

Charles Tapper got hold of it in 1896, the only reliable aspect of Tory policy on which he could safely campaign was the success of the National Policy "infant industries" in bringing prosperity to the land. Most voters agreed but voted contrariwise, succumbing to the Liberals' promise to heal the wounds of race and region. Wilfrid Laurier took power. Initially recruited by Alexander Mackenzie, Laurier had baited the Tories in 1876 on their high protectionism, but now he was more sanguine. Many expected him in 1896 to select the "Blue Ruin Knight," the venerable Richard Cartwright, as his finance minister, but the new government instead appointed the more pliable William Fielding of Nova Scotia. Cartwright was relegated to the trade and commerce portfolio.

Once again in opposition, Tapper found himself looking across the Commons at the Liberals on budget day. During the 1896 campaign, the Grits had again professed their love of a "revenue tariff." Once in power, they had canvassed industrial opinion on the tariff issue. By budget day 1897, however, Tapper would not have troubled to prepare two texts in anticipation of Fielding's offering. The Grits were going to keep the tariff. They would tinker with it, adding a level of preference for British trade, but Fielding saw the folly of dismantling it and would not follow Cartwright's path. The indignant Tories cried political hypocrisy. After years of bashing protectionism, the Grits were now its champions. Former Tory finance minister George Foster resorted to Biblical language: "They have lifted up their voice, and behold! they have blessed it".[3]

Political opportunism had carried the day. Cartwright retired to a cranky existence on the margins of Liberal power. His outspoken adherence to free trade had become a political liability for a prime minister intent on building national unity, and strident trade politics divided the nation. Cartwright saw other, hidden interests at work. The tariff, he later wrote in his memoirs, had exerted an "evil effect" on Canadian politics. It had fathered "a class of influential men" whose primary interest was to "cook and mystify the tariff as to make their dupes, especially if they belong to the agricultural classes, believe that they are getting some share of the plunder".[4]

Predicting Trade Policy: Some Abiding Determinants

In fact, the tariff in Canadian political history has been not so much "evil" as a telling indicator of the twists and turns of a complex society and economy in democratic action. As Cartwright's woe-begone career suggests, long-term adherence to principle, free trade or protectionism, offers a poor point of entry into this history. Trade has brought out the quintessential pragmatism of centrist Canadian politics. The nation has proved governable by the party best able to straddle divergent social, economic, regional and cultural values. Unbending adherence to narrow doctrines or causes can irreparably damage chances of holding broad political support and winning. Cartwright never came remotely near the prime ministership. Macdonald, Tapper and Laurier all developed an instinct for pliable trade politics, and all came to occupy the office.

The history of Canada's two centrist parties has thus been periodically punctuated by astonishing role reversals, "flip-flops" in contemporary political parlance. Our political history has been mile-posted by federal elections in which trade policy has monopolized the agenda: 1878, 1891, 1911, 1921, 1925, 1930 and, like a grand finale, 1988. The Liberals have "flipped" with the greatest regularity but also only partially until the late twentieth century. Laurier's search for the center of Canadian politics led him, perhaps, on the most circuitous journey: from free trade in 1891 to protectionism in 1896 and back to free trade in 1911. The Conservatives have been more consistently protectionist, except for one grand back flip in 1988. Yet, the Tories never lost sight of the free trade option, what may be called the "Washington option" was seldom out of their political calculations. For instance, while the 1935 Canadian-American trade treaty was held by Mackenzie King as evidence of the Liberals' abiding faith in freer trade, the Tory protectionist R. B. Bennett had set the process in motion. Defeat at the polls removed him from the final negotiation.

Straightforward political opportunism offers an expedient explanation, at first sight, for the meanderings of the Tories and Grits on trade policy. But opportunism begs the question of what drives such self-interest. Lacking any powerfully unifying notion of national mission, such as has shaped U.S. nationhood, Canada has had to construct a delicate nationality that constantly balances and adjudicates its constituent parts. Notions of "trade following the flag" or "Made in Canada" campaigns have had little resonance in Canada; Canada's trade agenda has been set by a hodge-podge of more discrete pressures. Its overall pulse has been dictated by the abiding verities of a nation that has carved out an existence as a sparsely populated, attenuated country on the margin of powerful metropolitan economies. To understand Canada's trade politics, one must first recognize these fundamentals, which perennially emerged when Canadian Conservatives and Liberals gathered in convention, caucus and cabinet to plot Canada's trade direction. The opportunism emerges from the way in which each party orders and acts upon the interplay of these varied economic, social and cultural influences.

Canada has always had a trade-oriented economy. As a rule of thumb, Canada has generated 30 percent of its GNP from trade. Since

European discovery in the sixteenth century, Canada has staked its economic vitality on its ability to export its natural resources [fish, fur, wheat, present day electricity] to sustain a high standard of living reliant upon the import of finished goods. One of the distinctive contributions of Canadian economics has been the "staples thesis," elaborated in the 1920s and 1930s by scholars like Harold Innis.[5] Canada, Innis argued, is best understood in terms of the social, political and economic implications of the country's reliance on staple exports. Other Canadian economists, notably N. S. B. Gras at Harvard and W. A. Mackintosh at Queen's, demonstrated how staple development was orchestrated by relations with the "metropolitan" markets of Europe and the United States.

Trade dependency has made Canada highly vulnerable to cyclical downturns in world commodity trade. Access to reliable markets has been an obsession for Canadian commodity producers and merchants. The rhythm of trade policy is often best understood in terms of periodic downturns or collapses in the markets for Canadian commodities: the end of assured access to the British market in the 1840s or the crash of 1929.

As a developing nation, Canada has always been capital and technology poor. Access to assured markets has historically paralleled access to foreign capital and technology. For instance, trade earnings have offset the balance of payments implications of tangible imports, and also the costs of servicing foreign borrowing and technology transfer.

Canada's sense of its national identity has often been at cross purposes with the reality of its economic dependency on external markets. Canada's otherwise amorphous national identity can quickly and powerfully coalesce around anti-American sentiment or a rejection of what is seen as the vestiges of "colonial" control from Europe, particularly Britain. The "loyalty" issue can act as the potential trump card in any national debate, loyalty being construed as a loose set of national values (such as the rule of law) that might be put at risk by closer ties with a major trading partner.

Canada has traditionally invoked the state power as a means of offsetting the implications of its precarious nationhood. Canadians have traditionally looked to the state to ease the risk of building a nation. In the nineteenth century, government aided the construction of canals and railways in order to expedite staple exports. More recently, Ottawa has relied on publicly-owned crown corporations, for uranium and aircraft production for instance, to assert a Canadian presence in the marketplace. Such state intervention has often touched trade policy through procurement quotas, industrial subsidies and regional development practices.

Canada is a nation with keen and well articulated regional and sectional identities. The idea of Confederation was born out of the factiousness of the legislative union that had bound Upper and Lower

Canada since 1841; the active assertion of local identity had frustrated the emergence of national political cohesiveness. Mindful of the American Civil War, Canada's Fathers of Confederation fashioned a constitution they hoped would place the powers of the federation ahead of those of the regions. Trade was thus made a federal power. Macdonald wanted the provinces to be little more than "glorified municipalities," but the regions refused to surrender their identities and, through the courts, reasserted their power in culture and economics. They can, for instance, construct inter-provincial trade barriers (e.g. in the brewing industry). Provincial control of natural resources has meant that Canada's all-important natural resource exports are subject to two levels of political jurisdiction. Quebec's resilience as a "distinct society" in a broadly defined sense of "culture" has added complexity to this national scenario.

Successful federal governance by either of the two traditional parties has invariably hinged on their ability to win majority control of central Canada. Macdonald demonstrated his political acumen by welding together a centrist blue/*bleu* axis which gave both Ontario and Quebec a strong voice in Ottawa. In the twentieth century, the Liberals under King, St.Laurent, Pearson and Trudeau mastered this formula. It has been virtually impossible to form a government solely out of support drawn from what Cartwright once sourly described as the "shreds and patches" of Confederation, the Maritimes and the West.

Canada's system of parliamentary parties concentrates political power in the hands of party leaders. The centrifugal power of region and race in Canada has denied federal politics the luxury of an open and tolerant party system. From the days of Macdonald, the "Old Fox," Canadian party leaders have appropriated to themselves the right of divining what is in the best interests of the party and, by inference, the nation. If Americans can gain political influence through the door of any congressman, Canadians look only to the cabinet room door or those of its ministers, particularly their *primus inter pares*, the prime minister. Canada has elevated the role of the party "whip" far above that of its British progenitor. Former Prime Minister Pierre Trudeau once cruelly described backbench members of parliament as "nobodies." The party leader is thus the prism of policy.

Changing ideological and economic imperatives have washed over these characteristics, altering their intensity and relevance over the last century. Macdonald, for instance, would hardly have countenanced the direct intervention of crown corporations, but he was quite prepared to subsidize private railway promoters. Other factors might arguably be added to the list. But it is characteristics such as these which form the menu Liberals and Conservatives have consulted whenever the winds of trade carry a scent of change. Through much of our post-Confederation history, the two parties have been guided by pragmatism to select the same, protectionist dishes from the menu. What, then, explains the departures from this harmony? What led the Liberals in 1891 and 1911 to read the menu upside down? What led Brian Mulroney in the mid-1980s to abandon the protectionism initiated by his illustrious predecessor Macdonald a century earlier? Could it happen again?

Protectionism by Default: 1840-1896

Canada's adoption of protectionism in the 1870s was a second-best scenario. Canadians had a strong predilection for close bilateral trade ties since long before Confederation. Only when these have been denied has the nation resigned itself to an effort to build a protected home market. If Canada has ever had a trade ideology, it was its persistent infatuation with free trade with a major trading partner. The dramatic elections of 1891 and 1911, when the Grits embraced free trade but failed to win the nation, and 1988, when the Tories forsook protectionism and won the nation, were simply a return to Canada's long-stalled hope of free trade. Protectionism in this light has been the outcome of the opportunism of whatever party was quick enough to seize the reality of blocked access to wider trading fields and adjust accordingly. In the 1870s, Macdonald played this shifting role with panache, leaving the Liberals upholding free trade principles that might have been popular if they had looked practicable at the negotiating table in Washington.

Before the 1840s, Canada did not have a trade policy, at least a trade policy over which it had any autonomous control. In the sorry wake of the American Revolution, Britain had passed the Declaratory Act in 1778, acknowledging the colonies' right in principle to retain the revenues from any duties imposed by the mother country in the regulation of trade. The colonies of British North America were part of Britain's great mercantilist empire. They were captive suppliers of staples (fish, timber and grain) and avaricious consumers of English finished goods. Britain went to elaborate lengths to frustrate the development of trade with the new American republic; Canada's trade was conceived in east-west, transoceanic terms. The political elites in the BNA colonies predicated their "policies" on this world view. Petitions to the Colonial Secretary and pressure brought to bear on colonial governors emphasized the need for improvement by the state of trade arteries (the building of canals, roads and harbors) to facilitate the flow of staple exports. The Canada Trade Act of 1822 was passed in London, confirming the colonies' full right to their customs revenues but at the same time prohibiting the import of many American finished goods. This strategy was ineffectively resisted in the 1830s by early champions of the farm. Upper Canadian [Ontario] dissent bore a Jacksonian cast. Unimpeded trade, north, south, east or west, and the rights of those on the land began to find an echo in the platform of the Reform Party. Similar sentiments were echoed by Lower Canadian [Quebec] *patriotes.* These were hardly political parties. They were more loose coteries of political "outs." The tragi-comedy of the 1837-8 rebellions fractured the Reform cause and for the time being left the commercial elite free to pursue its mercantilist trade.

The triumph of "Little Englandism" in the 1840s shattered this framework and soon had significant political repercussions. Britain's hasty abandonment of its Corn and Navigation Laws diminished almost overnight Canada's access to what for so long had seemed a solid and assured market. The revised British Possessions Act of 1846 reiterated this message by delivering into the hands of colonial politicians the autonomous power of altering customs duties once set by London alone.[6] For the first time, Canadians were in a position to shape their own trade policy. But, with responsible government barely recognized and political parties little more than schools of "loose fish" liable to pursue personal or local interest before party policy, an alternative to mercantilism was slow to emerge. The end of imperial preference thus left the colonies contending with a "chaos of suggested panaceas, which included protection, free trade and annexation to the United States".[7]

Out of this chaos was molded Canada's first conscious trade policy. Desperate to re-establish access to an assured market, merchants from central Canada began to agitate for reciprocity with the United States. A volatile minority still smarting from England's *volte-face* briefly advocated annexation to the United States, but this instantly triggered a "loyalist" reaction which discredited the idea. Instead, more moderate business leaders, such as St.Catherines miller and publisher W. H. Merritt, agitated for reciprocity as a means of opening the U.S. market to Canadian grain and of diverting U.S. trade through Canadian arteries. Aided and abetted by U.S. sympathizers (who were able to curry U.S. favor for reciprocity through reputable voices such as *The North American Review*), Merritt provided an early example of an organized business lobby being able to effectively place its priorities on the national trade agenda. Merritt's influence reached the governor's office and by the late 1840s both of central Canada's embryonic parties, the Tories and Reformers, were pro-reciprocity. Merritt had found an issue around which "loose fish" could coalesce. A politician himself, Merritt also provided an effective example of central Canadian businessmen reaching out to other colonies (the Maritimes) to draw their support for a "national" policy of free trade.

The Reciprocity Treaty of 1854 was the fruit of all this mercantile agitation. In the wake of a major external shock, trade policy had been largely prescribed by the business class. The pursuit of reciprocity had helped to harden Canadian party politics as they emerged in the early 1850s. Porous party discipline was increasingly superseded by leader-led parties with an enforceable party "line."[8] But other interests interjected themselves into the trade calculus. A sharp commercial depression in 1857 pinched provincial revenues and tempted the government to raise customs duties to fatten its coffers. This it did in the famous Cayley-Galt budgets of 1859, the birth of the "revenue tariff" to which Cartwright would later so dearly cling. The same tariff also contained a hint of other things to come: protectionism. As a side effect, the Galt-Cayley tariff would offer "incidental protection" to Canadian manufacturers.

Canadian "business" has never been homogeneous. Today, "big" business has a distinctly different agenda from that of "small" business on issues like tax reform and free trade. In the 1850s, the commercialists who had championed reciprocity as a gangplank to American markets soon found themselves at odds with the country's nascent industrialists, who in the spirit of European theorists like Frederich List looked to the state for protection of their infant industries. Centered on Toronto and led by merchants such as Isaac Buchanan, the early protectionists formed an expedient alliance with "revenue tariff" politicians.

The economic ethos of the colonies remained low tariff and free trade oriented. From the outset, protectionists ran the political danger of having their demands for higher tariffs painted as narrow self-interest, a tax on the free trading farmer and fisherman. Even as the reciprocity treaty of 1854 crumbled under the pressure of U.S. resentment of rising Canadian tariffs and Civil War support for the Confederacy, the Reform-Liberal party continued to espouse free trade. Its leaders, George Brown and Alexander Mackenzie, saw the tariff as government meddling in a *laissez-faire* world. The Tories, led by John A. Macdonald and a series of Quebec *bleus*, also avowed free trade, but were not averse to the adept use of some protection, particularly if it raised some revenue for the government. Both parties were desperate to construct a centrist coalition that could govern the two culturally divided BNA colonies of the interior. Too extreme an attitude to trade jeopardized this strategy. Moderation was the key, one that ideally fit the door of free trade.

The achievement of Confederation in 1867 may be viewed in many lights. The need for a workable bicultural political union was certainly fundamental. The agreement was also driven by the need to replace or at least augment the market once afforded by the collapsed reciprocity treaty (which ceased in 1866) with an alternative broad market. Efforts were made to open markets in the Caribbean and Latin America. The undeveloped Canadian west also beckoned to Ontario traders. But the more immediate opportunity of union with the Maritime colonies in effect offered the two central Canadian colonies a free trade zone. On this, the Great 1864 Coalition of Tories and Reformers which carried Confederation were of one mind. Even the redoubtable George Brown could champion the pact; four colonies combined gave Manchester Liberalism that much more chance of success in North America. There was little talk of protectionism in 1867. Ardent promises of railway construction and federal aid to the nascent national economy might, by today's standards, be construed as a kind of early non-tariff protection. But that was all.

The onset of recession in the early 1870s reintroduced protectionism to the stage of Canadian politics. Canada's traditional staple trades and its would-be manufacturers both struggled; the recession would prove to be persistent, stretching down to the 1890s. It is important to note that even in darkest days of this slump free trade remained the preferred option of both of Canada's political parties. Macdonald, the most pragmatic of the party leaders, might toy with a shift towards protectionism, but only *after* he had ferreted around Washington in the hope of arousing American interest in free trade. Nonetheless, Macdonald and the Tories proved the moveable fixture in Canadian trade politics in the years down to the 1890s. As Peter Waite has so aptly put it, Macdonald "had an instinct for when it was time to lay out lines towards new policies, and so warp the ship along to a new berth."[9]

Macdonald's shift to protectionism in the late 1870s was the product of his determination to preserve a centrist coalition as his power base and the ability of Canadian business to convince him that protection could act as an important bonding agent for that coalition. Slow growth and U.S. dumping onto the Canadian market had revitalized the demand for "infant industry" protection among Canadian manufacturers. The twist now given the demand by its advocates was that tariffs served the *national* interest rather than the exclusive interest of business. Just as the role of their being "hewers of wood and drawers of water" in the old mercantilist scheme had tapped into Canadians' sense of self, now protection could be held up as a policy that furthered Canadian nationhood, not impeded it. As historian Ben Forster has so convincingly demonstrated, protectionism's ascendancy was the product the ability of central Canadian businessmen to organize and present themselves as national spokesmen. Long before any other interest group transcended the bonds of parochialism, business mastered the art of national lobbying, drawing on its innate organizational skills.[10] The creation of the CMA (Canadian Manufacturers' Association) in the 1870s gave business an effective means of molding and then transmitting a *national* message to politicians. The CMA perfected a system of standing sub-committees which could broker regional and sectional interests within business into a common stand before Ottawa politicians. Similarly, Canadian trade associations invariably prefixed their names with the word Dominion. It would be decades before Canada's farmers and laborers mastered the art of wrapping their interests in a flag of national purpose.

In the mid-1870s, the business community's protectionist urge piqued Macdonald's sense of political expediency. Still sullied by the Pacific Scandal and outflanked by Cartwright and the Grits on the issue of free trade and the revenue tariff, he needed a policy to clearly distinguish his party from the Grits in the next election. Protection, Macdonald knew, appealed to business and was relatively neutral in terms of religion, language and race, the usually divisive forces in Canadian politics. The tariff thus offered a potential central plank to build a national following drawn from every region. It also offered the reward of bringing the support, financial and organizational, of the business community to the Tories. The danger lay in making the Tories a narrow party of business.

Macdonald's masterstroke was in convincing the public that the tariff was an elixir for *all* Canadians. For instance, it protected manufacturing, creating city jobs which in turn created demand for farmers' crops. In one of Canadian politics' best labelling jobs, Macdonald brilliantly dubbed his offering to the voters in 1878 the "National Policy." After the 1876 budget had revealed the Grits' true colors, Macdonald cautiously tried out his protectionist pitch at political picnics. The response was positive. Macdonald was offering jobs in Canadian towns at a time when the door to free trade seemed tightly closed. Protectionism had found a political home in Canada by default, not through lofty, principled conversion.

The equation of protection and prosperity won the day for the Tories in 1878, and again in 1882 and 1887. Economists have subsequently argued that Macdonald was "the first great Canadian non-economist," that the National Policy produced at best stunted growth in the 1880s and 1890s and penalized the average Canadian with a higher cost of living.[11] Conscious of protection's appeal, the Liberals pursued a quiescent trade policy in the 1880s, paying lip-service to the "revenue tariff" but always tempted by "incidental protection." Laurier's election as Liberal leader in 1887 pulled the Grits back towards free trade. Advised on the need of a distinctive policy, Laurier opted for "unrestricted reciprocity," a muted way to reawaken memories of prosperity under the reciprocity treaty. With Canada stuck in the economic doldrums, Macdonald sensed that Laurier had scooped him and quietly despatched emissaries to treat with U.S. Secretary of State Blaine. The staunch protectionism of the Harrison administration snuffed out this prospect, and Macdonald re-embraced the National Policy. Backed by the business community, he attacked the Liberals' U.R. platform as "veiled treason," a betrayal of Canadian identity. True Canadians would vote for "the Old Man, the Old Flag and the Old Policy." The strategy worked, but only just. In central Canada, where protectionism was supposed to pay political dividends for the Tories, voters swung back to the free trading Grits. It took the concerted efforts of business (the Canadian Pacific Railway in Montreal) to shore up the Tory vote in the cities. Even then, Macdonald needed Maritime and western support to clinch victory. The "shreds and patches" cf Confederation, Cartwright snorted, had won the day for Macdonald.

In the wake of 1891, the Liberals back-pedalled. At an 1893 policy convention (itself a political novelty), they reasserted belief in a "revenue tariff" but steered clear of any avowal of thoroughgoing free trade. During the 1896 election, Laurier obfuscated the trade issue for fear of alienating support in all-important Montreal and Ontario's rural ridings. The Liberals' success in winning a double majority in the two central provinces meant a *de facto* continuation of this tack. A hurried mission to Washington in February 1897 returned with news that the protectionist McKinley tariff of 1890 (soon to be followed by the equally formidable Dingley tariff) offered solid evidence of the folly of pursuing free trade.

Cartwright's subsequent rejection as finance minister may have dejected the farmers along the Grit concession lines of Ontario, but it also send a reassuring message to the proprietors of innumerable "infant industries" in the towns and cities of Ontario and Quebec. Nonetheless, an attempt was made to sound the Americans out on free trade before the budget was actually brought down. This luckless gambit led to a stand-pat federal budget from Fielding. The farmers were given a few morsels, such as a lower tariff on fence wire. In an effort to temporize, the Liberals began to devise ways in which to blunt the sharp edges of tariff politics: they introduced an intermediate level to the tariff schedule, they sent out commissions of inquiry and they fine tuned the tariff accordingly. But, in light of continued American protectionism and the first signs of an economic take-off in Canada, they eschewed any dramatic trade initiatives. In short, they learned to tinker with the tariff.

Tinkering with the Tariff: 1896-1950

The Liberals soon became pastmasters at tinkering with the tariff. They devised all sorts of ways of easing the sectional pain that it created. They consulted. They revised the schedule. To placate Anglo-imperialist nationalists and to protect access to the British market, they offered a preference on British trade. They developed surrogates, such as subsidies and bounties for producers, for the direct imposition of tariffs. They sought to break down trade barriers abroad by negotiating trade treaties (e.g. with Italy in 1910). Eventually, they began to invoke the cult of the "expert" in the interest of divining a "scientific" tariff, in effect of removing the tariff from politics. This naive notion would eventually take bureaucratic form in the 1920s in the Tariff Advisory Board, a panel of supposedly independent arbiters of tariff disputes.

The Liberals were able to sustain this balancing act in the Laurier years to 1911 because the nation was enjoying a period of boisterous prosperity. Farmers and manufacturers alike could find markets. Prairie sod buster and captain of industry found representation in the Liberal government. High tariff interests in central Canada still aligned themselves with the Tories, but this disaffection was never enough to endanger the centrist coalition keeping Laurier in power. Similarly, Canada's growing farmer population tended to see the tariff as a penalty paid by them to protect easterners, but they nonetheless voted Liberal. The Conservative leader since 1900, Robert Borden, was left to pursue a "singularly feeble" tariff policy, one most voters saw as threatening to Canada's prosperity.[12]

This success of the Laurier juggernaut at the polls tended to mask two developments soon to disrupt Canadian trade politics. As the 1891 election had shown, the National Policy had become more than a trade policy in many Canadian minds. Its high tariff walls protected more than "infant industries," namely, a Canadian identity now sheltered behind it. Macdonald's "old policy" had become "an expression of Canadian national sentiment,"[13] a sentiment reinforced by a series of diplomatic scrapes, such as the Alaska Boundary dispute, in which Canadians perceived that they had been bettered by their U.S. neighbors and forsaken by their erstwhile British allies. Any party wishing to return to the issue of free trade would run the risk of exciting this sense of national identity.

A second crucial development was the development of new groups and regions with distinct views on the tariff issue and the organizational clout to transmit them. The National Policy had been framed according to the political dictates of the central Canadian business community, which possessed the skills and wealth to impress its protectionist message upon the Conservative Party. The very success of the National Policy in developing the nation had, however, by the new century begun to incubate new regional and sectional identities. The agrarian West was the first to exhibit such distinctiveness: in 1905, the new provinces of Alberta and Saskatchewan were created. Their farmer populations were quick to identify the tariff as an added charge on their cost of living. Ontario and Maritime farmers continued to carry their nineteenth century grudge against the tariff builders of the cities. By the 1900s, this discontent was beginning to find organized form in grain-growers' associations and national umbrella organizations such as the Canadian Council of Agriculture. Business was still the predominant force behind economic policy, but the farmers now had to be listened to in Ottawa.

In 1911, Laurier succumbed to the old Liberal virus of free trade. Given the disastrous outcome of the ensuing election for his party, his tactical blunder lay in underestimating how deep rooted the "nationalism" of the National Policy had become in Canada and in overestimating the anti-tariff protest which had manifested itself in rural Canada. Several factors swayed Laurier's decision. The Taft administration in Washington found itself under pressure from low tariff Democrats eager to gain access to Canadian resources. The deal that American protectionism had made seem unobtainable in 1891 now seemed within reach: "the air from the south was sweeter."[14] Back in Ottawa, Laurier was at the same time getting his first taste of farmer political activism. In 1910, farmers had organized the March on Ottawa which had brought western discontent with the tariff right to the lawn of parliament. Surely, Laurier calculated, a reciprocity deal that focused on natural products and only marginally affected manufactured goods would appease the farmers and not alien the business community? After all, the nation was bathed in prosperity.

Two facets of the Liberals' quick flip to free trade in 1911 are worth noting. First, the decision was made in the prime minister's office and on his instinct, with little attempt to canvass sentiment of caucus or party. Laurier judged the moment and acted. Second, with the decision made, the 1911 trade deal was put together in a matter of weeks by Fielding and the minister of customs Patterson in Washington. This provided the first hint of another leading indicator of shifts in Canadian trade policy: the necessity of cordial and effective relations between Canada's prime minister and the White House. Without this kind of official friendship, any movement toward trade liberalization lacked a primary facilitating impetus. Macdonald never had this; King and Mulroney would.

Opposition leader Borden was caught flat-footed by Fielding's late January announcement of the deal. The Liberals seemed to have come up with the right deal at the right time. Nine months later, however, Laurier was drubbed at the polls. The loss of 72 Ontario seats and 27 Quebec seats pulled the rug from under his feet. At least the farm vote stayed predominantly Grit. This dramatic reversal underlines several abiding lessons about trade politics. First, Laurier committed a telling tactical error. He unveiled the quickly negotiated deal in January but let it simmer until a late summer election. In the interim, the opposition had time to regroup, map a strategy and form alliances. Second, and more importantly, the business community demonstrated that it still had the financial and organizational clout to stymie any trade initiative construed as against their interests. An influential faction of the Toronto-Montreal business community publicly denounced the deal and defected to the Tories in February, bringing along the formidable publicity and financial apparatus of the manufacturing, retail and corporate law communities. The revolt of the "Toronto 18" was one of the great defections in Canadian political history. The reunion of renegade Liberal businessmen with the high tariff interests who had stayed with the Tories in 1896 once again made the Tories the party of Canadian business and protectionism.

Realizing that a protectionist business critique of free trade would not in itself turn the tables on Laurier, Borden returned to Macdonald's 1891 political playbook and revived the "old flag" issue. Aided by ill-advised statements made by some U.S. jingoes, Borden brought to the fore the notion that Canada's social and political fabric was at risk under free trade. The Liberal party that limped away from the election loss of 1911 thus carried with it several stinging lessons. It seemed unlikely that any measure of reciprocity with the United States could be achieved without the wholehearted endorsement *and* actual support of Canadian "big business." The ongoing implications of the National Policy had wedded Canada's most influential businessmen to protectionism. The country's largest, best heeled corporations were clearly in the Tory camp. Arthur Meighen, Borden's successor, was as outspoken a high tariff advocate as Canadian politics had ever seen. The old saw that the Canadian Pacific Railway was "the Tory party on wheels" never seemed to be truer.

Another corollary of 1911 for the Liberals was that any precipitous shift in its trade platform bore the distinct risk of splitting party ranks. It took the party years to rebuild its credibility in the Toronto and Montreal business communities. It proved to be an awkward task because any move toward protectionist central Canada might jeopardize its appeal in the free trading West. This danger was real enough. In the 1921 federal election, Canadian farmers cast their votes for the country's first third party in politics.[15] The Progressive Party swept into Ottawa with 65 MPs who held the balance of power and put the Liberals on their low-tariff best behavior. Thus Laurier's goal of making the Liberals Canada's party of national party of reconciliation and compromise was left in jeopardy (a predicament further exacerbated by its stand against conscription in the fractious election of 1917). Not surprisingly, the leadership convention of 1919 that choose Mackenzie King to succeed Laurier made plenty of low tariff noise in convention but the party learned to play a more deft game once it won power back from the war-strained Tories in 1920. Victory in 1921 did not erase the memory of 1911; its ghost walked the caucus room for decades.

The three decades after the 1921 election may be seen as the twilight of traditional tariff politics in Canada. The party that tinkered best with the tariff tended to hold office longest. Mackenzie King's long years as prime minister (1921-25, 1926-30, 1935-48) eloquently spoke of his ability to temporize on the tariff. He pursued a "scientific" tariff with the Tariff Advisory Board. He inched one tariff down and notched another up. A major tariff revision was always just over the horizon. His was a party of "moderation and compromise," a government that "sought to find a course that will help to reconcile rather than to exaggerate the differences existing as far as the tariff is concerned."[16] With the Tories persistently pegged as unshakable protectionists, King determined to win the middle by following a muddled, vague tariff policy designed to win moderate tariff support in central Canada and not to shed farmer support. Any dramatic shift towards liberalized trade would upset the alchemy of this delicate fusion.[17] The existence of a free-trade oriented third party was the greatest threat to this strategy. King met the Progressive challenge of 1921 with a soft-shuffle of promises, patronage and tariff sleight of hand. The Tories obliged him with loud high tariff talk, making the Liberals seem like reasonable centrists. By 1925, returning prosperity and King's blandishments had dissolved all but a rump of the Progressives.

King continued to play this game right down to the Great Depression. Plummeting world demand for Canada's export staples, rampant U.S. protectionism and collapsing industrial demand inside Canada brought on a shock to the national economy that was similar, if more severe, than that experienced in the 1840s and 1870s. Like Alexander Mackenzie in the 1870s, King misread the situation, believing the depression a passing phenomenon. In the face of the highly protectionist U.S. Smoot-Hawley tariff, King's government simply tinkered Canadian duties upward. The nation expected more, and it was the protectionist Tories who supplied the required protectionism. In the run-up to the October 1930 federal election, Conservative leader R. B. Bennett promised to "blast" his way back into world markets by using a dramatically raised Canadian tariff as a battering ram. It was a powerful appeal, clinching the election for the Tories. Even traditionally Liberal Quebec gave Bennett healthy support. Like the 1878 election, the Tories triumphed in 1930 because they played on Canadians' sense of trade vulnerability at a time when trade liberalization was an impossibility. Just as Macdonald unveiled the National Policy in 1879, Bennett hiked Canadian tariffs, in some cases combining specific and *ad valorem* rates to build a formidable protectionist defence. Bennett tried to offset this walling of the Canadian market against U.S. protectionism by trying to expand Canada's preferential trade with the United Kingdom. Britain proved to be in a protectionist mood as well, and by 1931 was hastily abandoning its long-standing policy of free trade. Bennett did succeed at the 1932 Ottawa Conference in winning a five year agreement with Britain that enhanced Canada's access to the still crucial British market. Although Britain was still Canada's second best export market and second largest import supplier, Bennett realized that access to the United States, Canada's best export market, was crucial to any resuscitation of Canadian trade.[18] The opposition Liberals under King attacked the Ottawa Agreements with London as too rigid to permit give and take elsewhere on the trade front.

Bennett also sensed that the sealing up of the U.S. market was an aberration from the Canadian norm. News in 1934 that the U.S. president had received authority under the Reciprocal Trade Agreements Act to negotiate trade agreements that might roll back tariffs by up to 50 percent prompted Bennett to action. Late in 1934, he sent a note to Washington requesting initiation of talks, but he was poorly positioned to negotiate. His political popularity at home was severely eroded and he was facing a newly-elected and popular Democrat in the White House. King was better placed to carry the freer trade banner: he had stuck to his low tariff line of the late 1920s and had opposed the special status treatment of Britain in 1932. He nonetheless avoided any impression of throwing himself into the Americans' arms, the memory of 1911 would always serve to stabilize King's judgement in trade matters.

In the election of 1935, trade was a central but not primordial issue. Bennett was wounded in too many other respects for trade to save the day for him; King simply presented himself as the advocate of *freer* trade. Ironically, by the time King triumphed at the polls in October 1935, much of the groundwork for an agreement with the Americans had been laid. King largely inherited the deal and proudly signed it in Washington a month later. It was an agreement of moderate proportions, lowering duties on Canadian natural resources and granting the United States most-favored-nation status. Significantly, the agreement took the form of a treaty, obviating any potentially awkward recourse to parliament.

His appetite whetted by this initial success in trade liberalization, King determined to push on with other negotiations with Canada's leading trade partners, the United States and Britain. King's impulse to negotiate was shaped by a belief that the tangle of early Depression protectionism could be undone, "appeased," by steady broad front negotiations. This trilateral campaign did bear some small fruit: in 1937 a new agreement was signed with the British and in 1938 the United States agreement was expanded. The persistence of depression into the early stages of the war indicated the glacial effectiveness of the strategy.

Other lessons emerge from the Liberals' campaign for freer trade in the late 1930s. The period may be seen as the beginning of the end for traditional tariff politics in Canada. The economy was becoming too complex, too differentiated by region and too fragmented into splintered social and economic groups to permit the tariff to cut neatly through partisan politics. There was no longer a straightforward pegboard on which each move in Canadian tariff politics could be played out. Given the involved trilateral nature of Canada's foreign trade, there were no simple tariff concessions or retaliations. Flat portrayals of the Tories as "high tariff" and the Grits as "low tariff" were still credible, but were increasingly difficult to act out in political reality. Trade negotiation had become an intricate, bureaucratic affair, directed from the prime minister's office and dependent not so much upon sentiment from the party rank and file but more on the skills of astute trade negotiators such as Norman Robertson, Hector McKinnon and Dana Wilgress. If Canadian politicians were finally able to ease the tariff "out of politics," it was largely because the country was so well served by its senior civil service advisors, the so-called "mandarinate," from the late 1930s right through the post-war liberalization of world trade.[19] King was by nature inclined to this kind of controlled gradualism; it diminished the chance of a divisive national debate over trade policy and at the same time inched Canadian trade in the liberalized direction he believed the Liberals had long championed.

The overall import of trade negotiation in the late Depression was, nonetheless, that the bilateral and trilateral negotiation route was a slow, often acrimonious approach to freeing trade. As Ian Drummond and Norman Hillmer concluded of the Canada-US-UK talks of the late 1930s:

> All three participants had learned that it was very hard to negotiate tariffs downward, especially when their economies were interlocked not only by trade agreements but by the underlying and over-riding economic realities. To move the North American democracies forward there would have to be new ground rules, a new framework for negotiation, a new willingness to give concessions and receive imports, and a new readiness to allow for the generalization of concessions through an honest operation of the mfn [most favored nation] principle.[20]

The Second World War provided these "new ground rules." The exigencies of war produced a multilateral willingness to build a unified war economy amongst the Allies. Guided by the close personal ties between King, Roosevelt and Churchill, the Canadian economy found itself part of a continental and transatlantic trading block. Again, this strategy was directed by the prime minister and his advisors and had little resonance in party politics. The ethos of war tended to reduce any chance that a production sharing agreement such as the Hyde Park Agreement of 1941 might be construed as a "sell-out" of national interests. The Liberals won both wartime elections in 1940 and 1945 by resting on the image that they alone had the political and economic expertise to run the country efficiently. Out of all this emerged the Liberals' post-war commitment to multilateral trade negotiation. Just as Canada became a charter member of the World Bank and IMF, it also committed itself to multilateral tariff reduction through the General Agreement on Tariffs and Trade (GATT). Here, King perhaps reasoned, was the ideal vehicle to get the tariff out of politics. Canada could preserve the residue of the protection afforded it by the National Policy, and simultaneously bargain through the GATT for greater advantage in world trade. Politically, it defused the tariff, removing the danger of having to present the electorate with "take-it-or-leave-it" bilateral deals which history had shown could so easily divide the nation. When pressure was exerted by the business community, the government could simply defer to the GATT process.

King's attraction to multilateralism was convincingly demonstrated in the spring of 1948 when several of his closest economic advisors reported that the United States was ready to discuss bilateral free trade. The times were prosperous, and success thus was likely. Although tempted, King's political judgement was ultimately swayed by the memory of 1911. There would be "instant opposition" from the Tories, who would portray the deal as "King's toy," a first step to annexation by the United States. Without "the most careful, educational effort in advance," such talks could lead to the possible "oblivion" of the Liberal Party.[21] The idea was quietly scrapped. Unlike Laurier, King left politics later that year from the prime minister's office, not the opposition benches.

Multilateralism and the Persistence of Bilateralism: 1950-88

The 1950s, 1960s and 1970s were marked by a certain monotony in trade politics. Canada quietly participated in the Dillon, Kennedy and Tokyo Rounds of the GATT. Successive ministers of finance declined the possibility of any significant domestic adjustment of the tariff while the negotiations labored onward in Geneva. An interlude of Conservative rule under John Diefenbaker coincided with the economic downturn of the early 1960s during which the Tories temporarily hiked manufacturing tariffs in an attempt to promote a "made-in-Canada" economic strategy. Trade and commerce minister George Hees, for instance, declared in 1961 that free trade with the United States would result in the closing of "a great many Canadian factories" and "mass unemployment."[22] The Liberals' return to power in 1963 saw multilateralism's sway restored.

The net effect of the GATT Rounds through these decades was a steady draining of the reservoir of the protectionism that had surrounded the Canadian economy since the National Policy. The political significance of any future move toward bilateral trade liberalization was also being steadily reduced; more and more trade now moved between Canada and the United States free of protection. Bilateral free trade was being slowly realized through the back door of multilateralism. Indeed, some bilateral progress was made with negotiation of the 1959 Defence Production Sharing Arrangement and the 1965 Automotive Products Trade Agreement. Since these agreements, Canada in effect has enjoyed free trade in military equipment and autos with the United States. Their seeming success also kept alive in the Liberal party the lure of bilateral free trade with the United States. In the early 1960s, Liberal policy advisors such as John Deutsch (whose advice King had spurned in 1948) came before the Liberal Study Conference on National Problems to advocate Canada's integration into the U.S. market. Others, like Walter Gordon, demurred and argued for a kind of neo-protectionism against the incursion of the U.S. economy into Canada using non-tariff barriers.

The business community in these years divided its political loyalties. Given Canada's prosperity, business was little troubled by broad trade issues. The Tories retained a good deal of business support, although Diefenbaker's western populism tested this allegiance. The Liberals, on the other hand, tended to build their ties with corporate Canada in these decades. The Liberals found themselves in charge of a steadily growing national economy and business leaders naturally gravitated to them. In 1968, Pierre Trudeau only narrowly beat out business executive Robert Winters for the Liberal leadership. Winters retired to corporate Toronto. John Turner, a corporate lawyer, also contested the leadership.

The post-war era saw the perfection of non-tariff barriers as weapons of trade as well. As the tariff began to yield lessening economic leverage, nations increasingly turned to non-tariff means to achieve their economic ends. Government procurement policies, subsidies on exports, legislative controls on investment, all acted as surrogates for tariffs. Canada was no exception. The Pearson and Trudeau Liberal governments from 1963 to 1984 frequently resorted to non-tariff barriers to trade. Pearson's first finance minister, Walter Gordon, acknowledged the increasingly close tie between trade and investment by unsuccessfully applying a take-over tax on foreign acquisitions of Canadian companies. Similarly, the Canadian government fell into the practice of "rescuing" ailing Canadian companies in the hope of shoring them up. Since these activities affected export performance, Canada often found itself defending its policies before GATT tribunals or against U.S. countervail hearings. From the Canadian political point of view, these were containable skirmishes which seldom spilled over into national politics. Trade politics had become a matter of periodic brushfire wars, touching specific regions or industries, taking place against the general backdrop of GATT liberalization. The tariff itself ceased to be a blockbuster in Canadian politics.

There were still external shocks capable of upsetting the equilibrium of Liberal trade policy. As U.S. importance as Canada's primary trade partner grew, Canada's vulnerability to contractions of the U.S. economy or protectionist outbursts grew commensurably. In August 1971, for instance, Nixon's surprise imposition of a temporary 10 percent surtax on imports not only erased the gains of the last GATT round but severely hurt Canadian access to its most important market. The Nixon Shocks jolted the Canadian government into reconsidering its three decade drift towards the U.S. market. In 1972, it announced that it would now pursue a "third option" that would "develop and strengthen" the Canadian economy's independence and reduce its "vulnerability" to U.S. factors.

The "third option" took Canadian prime minister to Europe in search of new markets and was reflected in other initiatives such as the Foreign Investment Review Agency (FIRA), a screening agency designed to limit the "take-over" of Canada by foreign investors, a majority of whom were American. To some degree, these shifts were also a reflection of the ability of the New Democratic Party, which found itself holding the balance of power after the 1972 election, to impose its nationalist views on the Trudeau minority government. For the first time since the Progressive challenge of the Twenties, a third party had some impact on trade politics. Similarly, the advent of frequent and pervasive public opinion polling began to sway politicians' actions. For much of the 1970s, the polls revealed that Canadians were wary of America's pretensions.

For the decade the idea of bilateral free trade with the United States therefore languished. Industry, Trade and Commerce minister Alastair Gillespie told a Johns Hopkins University audience in 1973 that Canada wanted a new approach to solving its bilateral problems with the United States. "Solutions," he concluded, "should be sought to each problem on its individual merits rather than trying to lump them all together in some sort of a packaged settlement."[23] A 1975 Economic Council of Canada report, *Looking Outward*, which stressed the need for access to a larger trading block, fell on deaf ears. A year later, the first vice-president of the CMA declared that the "touted benefits of free trade are not so attractive to the businessman, industrial workers and politicians who must deal with the practical consequences and human implications of what the economists recklessly refer to as the adjustment period."[24] In 1979, another round of GATT tariff cuts began to be phased in, a seeming alternative to any bilateral adventure.

The "third option" none the less ultimately fizzled. Throughout the 1970s, Canada's trade dependence on the United States, and the list of trade irritants, mounted. These climaxed in the early 1980s in a dramatic deterioration of Canada-U.S. relations which served to remind Canadians that their access to the all-important U.S. market could not be taken for granted. Several of the "givens" of the relationship fell out of place. There was no love lost between Prime Minister Trudeau and President Reagan. As Stephen Clarkson has noted, there was a clash of "divergent nationalisms." Reagan's militant conservativism, intent on restoring American self-esteem at home and abroad, met head on with Trudeau's interventionist statism, a policy which saw the Canadian government intervene in the marketplace in the interest of national autonomy. The National Energy Program and a more vigilant FIRA made Washington see red. U.S. challenges to Canadian trade under GATT had similar effects in Ottawa. Trudeau and Reagan were barely on speaking terms.[25]

The bilateral crisis of the early 1980s was exacerbated by the onset of the 1982/3 recession. The necessity of easy access to the American market was made all the more apparent by a faltering economy. Unemployment and trade performance began to dominate the political agenda. Ottawa began to step back from the NEP and FIRA. The Department of External Affairs was given the additional responsibility of trade. In August, 1983, *Trade Policy for the 1980s* was issued by the department and it reflected the growing concern over access to the American market. Multilateralism was played down and the need to minimize Canada's exposure to US non-tariff barriers was played up. To achieve this, Ottawa brought forward the idea of sectoral free trade with the United States: free trade confined to precise industrial sectors, such as transit equipment and steel. Washington reacted positively, saying that it might be interested in "GATT-plus" agreements. Although it was to prove unworkable (principally because sectors could not be neatly defined), the Liberals had at least broken the free trade ice.

The trade issue did not become politicized or polarized in the 1984 federal election. It existed on a kind of bureaucratic, diplomatic level; there seemed an implicit consensus that the nationalist implications of continental free trade were best left alone. Prominent members of both the Liberal and Conservative parties, former External Affairs minister Mitchell Sharp and Tory leader Brian Mulroney, declared themselves against the idea. The election was instead fought along traditional economic lines, the Tories scoring effectively on the issues of job creation and declawing FIRA and NEP. The business community solidly backed the Tories as the party that would return the country to growth.

Much has been made of Brian Mulroney's pirouette on trade policy after the 1984 election. The man who ruled out free trade as opposition leader soon became its champion. When one considers the turn-around in light of the factors discussed in this paper, the decision becomes almost predictable. A window of opportunity opened for Mulroney and, once he had satisfied his political instinct that it would support a free trade gambit, he acted. Like Macdonald's shift to protectionism in the 1870s and Laurier's 1911 conversion to free trade, Mulroney's instinct told him that the political arithmetic looked promising. Like an astrologer, Mulroney believed that the stars had come into propitious alignment for a change of national attitude and that he must seize the moment.

The first favorable omen of change was the solidity of Mulroney's support. The Tories swept the country in 1984; Mulroney inherited the centrist formula that had served the Grits so well for so long. He had support from coast to coast, including Quebec. He was thus in a position to affect a change in policy in an area that had traditionally been decided by the central Canadian power block. In fact, as the free trade idea matured the Tories were able to counter industrial Ontario's misgivings by pairing Quebec and Alberta in support of free trade. He sensed that he could swing the deal by building an unorthodox Canadian power base out of the West, a longtime free trade region, and Quebec, a region newly anxious to tap the American market for its hydro-power.

Trudeau's departure from Ottawa also left Mulroney in a position to reestablish friendly relations with the White House. Mulroney and Reagan, professional Irishmen both, seemed to have a natural affinity for each other. Like King and Roosevelt, the prime minister was able to pick up the telephone and talk directly with the U.S. president. The possibility of unpredictable blow-ups in a trade negotiation was thus greatly reduced. Internally there was also relative harmony in federal-provincial relations in the early Mulroney years. Premier Lougheed of Alberta in particular became a stalwart of provincial support.

Mulroney was also quick to detect a shift in the national climate of opinion towards free trade. The reality of impeded access to the American market in the early 1980s had jarred the Canadian business community into some fundamental rethinking of its attitude towards trade. Probably, the most fortuitous factor in the whole free trade calculation was the conversion of Canadian "big business" to support of free trade. Throughout the 1970s, corporate Canada had been groping its way back to an effective consensus. Confronted by the need of a common stand on public issues ranging from competition policy to tax reform, big business had come together in the Business Council on National Issues. The BCNI effectively combined research and lobbying. It carried a kind of blue ribbon legitimacy into the public policy ring and by 1983 was making it clear that Canadian business was no longer inseparably married to the vestiges of the National Policy. Mulroney was assured that he could proceed without the danger of a big business defection, such as had scuppered Laurier in 1911. The BCNI was invaluable because of its organizational and financial clout and public voice. The CMA and other business lobbies gradually fell into line. Small business, represented by the Canadian Federation of Independent

Business, remained dubious about free trade, but with big and medium business on his side, Mulroney could afford their disaffection.

Mulroney detected other shifts in the national mood. In 1985, a royal commission established by the Liberal Party on Canada's development prospects somewhat unexpectedly reported that it saw free trade as a acceptable alternative for Canada. Even though the commission's chairman, former Liberal finance minister Donald Macdonald, confessed that free trade would demand a "leap of faith" by Canadians, his support of the idea gave Mulroney important cross-party support for free trade, a kind of reverse defection. The government also received solid support from its senior trade bureaucrats, men like Derek Burney at External who helped to mould Ottawa's initial thoughts on free trade and later guided the government through the arduous negotiation process in Washington.[26]

As Mulroney moved toward free trade after his 1984 victory, none of the political alarm bells that had belatedly rung in Laurier's ear in 1911 and had paralysed Mackenzie King throughout his prime ministership had in fact rung. Also remarkable, it was a Conservative prime minister who had set out on a route that the Liberals had traditionally tried to travel. To many it appeared that Mulroney was betraying Macdonald's protectionist legacy to Canada. A closer reading of the historical record reveals that even for the Tories protectionism had always been a second best option, taken when the chances of free trade seemed slim. The National Policy was born out of opportunism, not economic ideology. Macdonald seized a political opportunity thrown up by the times: recession and Washington's lack of interest in free trade. Having fostered Canadian protectionism, the Tories found themselves long wedded to the concept, but the notion of bilateral free trade was never entirely out of mind. Similarly, the Grits had clung to the memory of Brown, Mackenzie and Cartwright, their belief in trade liberalization. But as Laurier had shown, the Liberals were prepared to accommodate the National Policy. In the end, the growth of vested interests ("infant industries") and the association of protectionism with national identity ("no truck nor trade with the Yankees") usually tipped the Canadian political balance. Expediency, not ideology, carried the day, particularly if it carried Canada back to its natural inclination for bilateral trade.

One element in the political dynamic of free trade was not entirely within Mulroney's control. Powerful vested interests were with him, but the potential for a nationalist reaction to free trade was less governable. This, after all, was what had held King back in 1948 and what had stymied Laurier in 1911. Timing would be of the essence. From the outset, it was clear that the actual negotiation of the pact would be long and intricate. Opposition would have ample time to form, much as Borden had done in 1911. The pro-free trade forces must therefore seize the initiative. A cohesive caucus, a government information blitz and continued good relations with Washington all contributed to this early start. The emergence of a pro-free trade umbrella group, the Canadian Alliance for Trade and Job Opportunities (largely coordinated by the BCNI), solidified the quick start strategy. Early opinion polls confirmed Canadians' generally favorable reception of free trade.

If Mulroney had one stroke of luck in the free trade campaign, it was that the move placed the Liberal opposition in a genuine quandary. Having backed sectoral free trade while in office in the early Eighties, the Liberals had signalled their willingness to at least play with the idea. Furthermore, there was good evidence that the strong corporate backing the Liberals had enjoyed in the previous two decades was now inclined to accept the BCNI perspective on free trade. Liberal leader John Turner, who spent a political exile on Bay Street in the late Trudeau years, was widely seen as a businessman in politics. Added to the Liberals' indecisiveness was the fact that, in the wake of the party's lopsided loss in 1984, Turner's leadership was much questioned in party ranks, and it was uncertain if he could impose a unified party line in any direction.

Opposition to free trade was thus fragmented from the start. Despite Turner's earlier declaration that, if elected, he would "rip up" the Free Trade Agreement, the New Democratic Party in fact seized the early initiative in opposing the deal when an election was finally called in the fall of 1988; the deal was a "sell-out" of Main Street Canada. Labour, the consumer and national identity were at risk. An umbrella group, the Pro Canada Network, provided a populist critique to the business dominated pro-free trade message. The Liberals were dogged by their own internal problems; memories of Turner's inept performance in the 1984 election eroded his leadership credibility. It was not until Turner wholeheartedly committed the Liberals to an emotional attack on the implications of the deal that the anti-free trade forces finally came alive. Turner's spirited portrayal of free trade as a Bay Street policy and his ability to arouse doubts about Mulroney's sincerity turned the election into a vigorous race in its last weeks. But it came too late. The anti-free trade vote was split. Had Turned moved earlier he might have monopolized the anti-free trade sentiment. Instead, it was split between the NDP and the Liberals. At the same time, Turner's perilous adoption of an anti-Bay Street persona eroded much of the Liberal party's business support. Unlike 1911, when the pro-free trade party had split apart, it was the anti-free trade party that in 1988 had hesitated and then divided before the electorate. Liberals will perhaps always debate what might have happened if Turner had felt surer in the starting blocks in 1988 and had dashed, somewhat like Borden in 1911, out to an early lead and then turned the race into a contest of national emotion not economic orientation. As it was, Brian

Mulroney had read his cards well, and the one wild card he feared was played too late. In November, 1988 he became the first Canadian political leader ever to win a free trade election.

Has the Curtain Fallen Forever?

Will Canadians ever again be faced with an 1878 or 1930 style protectionist election? Could the National Policy ever be resurrected from its political grave? Can Sir Richard Cartwright finally find peace in the grave, his beloved free trade now enshrined as Canada's trade policy?

The continued march of global trade liberalization in the foreseeable future seems undeniable. Since the end of the last war, Canada has been a willing participant in multilaterally negotiated tariff reductions. It joined the Uruguay Round in 1986. Bilateral reductions have proven more elusive, but given the opportunities, Canada has succumbed to its long-standing inclination for assured access to the larger North American market. As the world reorganizes into larger trading blocks, and as Canadians accustom themselves to the idea of global competitiveness, it seems increasingly unlikely that we will ever slip back into the protectionist cocoon of the National Policy. Free trade is here to stay.

We have not, however, entered elysium. Protectionism is a persistent virus and Canada's immunity to it can vary with the general national and international climate. Just as Brian Mulroney capitalized on a propitious alignment of factors favoring free trade in 1988, so too could a future prime minister or opposition leader seize a protectionist moment. The possible variables are now familiar: a sharp economic downturn, a breakdown in cordial relations between Sussex Drive and the White House, protectionist gambits thrown up in an election year on either side of the border or an arousing of Canadian national sentiment. The combination of some or all of these forces could dramatically change the willingness of the Canadian government to defend free trade.

At present, free trade's future well-being is troubled by protectionist growling in the United States. Recent decisions on the "national content" in Canadian-made Hondas and alleged stumpage subsidies on Canadian softwood lumber have created new tensions between Washington and Ottawa. To some degree, this is a predictable accompaniment to any U.S. presidential election year. Such tensions assume a more worrisome context when set against the ongoing structural problems of the U.S. economy and the fact that for many Americans protectionism is the easiest tonic for such pressures. The November election did not banish this mood. If such protectionism reaches critical mass in the eyes of many Canadians, particularly opinion and business leaders, conceivably one of Canada's mainstream parties might seize the moment and attack free trade. In recent years, structural problems have bitten deep into the Canadian economy too, creating high unemployment and bankruptcy. A heated debate has taken place over the degree to which free trade is responsible for these losses. The opposition Liberals issued the vague threat to "renegotiate" the Mulroney trade deal if they won the election. Note that both opposition parties try to personalize dissatisfaction over the 1988 pact by constantly referring to it as the "Mulroney deal."

From the U.S. perspective, there is cause for concern that Canada's current constitutional woes may eventually lead to a federation so economically decentralized that Canadian trade policy may become perpetually precarious as various provincial regimes vie for turf in the national economy. Should Quebec separate, the whole structure would be thrown into disarray. Would the United States wish to renegotiate free trade with two relatively small and ultimately insignificant post-break-up economies? What sort of a hard-line deal would the United States then be in a position to exact? How far would Quebec go to gain access to the U.S. market for its hydro-electricity?

A total abandonment of free trade seems unlikely. More probable is the persistence of protectionist brushfires. Canadians are very sensitive to the ravages of fire in the great north woods. If the conditions are just right, much damage can be done. Canadians, as the junior partner, will remain vigilant for their rights under free trade. The cry of "no truck nor trade with the Yankees" will never be completely removed from the Canadian political playbook. Whether real or perceived, an unfortunate coincidence of adverse turns in the trade relationship, perhaps not dissimilar to the recent developments over Honda cars and softwood lumber, could send a Canadian political party back to the protectionist hustings. Sir Richard may one day have to rise from the grave.

Notes

My thanks to Robert Bothwell and David Farr for their comments on this paper.

1. See *Debates of the House of Commons*, March 10, 1876. Ben Forster's *A Conjunction of Interests: Business, Politics, and Tariffs 1825-1979* (Toronto: University of Toronto Press, 1986), Chapter 7, provides an excellent account of the trade policy agonies of the Mackenzie government.

2. For one version of this anecdote, see Edward Porritt, *Sixty Years of Protection in Canada 1846-1907 - Where Industry Leans on the Politician* (London: Macmillan, 1908), p. 287. Porritt, an English journalist, was a Manchester liberal who championed Cartwright's adherence to free trade.

3. See Joseph Schull, *Laurier: The First Canadian* (Toronto: Macmillan, 1966), p. 366.

4. Richard Cartwright, *Reminiscences* (Toronto: William Briggs, 1912), pp. 160-1.

5. See H. A. Innis, *Essays in Canadian Economic History* (Toronto: University of Toronto Press, 1956).

6. See O. J. McDiarmid, *Commercial Policy in the Canadian Economy* (Cambridge, MA: Harvard University Press, 1946), Chapters 3 and 4.

7. D. C. Masters, *The Reciprocity Treaty of 1854* (London: Longman, Green, 1937), p. xi.

8. See J. M. S. Careless, ed., *The Pre-Confederation Premiers: Ontario Government Leaders 1941-67* (Toronto: University of Toronto Press, 1980).

9. P. B. Waite, *Canada 1874-1896: Arduous Destiny* (Toronto: McClelland and Stewart, 1971), p. 83.

10. See Forster, *A Conjunction of Interests*.

11. See J. H. Dales, *The Protective Tariff in Canada's Development* (Toronto: University of Toronto Press, 1966), p. 144.

12. R. C. Brown, *Robert Laird Borden: Volume 1 1854-1914* (Toronto: Macmillan, 1975), p. 117.

13. R. C. Brown, *Canada's National Policy 1883-1900 A Study in Canadian-American Relations* (Princeton, NJ: Princeton University Press, 1964), p. 402.

14. Schull, *Laurier*, p. 502.

15. See W. L. Morton, *The Progressive Party of Canada* (Toronto: University of Toronto Press, 1950), and V. C. Fowke, *The National Policy and the Wheat Economy* (Toronto: University of Toronto Press, 1957).

16. H. B. Neatby, *William Lyon Mackenzie King 1924-1932: The Lonely Heights* (Toronto: University of Toronto Press, 1963), p. 71.

17. See T. Traves, *The State and Enterprise: Canadian Manufacturers and the Federal Government, 1917-1931* (Toronto: University of Toronto Press, 1979) for an analysis of how intractable the tariff question had become by the 1920s.

18. See Ian Drummond and Norman Hillmer, *Negotiating Freer Trade: The United Kingdom, the United States, Canada, and the Trade Agreements of 1938* (Waterloo: Wilfrid Laurier University Press, 1989) and McDiarmid, *Commercial Policy*, Chapters 12-13.

19. See J. L. Granatstein, *The Ottawa Men: The Civil Service Mandarins 1935-1957* (Toronto: Oxford University Press, 1982).

20. Drummond and Hillmer, *Negotiating Freer Trade*, pp. 162-3.

21. J. W. Pickersgill and D. F. Forster, eds., *The Mackenzie King Record*, Vol.4 (Toronto: University of Toronto Press, 1970), pp. 262-73.

22. J. T. Saywell, ed., *Canadian Annual Review of Public Affairs* (Toronto: University of Toronto Press, 1962), p. 141.

23. *Canadian Annual Review*, 1973, p. 233.

24. Ibid., 1976, pp. 372-3.

25. See Stephen Clarkson, *Canada and the Reagan Challenge: Crisis in the Canadian-American Relationship* (Toronto: Lorimer, 1982).

26. By far the best treatment of the Mulroney government's embracing of free trade has been provided by Bruce Doern and Brian Tomlin in *The Free Trade Story: Faith and Fear* (Toronto: Stoddart, 1991).

6

The NDP and Free Trade: Facing the American Capitalist Empire

Douglas Owram

This isn't so much about free trade as it is about the heart and soul of this country. It's about the definition of Canada.
—Stephen Lewis, Winnipeg 1988

Two general and perhaps controversial propositions introduce this chapter. First, issues of Canadian trade relations with the United States should not be seen primarily as an economic question. Canadian-American relations are so laden with history, symbolism and fear that the issue of free trade is more like a religion than economics. This view, with a little imagination, can be taken back to the immediate aftermath of the War of 1812 when a strong anti-Americanism set in and restrictions were put on American immigration and land-holding in Canada.[1] It is hardly surprising, therefore, to say that political party positions on free trade reflect this perspective. Economic rationalism is mixed with history, nationalism, and stereotypes of the great power to the south.

The second proposition is that the New Democratic Party (NDP) is the most fixed of all the parties in its anti-free trade position. The reasons for this protectionism, however, are far from simple. For the party is made up of a diverse constituency, and has various competing ideological concerns and regional interests. The NDP's development of such a strong anti-free trade position therefore requires some explanation, which can only be undertaken historically.

In this chapter, I examine these presumptions in three ways. First, I develop the argument that trade policies with the United States have never been primarily economic and therefore should not be understood in those terms. Second, I look at the evolution of party positions on trade policy in the twentieth century, focussing on the New Democrats from their origins as the CCF in the 1930s through their turnabout on the United States generally in the post-war years. Third, I examine some of the complex forces which shaped New Democratic thinking in the latest round of negotiations. How unified is the party? What is their likely influence on the current debate about NAFTA?

Trade and Nationalism

Internally, the Canadian sense of identity is shaped by the nation's geographic regionalism and bilingual history. Externally that sense of identity is determined above all else by what the late J. B. Brebner and others have termed the North Atlantic triangle: Great Britain, the United States and Canada.[2] While the internal aspects are relevant to this discussion, it is really the Canadian understanding of its place within the triangle that is crucial to any discussion of Canada-U.S. trade relations.

Canadian history, at least until after World War II, can be read in terms of the pull between the North American environment which Canada shared with the United States, and the membership in and loyalty to a British Empire centered in Great Britain. Moreover, though there were always counter-currents, orthodox opinion was soundly of the opinion that the attachment to Britain was good. Conversely, the temptation of the North American continent was bad, for that road led to absorption into the United States, something consciously rejected in the period 1776-1783.

This sense of the triangle means that in the nineteenth century, the evolving sense of Canadian distinctiveness rested to a considerable degree on celebrating the one element over the other. Anti-Americanism was thus the flip side of Britannic loyalism. "Imperialism," as one Canadian historian put it, " was a form of Canadian nationalism."[3] Equally a part of that nationalism was, in the words of another historian, the fact that the nineteenth century Canadian "appears to have leapt from the womb fully equipped with a lifetime's antagonism toward the United States."[4]

Part of this anti-Americanism flowed naturally from Canadian history. The American Revolution had led to the invasion of British North America in 1776. The Loyalists (Tories in the United States) fled as the losers in the struggle and became the founding elements of two new colonies, Upper Canada (now Ontario) and New Brunswick. Then, in

1812, Canada's membership in the Empire meant that it was again invaded in the ongoing struggle between Britain and the United States. Over the next decades, excursions, incursions, alarms and diplomatic crises, and a general tone of hostility maintained and deepened the Canadian fear of the United States. Not until after World War I did Canadians really cease to see the United States as their enemy. The Canadian military did not scrap its plans for defence of Canada against the American foe until 1931![5]

If there was real hostility and fear, there was also much bombast and rhetoric. Canadians, as S. F. Wise has emphasized, jumped on the "narcissism of small differences" to attack every American weakness they could find. American politics were viewed as corrupt and dominated by the rule of the mob. American morals were thought far too loose, dominated by the cheap magazine and the divorce court. American justice was seen as farcical, ruled by "Judge lynch" and violence. American society was condemned for slavery and treatment of Indians.[6] All of these criticisms were valid ones, raised by many Americans as well. The difference was that in Canada they were part of a nationalist reaffirmation. It is good we are separate, the unwritten theme went, because of the weaknesses of the society to the south.

Continual reaffirmation was necessary because of another, competing image of the United States. The Yankees may have been immoral, but they were rich. Canada, though wealthy in world terms, has usually had a lower standard of living and slower growth rate than the United States. The lower standard of living worked at odds with Canadian nation building. The vast moving frontier of the United States drew Canadian immigrants throughout the nineteenth century. Also a temptation were the plentiful factory jobs of the newly industrialized northeastern states. In times of economic slowdown or stagnation, the fear of U.S. temptation became especially acute. Canada was often characterized as a great way-station. Immigrants poured in from Europe, but there was an almost equally great outflow southward through the century. In times of depression, Canada occasionally became a net exporter of people. At one point in the late nineteenth century, it was estimated that one quarter of all those born in Canada ended up as American citizens.[7]

The economic temptation of the United States reinforced the tendency to moralize. Only the superior moral qualities of life in Canada could serve as a barrier to a mass outflow of Canadians southward to the land of milk and honey. J. Murray Gibbon's novel *Eyes of the Stranger* published in 1926 is typical of Canadian attempts to emphasize moral superiority. In it, the hero is a rural (naturally), clean-cut (naturally), God-fearing (naturally) youth. He decides to leave the family farm and seek fame and fortune in the glittering city of New York to the south.

Initially things work out well. He gets a job, meets a girl and seems to be on the verge of success. There is a villain however. A U.S. Senator, bootlegger and war profiteer, threatens both the youth's future and the virtue of the heroine. The hero soon comes to realize that he was meant for Canada. He returns and settles in the Canadian Rockies where, presumably, he lived a cleaner and happier life than could be found in that sinful city to the south.[8] The story stands as a metaphor for the Canadian sense of identity. It might even have a motto: poor but pure.

It was not long before nationalist and anti-American concerns became an element in the discussion of trade patterns as well. Just as individuals might be tempted southward, so too might the whole nation. If Canada was to resist the siren song of the United States, it had to promote trade patterns that would diminish the influence of the United States and enhance the role of Great Britain. This implied an east-west trans-Atlantic flow of goods rather than a north-south one. London was to be preferred as a market to New York. After Confederation, an internal dimension was added and this is extremely important to note. Not only was east-west trade good because it tied us across the Atlantic but, in a nation divided by vast geographical barriers (the shield, the rockies), the development of east-west trade also promoted internal unity. The popular imagery of the Canadian Pacific Railway as a great nationalist institution derives in large part from this line of thought.[9] It linked the regions and made trade between the manufacturing center and the prairie hinterland a possibility. The idea of an east-west trade flow thus has deep roots in both Canadian history and Canadian nationalism.

There has been a long-standing tension, therefore, between the wealth of the United States and the fear of American temptation. To put it another way, Canadian politicians recognized that themes of moral superiority could only go so far, as emigration figures continually reminded them. The real answer was to diminish or even eliminate the disparity in wealth between the two countries. This created a paradox however. For the road to greater wealth often implied closer trade connections with the United States. Could one move closer to the devil and at the same time avoid going to hell? The particular interpretation that held sway at any given time has, over the decades, done much to shape Canadian-American trade policy.

There have been several swings of the pendulum. The first real attempt to resolve the problem came in 1854 when British North America, through Great Britain, negotiated a Reciprocity Treaty with the United States. In this case, the motivation was explicit. Canada had just survived a movement for annexation to the United States, and Governor General Lord Elgin saw improved trade as heading off this sort of political extremism.[10] In 1866, however, bad Anglo-American relations coming out of the Civil War and rising U.S. protectionism killed the treaty. The United States headed into a high protectionist phase that lasted well into the twentieth century.

Canada replied in kind. When John A. Macdonald's Conservatives came back to power in 1878, they did so on the basis of the National Policy. This emphasized the other side of the trade equation: an east-west system based on the railway, western immigration and high tariffs.[11] It remained the basis of Canadian trade policy for the next two generations. As late as the 1930s, the Conservative administration of R. B. Bennett sought to revive the notion of the National Policy through high tariffs and special trade agreements with Great Britain. The old pattern was no longer viable however. Whether as importer of Canadian goods, exporter to Canada, or investor in Canada, the United States was by the 1930s more important than Great Britain.[12]

The National Policy of 1878 and after turned Canadian instincts into national dogma. Henceforth the concept of national existence, anti-Americanism, and an east-west trade access were securely linked. To challenge the trading pattern was to challenge the whole nationalist ideology.[13] Sometimes this challenge was explicit. When the Liberals proposed unrestricted reciprocity in 1891, Toronto intellectual Goldwin Smith openly advocated annexation to the United States. To Smith, it was a clear case of accepting the reality of the continent, abandoning the silly cultural resistance, and moving to a north-south trade axis. "In the present case there are on one side, geography, commerce, identity of race, language, and institutions." All there was on the other side was emotion, "Imperial sentiment."[14] Smith's explicit annexationism only reinforced the tendency to equate east-west trade and national survival however. John A. Macdonald's reply, "a British Subject I was born and a British subject I will die," proved a successful riposte. Macdonald won the election and retained its high tariff system.

In other instances the threat was manufactured. In 1910 Wilfrid Laurier's Liberals were able to reach the first agreement with the United States since the Reciprocity Treaty of 1854. The opposition Conservatives, supported by some renegade Liberal businessmen, however, successfully diverted Canadian attention from economic benefits to cultural threat. Their appeal to nationalist sentiments was so effective that they overcame a considerable early handicap and defeated Laurier. The agreement died.[15] It was the last comprehensive Canadian-American trade agreement to go to the electorate for nearly seventy years.

Almost as important as the trade battles themselves was the creation of historical myth around them. This had always been present to a degree but really became a part of the national canon only in the interwar years. At that time the "staples" school (Harold Innis, W. A. Mackintosh,

Donald Creighton and others) formally developed the idea that trade and nationalism were closely interlinked in Canadian history. This was further sanctified when the Royal Commission on Dominion-Provincial Relations of 1937-1941 (the Rowell-Sirois Commission) adopted the same analysis of the Canadian economy.[16] Canada, the argument went, was a story of the struggle of the northern part of the continent to achieve its destiny in the face of tremendous competition and even threat from the south. That success rested on the use of the St. Lawrence-Great Lakes system as a springboard to east-west trade. Sequentially the fur trade, timber trade, agricultural settlement and western development followed the same pattern. Canada survived because it followed these east-west dictates. Those who comprehended the implications of the Canadian empire and pursued them became heroes. Those who did not became the villains. Behind it all, though, was the lurking presence of the United States.[17] The powerful intellects and productivity of Innis, Creighton and others meant that by World War II this vision of Canada's history had triumphed. It would remain dominant in the public imagination even as Canada drew ever closer to the Untied States.

These events, fought before the CCF or NDP was even created, are relevant because they establish the parameters of debate and introduce the contending forces. As party platforms have been framed and reframed through the twentieth century, they have always done so with these basic historical myths in mind. Canada continued to see itself as poorer but distinctive. North-south trade seemed a recipe for improving economic well-being, but only at the risk of fragmenting the country or exposing it to excessive American influence. Anyone who ventured into Canadian-American trade relations had to have a stout heart and perhaps a political death-wish.

The CCF and Free Trade

When the Cooperative Commonwealth Federation (CCF)[18] was formed in 1932-33, it brought together several disparate strands of Canadian radicalism. The groups that assembled in Calgary in 1932 and Regina the next year to create the new movement included religiously motivated social gospellers, militant union groups, one-cause reformers and obscure splinter organizations. All had an effect on the party. Two groups were most influential, however, and it was these two groups that determined the party's early outlook toward Canadian-American relations generally and the tariff specifically.

The largest initial base of support for the new CCF came from the beliefs and political values created by an agrarian reformist movement that had developed in Western Canada over the past thirty years. The Canadian prairies had been developing slowly from the 1870s and rapidly from the turn of the century. From the beginning there were sporadic protests by farm organizations against what they saw as unfair political or economic forces. These protests really only became organized around the turn of the century when farmers began to form associations to protest against freight rates, elevator monopolies and other matters of interest.[19] It was not until after World War I, however, that the agrarian movement really exploded into politics. Growing discontent brought various provincial farm organizations together to form the Progressive Party. In 1921 the Progressives shocked the nation by capturing 65 seats in Parliament, a number second only to the victorious Liberals.[20]

Though Progressive ideology had many variants, the mainstream of the party were classic agrarian reformers. Many of their ideas were borrowed from American groups like the Non-Partisan League, state Progressive Parties, and Populism. Detailed discussion of their views is beyond the scope of this paper. What is relevant, however, is that as commercial farmers oriented toward the world market, Progressives were hard-line free traders. The 1921 platform referred to the tariff as the "most wasteful and costly method ever designed for raising national revenue," and urged a "substantial all-round reduction of the customs tariff." Nor were the Progressives afraid of closer American ties. While they called for lower tariffs on British products, they also demanded "unrestricted reciprocal trade in natural products with the United States along the lines of the Reciprocity Agreement of 1911," and the placement of all agricultural machinery on the free list.[21] During the election campaigns of 1921, 1925 and 1926, the theme of the unjust tariff was key to the arsenal of the party. Promises to lower the tariff were equally key to the success of William Lyon Mackenzie King's Liberals in drawing off farmer support by the end of the decade.[22] Though the Progressive party fell apart, the tradition of farmers as free traders and as political activists was well-entrenched in Canada by the time of the Great Depression.

The other group central in forming the CCF, and especially influential in drafting early policy, consisted of Canadian academics, mainly from Toronto and Montreal. Organized in an initially non-partisan League for Social Reconstruction (LSR), many of these social democrats were British educated and admirers of the Webbs' Fabian Society. The League's ideas were extremely influential when the CCF's founding document was drawn up in 1933.[23] The group published the massive *Social Planning for Canada* in 1935 as a quasi-official statement of party purpose. Throughout the decade they remained crucial to the formation of party policy.

This group of academics possessed two related beliefs that affected CCF policy toward the United States. First, they were nationalists. Most of them had fought in World War I and had been disillusioned by the experience. Like many of their counterparts south of the border, they questioned the need for North Americans to be involved in resolving Europe's quarrels. They remained attracted to many things in Britain, but were as a group suspicious of British influence over Canadian politics and saw themselves as North American.[24] The United States was not their ideal land (after all they were socialists), but they saw Canadians as having much in common with their neighbors to the south.[25]

Aside from being generally pro-North American, these intellectuals was supportive of free trade. This was not surprising nor particularly radical among academics in the 1930s. The sorry history of international protectionism led to denunciations of the practice from political economists of practically all political stripes. In this sense the League members were more or less conventional in their criticisms. "The history of tariff legislation," concluded *Social Planning for Canada*, "presents a nice picture of the way in which a group of enterprising citizens can set up exotic industries and reap vast fortunes from the exploitation of miserably paid workers and fleeced consumers."[26] Nevertheless, when their free trade outlook was combined with their sense of being North American it had a potent effect. For many Canadians, free trade was fine on economic grounds but there was the political impact to consider. East-west trade, attachment to Empire, and other issues intruded upon the decisions of many. For the League, however, it seemed natural to look to the United States. They curtly dismissed the anti-American arguments with the comment that "for our part, we do not believe Canadians will love their country only if they are kept poor."[27]

Though the CCF in the 1930s was a free trade party, however, its policies should be kept in perspective. Unlike the Progressives, the CCF saw the tariff as a marginal issue. M. J. Coldwell, a Member of Parliament and future leader of the party, summed it up in 1936 when the Liberal government brought a Canadian-American trade deal to Parliament. "We hear a great deal about tariffs," he began. "I am not a high tariff man; indeed, I do not believe in tariffs." At the same time he thought the Liberals were fooling themselves. "The tariff controversy is out of date. The question today is not about tariffs but about exchange of goods. . . . Tariff policies are not the solution of our difficulties."[28] The leader of the party, J. S. Woodsworth, said basically the same thing. The trouble with Canada, he said, goes "deeper than the question of protection or lower tariffs."[29]

This was a change of considerable significance. In Canadian history, the tariff issue had been perhaps the single greatest source of controversy on economic issues from Confederation to the 1930s. This was natural given the nature of government at the time. The tariff was the greatest single economic imposition of government upon its people. Indeed, until World War II, Customs and Excise taxes comprised the largest revenue source for the Canadian government. The tariff also had dramatic redistributive effects between those who could benefit from protection and those who suffered because they had to buy goods in a protected market. Critics in Canada as in the United States argued that high tariffs redistributed things all the wrong way: from farm to city and from poor to rich, from workers to owners. Just as important as the direction of redistribution was the simple fact that there were few other levers for Canadian government to employ. The modern social safety net of medicare, unemployment insurance and job training programs did not exist. In other words, at a time when other government fiscal and redistributive policies were constrained or non-existent, the tariff issue often became a surrogate for broad questions of social principle. This contrasts sharply with the post-1945 political scene when tariff issues became much less controversial in the face of a broader conception of government fiscal and social management.

But even in the 1930s the CCF believed that governments should move into a whole new range of social and economic areas. The party believed that the limited state only served the "predatory interests" of capitalism. Only when the "natural resources and the principal means of production and distribution are owned, controlled and operated by the people," concluded the party's founding manifesto, would capitalism and the predatory system be controlled. In order to achieve this the party called, among other things, for large scale nationalization and extensive government planning. Its aim was to "replace the present capitalist system, with its inherent injustices and inhumanity, by a social order from which the domination of one class by another will be eliminated."[30] International trade, for its part, would be regulated by a series of Import-Export boards. Central planning would replace both the market system and the old debates between free traders and protectionists would become "obsolete." Given such plans, it is no wonder that the tariff seemed a relatively minor issue.

In the first years, therefore, the CCF attitude toward trade with the United States was shaped by three things. The first two of these, the party's agrarian roots and the pro-North American attitude of its intellectuals, pushed it toward a free-trade anti-tariff position. The third force, a belief in the need to go beyond capitalism, mitigated the importance of free trade as a party issue. As the 1936 debate, and a subsequent one in 1938, indicated, the party would support free trade but did so while reminding people of the futility of such agreements. By

World War II, the question of tariffs practically disappears from party policy. The publication in 1943 of *Make This Your Canada* was an attempt to set out the CCF's vision for the post-war world. The book emphasizes the importance of a positive relationship between the North American wartime allies. It also retains a focus on agrarian issues. The tariff, however, has become inconsequential. Instead the discussion of farm policy centers on issues like marketing boards, farm subsidies and control of the agricultural implements monopoly. The tariff is not mentioned.[31]

This trend continued for the next several years. The tariff became less of an issue among all parties after the 1933 Imperial Economic Conference, the 1935-36 Canada-U.S. Trade Agreement, and 1938 trilateral agreement significantly reduced tariffs from the levels of the early thirties. Moreover, as is well known, the lesson of the depression was not lost on the international community. By the end of World War II, a series of steps at places like Bretton Woods created a reasonably stable system for international trade. The extreme protectionism of the inter-war years was now replaced by an agreement in principle that trade should both be fairer and freer. Thus in the elections of 1945, 1949, and 1953, the CCF devoted practically no attention to the question of tariffs while continuing to advocate general support for the new GATT and IMF frameworks. Indeed, tariffs would not be a significant issue again for some time to come.[32]

The tariff had been relegated to a quiet corner of CCF policy. The party remained vaguely free trade but the fact was that as the issue hardly ever arose nobody ever really thought about it. When other, non-economic issues began to challenge the old assumptions of free trade it quickly became apparent just how weak the party's attachment to the old agrarian issue really was.

Anti-Americanism and Nationalism in the Post-War Years

Canada's sense of security had always depended on what it viewed as a proper balance of influence among the two great powers of the North Atlantic triangle. In the 1930s, LSR members remembered World War I and stressed the need to move to a North American position. By the 1950s, however, the British Empire was much weakened and Canada's independent status had been emphasized by a series of diplomatic and legislative actions during and after the war. Only the most dedicated Anglophobe could have perceived Britain as a threat to Canadian independence by 1950.

In contrast, some Canadians, mainly intellectuals and politicians, were growing wary of the new superpower, the United States. Typical was Prime Minister Mackenzie King who, by the end of the war, was more worried about American influence than he was about his old foe, creeping British centralization. King was joined by the already mentioned Harold Innis, Canada's foremost economist, who wrote in 1949 of the power vacuum left by British decline and the overly great influence of the United States. He also coined a phrase that was to become famous. Canada, he said, had emerged from colonial status with Great Britain only to be drawn back to a new colonial relationship with the United States. "American imperialism has replaced and exploited British imperialism."[33]

Until the later 1950s these concerns were amorphous and confined to a fairly narrow, if elite, circle. Two events followed in relatively quick succession, though, which made the debate over American influence a public matter. First, in 1957 the Report of the Royal Commission on Canada's Economic Prospects (Gordon Commission) expressed concern about the vast growth in American investment in Canada.[34] This was something new. For until then, Canadians had spent a great deal of time and effort luring foreigners to invest in the country. Indeed, one of the great benefits of the tariff according to its advocates had been precisely this ability to create branch plants.[35]

The second event seemed designed to prove the point raised by the commission. In Parliament a nasty battle broke out over the construction of a Trans-Canada pipeline. Questions of government arrogance mixed with concerns about American financial influence, the selling of national resources and other nationalist concerns. In the election that followed, the government found itself dogged with charges of excessive continentalism. With these events the public mood toward Canadian nationalism changed perceptibly. Most Canadians remained generally pro-American, but the issue of American economic dominance, and especially American ownership of Canadian resources, was never far below the political surface.

Though these events had an influence on the CCF, they were not restricted to any specific party. There were other concerns peculiar to the left, however. In particular, the whole relationship to the United States as "leader of the free world" in the Cold War caused tension. It should be emphasized that the CCF was not pro-Soviet. Indeed, it had done its own small part to prosecute the cold war when in the later 1940s it purged its own ranks of known Communists.[36] Nor, so far as can be seen, was there one single thing which made the CCF restive with the Cold War. Small things rankled however. The arrogance of the United States and its claim to moral superiority was looked upon with doubt by people who still felt at odds with capitalism. The CCF also resented the tendency of Cold Warriors to brand all left wing regimes as Communist. In addition, many of the CCF's intellectual supporters were early proponents of ban-the-bomb and general disarmament activities. The United States as an atomic power and quite a belligerent one, now seemed an obstacle rather than a guarantee of world peace. Finally, the CCF in Canada had been from the beginning a party of civil rights, partly because its leaders were often subject to minor harassment by the establishment. The great McCarthy-HUAC witch hunt in the United States made many Canadians uncomfortable, but it made CCFers especially critical.

The CCF was hardly prone to radical anti-American rhetoric in this period. Any party with pretensions to mainstream electoral support could not afford to sound like an agent of Moscow. In the immediate aftermath of the Korean War, it was significant enough that the CCF repeatedly broke ranks on Cold War issues. By 1953, the party was calling for Canada to draw back somewhat from the United States. There was rhetoric critical of what it termed "war hysteria." There was also the specific argument that nuclear arms should be under U.N. control. Most importantly, the CCF began to call into question the whole moral basis of the cold war. While restating its anti-Communist position, it concluded that it was determined not to be prevented from criticism "by verbal denunciations and hysterical war propaganda. The best defence of democracy lies in social justice and in respect for fundamental freedoms."[37] Any particular pro-Americanism of the early CCF had, by the mid-1950s, given way to a more distant and somewhat critical view of the United States. This was just the beginning.

The next fifteen years were turbulent times for the left in Canada. First, the party totally restructured itself. In the later 1950s, the CCF was in trouble. It had lost much of its earlier socialist fervor. The 1950s were not the same as the 1930s, and this was reflected in the relatively tame platform adopted in Winnipeg in 1956. The belief in planning, social engineering and a strong safety net were retained. Gone, however, was much of the apocalyptic rhetoric and the mass nationalization of the Regina Manifesto.[38] The changes did not revitalize the party. In 1957 and especially in 1958, the party's electoral results were abysmal. The second election was especially disastrous with leader T. C. Douglas defeated personally and the total representation reduced to 8 seats. As the historian of the party wrote, "the CCF's problem was no longer a secret."[39]

A long discussed idea seemed to provide a solution, however. For many CCFers, the dependence on a shrinking agrarian population was disastrous. Canada was an urban nation, and unless a means were found to improve the party position in urban centers, the future was dim. The answer was to follow the example of the British Labor Party and seek formal affiliation with the Canadian Trade Union movement. The major trade unions in Canada had long been torn between the British example of political activism and the American one of detachment and pragmatism. In the later 1950s, though, the mood was right within the union movement, and in 1961 the old CCF re-formed with a formal union presence under the title of the New Democratic Party. Though the party lost neither its western nor agrarian roots, it was now much more interested in and dependent upon unions. Indeed, one of the great benefits of the new arrangement was the access to union coffers during election campaigns. One of the costs of such dependence, however, was a much greater ability by unions to influence party policy; and manufacturing unions at least do not tend toward free trade. Nevertheless, in the prosperous and generally internationalist mood of the early 1960s, the union presence did not immediately affect tariff policy. The platform of the new party continued a tradition when it concluded that "tariffs are outmoded, patch-work attempts to protect domestic industry."[40]

The survival of an attenuated free trade orientation can be shown in the 1965 discussion of the Canada-U.S. Auto Pact. This pact was a sectoral policy of freer trade aimed at the auto industry. Its main purpose was to end the inefficiency of branch plant auto industries in Canada while safeguarding Canadian jobs. The NDP position on it was consistent throughout. It supported the idea of free trade, accepted the need for "rationalization" of an inefficient industry, and supported the principle of closer trade relations with the United States. It did have criticisms, arguing that not enough was done to retrain workers put out of a job and that car prices in Canada hadn't come down sufficiently. Nonetheless, as Toronto M.P. Andrew Brewin put it, "We in this party have made it very clear that we are not opposed to the basic purposes of the agreement."[41] The Auto Pact and other trade debates from the early to mid-60s imply that the unions did not immediately impose a protectionist viewpoint upon the NDP.

The key force reorienting the party lay not in the union halls but on the university campuses.[42] Canada as elsewhere saw a flowering of radicalism in the 1960s. This new movement was eclectic, youth oriented and brash. It began in university based organizations like the Committee for Universal Nuclear Disarmament (CUND) in the later 1950s. By the 1960s it had expanded into bodies like the Student Union for Peace Action (SUPA), the Canadian Union of Students (CUS), and other organizations. As in the United States and Europe, academics and others felt the pull of many of the ideas of the decade. Much of it was transitory and depended on the vast expansion of universities and the general affluence of the period. Nevertheless, from the later 1950s through the early 1970s, it had a profound political impact, shaping the rhetoric of political debate and redefining the nature of reform.

Initially, much of the Canadian new left took its cue from its counterpart south of the border. The civil rights movement of the later 1950s and early 1960s, the 1964 Port Huron statement of the Students for a Democratic Society, and the early anti-war movement were all influential in Canada. Thus, in many ways the Canadian new left was born in a continental mould, a free trade of ideas if you will. In fact, its critics have denounced the Canadian student left as essentially derivative, drawing inspiration from south of the border. Despite this, the Canadian new left was consciously nationalist and increasingly strident about its nationalism as the decade went on. Part of this was a natural extension of the movement's very continentalism. The left in the United States was making a criticism from within society. They were Americans and thus any critique implied a necessity for reform. In Canada the growing critique of the United States created the temptation to disengage from an Empire that was characterized in such dark terms.

There was more to it than a recoiling from Watts or Vietnam. The 1960s, after all, was an age when nationalism and the left were seen as linked. This was the age of national liberation struggles. Castro and Mao were extremely popular; so too was Che Guevara. The efforts of nations to throw off colonialism was looked upon with sympathy everywhere, and Communism was seen as the natural ideological center of such efforts. This is hardly surprising. In the United States, the new left did the same thing. The difference is that the left in Canada could, with a little stretching of the mind, portray their country as just another third world nation, albeit a rich one. Canada was, in the words of one influential critique of foreign ownership, just a "rich, industrialized, underdeveloped country."[43] As another put it, Canada was merely a "dependent capitalist state in the American Empire."[44] This country, it appeared, needed a little national liberation of its own.

This attachment to the spirit of left nationalism led to a renewed attachment to earlier Canadian nationalist intellectuals. Harold Innis, Donald Creighton and the other proponents of the east-west trade system gained adherents from a new generation. There is an irony in this, for Innis had been a liberal individualist and Creighton an active Conservative. Both were highly suspicious of state power and would never have accepted a socialist program for change.[45] Nonetheless, Innis and the staples school were attractive to the left for three reasons. First, it had been a Canadian school of economics. Second, it was very political in its orientation toward economics. Unlike the neo-classicists, it viewed economics as inseparable from political policy. Finally, Innis and Donald

Creighton were pro-British and anti-American. They had sympathized, occasionally romanticized, Canadian efforts to retain the British connection and thwart American manifest destiny. An earlier generation of CCFers had seen Creighton and his ilk as part of a dying colonialism. In this new age, however, they were viewed as nationalists. They became icons of the left.[46]

The combination of Canadian political economy and third world dependency theory had a decisive impact on left wing economic thought. Competition, comparative advantage, open trade and a host of other standard economic themes were not so much challenged as thought irrelevant to the Canadian situation. Canada, it was repeatedly argued, was not in a classical economic situation. As an underdeveloped and economically colonized country, the rules were stacked against it. American extraterritoriality, branch plant export of profits, the failure to develop Canadian markets and a host of other weaknesses seemed attributable, at least in part, to the tremendous U.S. presence in the Canadian economy. A favorite phrase was to describe the situation as "neo-mercantilist" or as part of an "imperial relationship."[47] Those who preached a pro-business line and talked in terms of rationalization and economic efficiency were increasingly looked upon with doubt. Whether consciously or unconsciously, they were in effect hastening the integration of the two economies and the disintegration of Canada.

The new left also recognized that nationalism was an appeal with a broad base. As one SUPA leader wrote in 1967, "the necessity of Canadian independence for radical change and the fact that majority opinion in Canada is in favor of Canadian nationalism can be seen as at least a temporary lever for social change."[48] He was right. By the mid-sixties, Canadians were susceptible to nationalist appeals. The findings of the Gordon Commission, the Pipeline debate and other early skirmishes had been followed by more and more political controversy surrounding Canadian-American relations. In the early 1960s, the Canadian government and much of the Canadian public had expressed unease and ambivalence toward the cold war politics surrounding the Bay of Pigs and then the Cuban Missile Crisis.[49] Most explosively, in 1962-1963 the issue of nuclear weapons on Canadian soil had become a major political issue. Neither the badly divided Conservatives nor the anti-nuclear NDP were able to prevent the election of a Liberal pro-American government and the acceptance of BOMARC nuclear missiles onto Canadian soil. For many it was the symbolism of Canada's fall into continentalist arms.[50]

Even the new pro-nuclear, pro-American Liberals could not avoid the controversy over Canadian-American relations, however. Walter Gordon, the former Royal Commission Chairman, was now a Liberal cabinet

Minister.   In 1963, as Minister of Finance, he introduced a series of measures to curb foreign takeovers of Canadian firms.   Controversy followed, and many of the proposals were withdrawn.   Nonetheless, the concern over U.S. investment had once again become front page news. Two years later, now as Minister without Portfolio, Gordon created a Task Force to study the whole issue of foreign ownership. Mel Watkins, a left leaning nationalist, was appointed to head it. The Watkins report was an official document and, as Watkins himself later noted, carefully avoided inflammatory language.   Nonetheless, it did proceed from the assumption that large scale foreign ownership impeded economic and political independence.   While mentioning the benefits of foreign investment, it stressed the need for that investment to be controlled if the state was not to lose its sovereign position.   Only government inter-vention and regulation, the report continued, could prevent a further deterioration of the situation.   From a perspective like this, protectionism took on a new nationalist hue.   "Tariffs for manufacturing in the host country are defended as necessary to maintain the vestiges of a national economy, but attacked as inefficient and eroded by pressures for rationalization and integration." [51]

All of these events reflect a major change in Canadian thinking on the United States.   In a way, the SUPA official was correct.   From the later 1950s through mid-sixties, the public had come to see the United States and U.S. influence in Canada as a threat to Canadian nationalism.   The various incidents mentioned above led to a fairly widespread critique of Canadian-American relations which challenged the standard post-war themes of co-operation, undefended border, and the like.[52] Each party responded to the theme in its own way, but all three took the nationalist issue seriously. The party that took it most seriously of all was the newly created NDP.

By the mid-60s, the NDP faced growing pressure from within and without to move leftward and to do so in an explicitly nationalist and anti-American direction.   The always powerful intellectual wing of the party was increasingly influenced by those associated with the new left. Mel Watkins, for example, left his stint in Ottawa radicalized and was soon arguing within the party that socialism would not succeed in Canada unless independence was first secured.   By 1968, the issue of nationalism and radicalism was sufficiently important that leader David Lewis invited a couple of radical economists to present their ideas on Canadian colonialism and U.S. ownership to the party leadership.[53] Influenced by this and by a growing radicalism among younger rank and file members, the 1968 platform explicitly accepted the policy of the economic nationalists.   "New Democrats have become convinced that recovering our economic independence is a crucial step in securing our future prosperity. This is not a matter of narrow nationalism nor does it hinge merely on the foreign or domestic ownership of our industry and commerce." At the same time, it explicitly broke with the Canadian practice of quiet diplomacy and advocated a withdrawal from the Cold War alliance system. "The time is overdue to dismantle the series of military alliances which were our foreign policy twenty years ago."[54]

Clearly the party was moving to the left and to a position increasingly critical of the United States. The real challenge of the next few years, however, came from those new leftists who wanted the party to go still further toward an anti-American and radical socialist position. In 1969, the always present academic influence on the party was divided. Older, traditional New Democrats were comfortable with the party's position, but a group of younger academics and students came from the new left and wanted to bring the party more fully into a radical-socialist position.

The group was led by historian James Laxer and by the already-mentioned Toronto economist, Mel Watkins. By 1969, they had coined themselves the Waffle group and set out to influence the party. Active, articulate and supported by the powerful student movement, they became a major influence on the party, at least briefly.[55] The Waffle was an avowedly radical movement made up mainly of students, academics and professionals.[56] It sought to return the apostate NDP to its more radical and socialist roots. Most important here is the particular ideology of the movement. Continentalism, not class, was the focus of attention. The Waffle saw the United States as the issue. Gone were the oblique references of earlier NDP documents. In their place was an explicit anti-Americanism. "The American empire is the central reality for Canadians," argued the group's manifesto. "It is an empire characterized by militarism abroad and racism at home." From there it was a short step to conclude that "the major threat to Canadian survival today is American control of the Canadian economy."[57]

The Waffle brought their ideas to the 1969 NDP convention in Winnipeg. Student radicals and academics lined up against the party's old-guard. Suddenly those who were used to seeing themselves in the vanguard for reform were accused of being reactionaries. In order to counter this charge and in order to stave off the Waffle resolution, the party executive moved a resolution that, though less rhetorically provocative than that of the Waffle, was equally nationalist. This so-called "Marshmallow Resolution" also portrayed the United States as a threat to Canadian nationalism and socialism. "The erosion of our national independence has reached alarming proportions," it read. "Effective measures to reverse the trend are necessary now before foreign control of our economic life reaches the point of no return."[58] In his speech introducing the resolution, party leader David Lewis said that

"Unless [Canada] is free economically, we cannot build a socialist society in this country." The link between American domination, Canadian nationalism and socialism had been accepted.

The next few years would be turbulent ones for the NDP. The Waffle continued to press the party leftward. In 1971, James Laxer was even able to mount a credible bid to take over the leadership of the party, losing only after four ballots. The rhetoric of the Waffle became increasingly intransigent, increasingly anti-American and increasingly awkward for a party that still wished to appeal to left-liberal middle class voters. Finally, the Waffle pushed too hard. A series of attacks on the union leadership as puppets of American international unionism led to a counter-attack. In Ontario in 1972, the Waffle was expelled. Thereafter the group lost influence as the more conventional membership faded into the mainstream of the NDP. The truly radical broke away to form a variety of short lived radical socialist movements.[59] The party regained some of its equilibrium.

Despite the eventual collapse of the Waffle movement, the 1960s and early 1970s were, I think, central to a reorientation of the New Democrats. First, at the beginning of the decade they had created formal links with a powerful union movement. That movement could not always deliver the votes, but it was of considerable influence in the party hierarchy. It was also crucial financially. By the mid-70s, it accounted for two-thirds of all party funds.[60] Then, during the 1960s, party ideology took on a strongly nationalist perspective. That nationalism, moreover, was increasingly tied to the perceived American threat. The focus in this decade was foreign ownership but the more general point was that continental integration was dangerous to Canadian independence and without true Canadian independence, it was further argued, there could be no victory for the left. In more heated times, as the rhetoric of the Waffle movement demonstrated, the rhetoric could be stridently anti-American. Even among the mainstream, however, a distrust of American power and influence had become a central part of the party's ideology.

After a decade of Vietnam and Canadian nationalist rhetoric, by the early 1970s the distrust of American influence was widespread, with a plurality of Canadians fearing increased U.S. domination of Canada.[61] The Liberals under Pierre Trudeau moved at least temporarily back to a mild nationalist position, adopting measures such as the Foreign Investment Review Agency in order to control U.S. investment.[62] As the decade went on, Canadian distrust of the United States receded. The end of the war in Vietnam, the replacement of Nixon with Ford and then Carter and, perhaps most of all, a bout of inflation and high unemployment, made many Canadians look more receptively upon American dollars. By the early 1980s, nationalism was in retreat among government officials and the major parties. This was not the case, however, for the NDP. Much of the party membership had first become involved in politics in the turbulent 1960s. The more extreme rhetoric was gone, but the general assumptions about Canadian nationalism, social reform and the threat of continentalism remained.

The background and early thinking of many contemporary leading NDP politicians demonstrate this point. To simplify things, however, it might suffice to point to the leader during that debate.   Edward Broadbent was born in 1936 and was during the 1960s a graduate student and then lecturer in Political Science. He had been a founding member of the Waffle movement and was involved in the drafting of the Waffle Manifesto and other early, radical statements.[63]   Eventually the intransigence and pseudo-revolutionary rhetoric of the group caused him to leave it. Nevertheless, in his early speeches and activities for the party, Broadbent clearly accepted the basic premises of the new nationalist outlook: that the United States was a problem and that Canadian reformism was endangered by too great a U.S. presence. To reinforce all of this was the practical fact that when Broadbent entered Parliament in 1968, he did so from the auto-union dominated riding of Oshawa. Nothing in his background or his direct political interests indicated that he would be in any way sympathetic to the doctrine of closer trade relationships with the United States. In this he was typical of much of his party. Canadian nationalism and a distrust of the United States was deeply imbedded and was certainly more important to party thought than any vestigial attachment to the notion of free trade.

The NDP and the Free Trade Debate

The idea of a broad trade agreement with the United States sneaked up on the Canadian public. In the 1970s, the Trudeau government had continued to propound what it termed the "third option." This sought to diversify Canadian trade away from the United States. At the same time many academic economists and civil servants were aware that the third option wasn't leading anywhere. Canadian trade with the United States was, through the 1970s and into the 1980s, growing in both absolute and relative terms. In 1956, when the Gordon Commission first report, the United States accounted for approximately 65% of all imports into Canada. By 1975 the figure was closer to 70%. The rhetoric about third options and concerns about nationalism had done nothing to reverse the long term trend.

The inevitability of dependence on American trade became a central part of the thinking behind the 1983 Royal Commission on the Economic Union and Development Prospects for Canada (Macdonald Commission). Noting the failure of the third option, the Commission concluded that the very vulnerability of Canada made close ties with the United States desirable. Our most important trading relationship, the logic went, had to be ensured through a special framework agreement.[64] The idea also had a strong resonance with economists inside and outside of government. For the great majority of them, free trade was an inherent part of their discipline. Most importantly, however, it fit the mood and political requirements of the new Conservative government. Prime Minister Brian Mulroney was by far the most pro-American of recent Prime Ministers and was, besides, in need of an economic strategy. Usually the ideas of Royal Commissions languish for many years or indeed never lead to action. This one was different, however. Even before the report was finalized, the Canadian government was moving toward free trade negotiations with the United States.

The well-known details of the free trade talks will not be discussed here. Nor is there a great deal to be said about NDP discussions or internal debates on the deal. For in spite of some reservations in the West, the party came out instantly and strongly against the pact. This time they were in a strong alliance with their labor supporters. Big unions like the Canadian Auto Workers and the umbrella Canadian labor Congress denounced the concept from the beginning. As the talks went on and the details became gradually clearer, the hostility grew. This was no trade issue in the mind of its critics. Instead, as Ontario NDPer Stephen Lewis put it in 1988, it was a struggle "about the heart and soul of this country. It's about the definition of Canada."[65]

The party's position against free trade rested on three basic points. In hindsight, perhaps the most pertinent criticism that could have been made was that the whole agreement missed the mark insofar as Canada was concerned. Left wing economist Marjorie Cohen noted in 1987 that free trade was not really the issue. Most of the trade between Canada and the United States was already free. Rather, Canadians feared American harassment through non-tariff barriers and countervailing duties. The American tariff on softwood lumber was, as is well known, instrumental in pushing forward the move to an agreement. The trouble, said Cohen, was that the United States "can continue to harass Canada over such issues as regional, provincial and local development schemes; aspects of its unemployment insurance program; government aid to resource sectors; research and development grants; corporate tax policies, and the operation of national railroads—whenever these involve exports to the United States."[66]

Second, the party and its supporters condemned the free trade agreement because it would interfere with key Canadian resource plans, a National Energy Policy for example. This didn't carry much weight however. Unlike the 1970s, the 1980s were not a period characterized by concerns over scarcity of natural resources. When a brief flurry did arise about selling water, the Conservative government moved quickly to say that this was not part of the negotiations. Moreover, the idea that free trade would prevent the government from meddling in a region's resources was, especially in the West, a positive not a negative aspect of free trade. The theme carried little weight.

The third argument was the one given by far the most attention. Drawing upon Canadian traditions dating back to the nineteenth century, this argument portrayed the United States as a flawed, even diseased society. Sometimes this was developed in more or less economic terms. Ronald Reagan and the neo-conservatism of the 1980s was seen as a last desperate attempt to prop up a failing economic system. For Canada to hitch itself to a falling star was doubly dangerous. First, it threatened Canadian sovereignty, and second, it did so by tying the country to a loser.[67] Instead, the third option scheme should be pursued with Canada pursuing multilateral trade relationships.

This fuzzy notion that somehow the United States was not worth dealing with had a good many holes in it. The United States was, after all, our largest trading partner by far. The argument became much more powerful, however, when used in reference to the comparable social systems. This was an issue on which a good many Canadians had strong feelings based on two popular notions. The first held that there was a substantial difference in the nature of the two societies. Second, the majority of Canadians believed without doubt or hesitation that Canadian society was superior. Sometimes this emotion was described in reference to specific social programs, especially medicare. Equally often, however, the belief encompassed a general image of the two nations and involved everything from gun use to religious hucksterism. Even the pro-free trade *Globe and Mail* argued that "if the United States were exporting its social programs no one in the industrialized world would buy them."[68] The threat of infection of Canadian society and social programs thus appealed in a powerful and visceral way to Canadian traditions. It became the center-piece of both NDP and Liberal ads during the 1988 election campaign. Pictures of nurses stepping freshly out of the operating theater to express worry about the future of Canadian medicare put the issue in the starkest possible form.

The question of course was why Canadian social programs would be affected at all. Sometimes the accusation was that the United States would demand a removal of "hidden subsidies" in the form of social programs.[69] The government repeatedly indicated it would not make such trade-offs, however, and the basic argument underpinning this depiction of social disaster was both more subtle and more difficult to explain to the electorate. It was first expressed in detail by Stephen Clarkson, a professor of Political Science, in a 1982 book. Clarkson argued that free trade was dangerous not because of what the Americans would make us do but because of what our businessmen would demand. Faced with the harsh competition of a North American free trade zone, they would be unable to compete while carrying the relatively higher taxes imposed by Canada's social system. The only answer would be to demand a reduction of Canadian social programs and taxes until we had essentially conformed to the American system.[70]

Clarkson's thesis allowed critics to move on to comfortable ground. The long-rooted Canadian sense of superior morality (if inferior economy) could now be presented in the modern dress of a defence of the social security system for which the NDP took special credit and had special affection. It also allowed a considerable element of anti-Americanism to be introduced into the debate. The powerful NDP figure and leader of the Canadian Auto Workers Robert White mixed the fear of loss of social programs with a popular stereotype of American society when he termed the agreement "ludicrous. . . . It'll mean we're moving toward a Rambo, dog-eat-dog, survival of the fittest society with no ability to maintain our social programs or ability to structure our own economy." This was followed a short time later by a full page Auto Workers ad which was even more specific in its portrayal of the dark maw that awaited us if continental integration was pursued. "Canadians have a medical system that guarantees everyone good health-care, not just those who can afford it. We have social programs that address the needs of the elderly, the needy, the homeless, the sick. Canadians believe that we are responsible for one another, that life is survival for all, not just the fittest. We have a flourishing multicultural environment. Our cities are safe. Our citizens live in security. "[71]

In the end, of course, the NDP failed to stop the Conservative tide and the free trade agreement went through. That in no way weakened the party's position however. In fact, if anything, it has strengthened it. It was always expected that there would be a period of "readjustment" after the conclusion of the agreement. new businesses would arise and certain old one disappear. Nobody had expected this to take place during a recession, however, and the hardship of lost jobs, plant closures and capital movement southward have all confirmed in the mind of NDP supporters, blue and white collar, that free trade was a ghastly mistake. Even had the economic shakedown been less severe, however, the party's position would not likely have changed. For as I have argued, the primary force of the NDP opposition to free trade lay not in a fear of loss of jobs but in deep-seated ideological developments over the past thirty years. Party members are not for the most part stridently anti-American any more. Party members hold strongly to the belief that a part of Canadian distinctiveness (and superiority) is a greater openness to social programs. Accordingly, closer Canadian-American ties present a danger of erosion of Canadian values and programs. It would take a major reversal of a good many assumptions for the NDP to find in free trade a positive force for their cherished beliefs and goals. There is nothing on the horizon to indicate this will happen.

Notes

1. Gerald Craig, *Upper Canada. The Formative Years 1784-1841* (Toronto: McClelland and Stewart, 1963), Chapter 6.

2. J. B. Brebner, *The North Atlantic Triangle. The Interplay of Canada, the United States and Great Britain* (Toronto: Ryerson Press, 1945).

3. Carl Berger, *Sense of Power. Studies in the Ideas of Canadian Imperialism* (Toronto: University of Toronto Press, 1970), p. 259.

4. S. F. Wise and Robert Craig Brown, *Canada Views the United States. Nineteenth Century Attitudes* (Toronto: Macmillan, 1967), pp. 18-19.

5. James Eayrs, *In Defence of Canada. Vol 2. Appeasement and Rearmament* (Toronto: University of Toronto Press, 1967), p. 176.

6. S. F. Wise and R. C. Brown, *Canada Views the United States. See also Carl Berger, The Sense of Power,* Chapter 6, "Critique of the Republic."

7. J. L. Granatstein and Norman Hillmer, *For Better or For Worse. Canada and the United States in the 1990s* (Toronto: Copp Clark Pitman, 1991), p. 20.

8. John Weaver, "Imperilled Dreams. Canadian Opposition to the American Empire, 1918-1930," PhD Duke University, 1973, p. 132.

9. The most popular example of this mythology is Pierre Berton, *The National Dream. The Great Railway 1871-1881* (Toronto: McClelland and Stewart, 1970). It is a common theme from the late nineteenth century on however. See, as examples, R. G. MacBeth, *The Romance of the Canadian Pacific Railway* (Toronto: Ryerson, 1924); John Murray Gibbon, *Steel of Empire. The Romantic History of the Canadian Pacific* (New York: Bobbs-Merrill, 1935); Donald Creighton, *John A. Macdonald. Vol. 2 The Old Chieftain* (Toronto: Macmillan, 1955).

10. Donald Warner, *The Idea of Continental Union* (Louisville, University of Kentucky Press, 1960), p. 31.

11. For a brief overview of the National Policy, see Kenneth Norrie and Doug Owram, *A History of the Canadian Economy* (Toronto: Harcourt Brace Jovanovich, 1990), Chapter 11. Ben Forster, *A Conjunction of Interests. Business, Politics and Tariffs, 1825-1879* (Toronto: University of Toronto Press, 1986) gives the background to high tariff arguments embodied in the National Policy.

12. Statistics Canada, *Historical Statistics of Canada,* 2nd edition (Ottawa: Supply and Services, 1983), Tables F334-41.

13. R. C. Brown, "The Nationalism of the National Policy," in Peter Russell, ed., *Nationalism in Canada* (Toronto: McGraw Hill, 1966).

14. Goldwin Smith, *Canada and the Canadian Question* (Toronto: University of Toronto Press, 1971; original published in 1891), p. 220.

15. R. C. Brown and G. R. Cook, *Canada 1896-1921. A Nation Transformed* (McClelland and Stewart, 1974), p. 179-85.

16. Canada. *Report of the Royal Commission on Dominion-Provincial Relations,* Book 1 (Ottawa: King's Printer, 1941).

17. W. A. Mackintosh, *The Economic Background of Dominion-Provincial Relations* (Toronto: McClelland and Stewart). See Harold Innis, "Great Britain, the United States and Canada," in Mary Q. Innis, ed., *Essays in Canadian Economic History* (Toronto: University of Toronto press, 1956), 394-412; D. G. Creighton, *Empire of the St. Lawrence* (Toronto: Macmillan, 1956; original published 1937).

18. The Cooperative Commonwealth federation or CCF was the direct forerunner of the New Democratic Party. The latter was not actually formed until 1961 when the CCF joined various labor union organizations and created the new party.

19. There is a long record of historical writing on this topic. Still important is the classic overview, Louis Aubrey Wood, *A History of Farmers' Movements in Canada. The Origins and Development of Agrarian Protest 1872-1921.* Introduction by Foster Griezec (Toronto, University of Toronto Press, 1975). See also Paul Sharp, *The Agrarian Revolt in Western Canada* (New York, Octagon Books, 1971). More recently an intellectual history has attempted to classify farm and other western politics in ideological terms. See David Laycock, *Populism and Democratic Thought in the Canadian Prairies 1910 to 1945* (Toronto: University of Toronto Press, 1990).

20. W. L. Morton, *The Progressive Party in Canada* (Toronto: University of Toronto Press, 1950), pp. 96-129.

21. This is from the United Farmers Platform of 1919 which was the founding document of the movement. See D. Owen Carrigan, *Canadian Party Platforms, 1867-1968,* (Toronto: Copp Clark, 1968), p. 91.

22. W. L. Morton, *The Progressive Party,* pp. 237-8.

23. Michiel Horn, *The League for Social Reconstruction. Intellectual Origins of the Democratic Left in Canada 1930-1942* (Toronto: University of Toronto Press, 1980), pp. 42-4.

24. Horn, *League for Social Reconstruction,* 11-12, 152; R. Douglas Francis, Frank H. Underhill. *Intellectual Provocateur* (Toronto: University of Toronto Press, 1986).

25. On CCF attitudes in the 1930s and 1940s, see Lawrence Aronsen, "The Northern Frontier: The United States and Investment in Canada, 1945-1953," Ph.D. thesis, University of Toronto, 1980, Chapter 5.

26. The League for Social Reconstruction, *Social Planning for Canada* (Toronto: University of Toronto press, 1975; original published in 1935), p. 32.

27. Ibid., p. 355.

28. Canada, House of Commons, *Debates,* February 24, 1936, p. 174.

29. Ibid., February 11, 1936, p. 104.

30. Carrigan, *Canadian Party Platforms*, p. 121.

31. David Lewis and Frank Scott, *Make This Your Canada. A Review of CCF History and Policy* (Toronto: Central Canadian Publications, 1943), pp. 170-1.

32. Carrigan, *Canadian Party Platforms*, pp. 176, 201-4.

33. Harold Innis, "Canada, the United States and Great Britain," p. 395.

34. Canada. *Final Report of the Royal Commission on Canada's Economic Prospects* (Ottawa; Queen's Printer, 1957), Chapter 3.

35. Michael Bliss, "Canadianizing American Business: The Roots of the Branch Plant," in Ian Lumsden ed., *Close to the 49th Parallel* (Toronto: University of Toronto Press, 1970), pp. 27-42; H. V. Nelles, *The Politics of Development. Forests, Mines and Hydro-electric Power in Ontario 1849-1941* (Toronto: Macmillan, 1974), pp. 62-9.

36. Walter Young, *The Anatomy of a Party: the National CCF* (Toronto: University of Toronto Press, 1969), pp. 277-84.

37. Carrigan, *Canadian Party Platforms*, p. 176.

38. "The Winnipeg Declaration, 1956" cited in *The Decline and Fall of a Good Idea. CCF-NDP Manifestos 1932 to 1969* with an Introduction by Michael Cross (Toronto: New Hogtown Press, 1974), pp. 30-2.

39. Desmond Morton, *The New Democrats 1961-1986. The Politics of Change* (Toronto: Copp Clark Pitman, 1986), p. 19.

40. "New Party Declaration" (1961) in *The Decline and Fall of a Good Idea. CCF-NDP Manifestos 1932 to 1969*, p. 36.

41. Canada, House of Commons, *Debates*, May 10, 1965, p. 1132. See also the speech of T.C. Douglas, pp. 1110-1115.

42. Philip Resnick's left wing analysis of this age, *The Land of Cain. Class and Nationalism in English Canada 1945-1975* (Vancouver: New Star Books, 1977), pp. 167-178.

43. Kari Levitt, *Silent Surrender. the Multinational Corporation in Canada* (Toronto: Macmillan, 1970), p. 127.

44. "Introduction," in Robert Laxer, ed., *Canada Ltd. The Political Economy of Dependency* (Toronto: McClelland and Stewart, 1973), p. 8.

45. Carl Berger, *The Writing of Canadian History. Aspects of English Canadian Historical Writing Since 1900*, 2nd edition (Toronto: University of Toronto Press, 1986), p. 85.

46. See Dave Godfrey and Mel Watkins, eds., *Gordon to Watkins to You. A Documentary; The Battle for Our Economy* (Toronto: new press, 1970), pp. 3-4.

47. C. W. Gonick, "Foreign Ownership and Political Decay," in Ian Lumsden ed., *Close to the 49th Parallel*, pp. 43-72, 46. See also McMaster University, Papers of the Student Union for Peace Action, "NDP Socialist Caucus Bulletin," for themes of this sort.

48. McMaster University, Special Collections, Papers of the Student Union for Peace Action, Box 5, "Canada in the Twentieth Century and the Future of Man," unsigned memo 1967.

49. Robert Bothwell, Ian Drummond, and John English, *Canada Since 1945: Power, Politics, Provincialism Revised Edition* (Toronto: University of Toronto Press, 1989), pp. 193-4.

50. George Grant, *Lament for a Nation. The Defeat of Canadian Nationalism* (Toronto: McClelland and Stewart, 1965).

51. Godfrey and Watkins, *Gordon to Watkins to You*, p. 68.

52. See, as an example of the moderate leftist literature of the era on this issue, Abraham Rotstein and Gary Lax, *Independence. The Canadian Challenge* (Toronto: Committee for an Independent Canada, 1972). For a left-of-center historical analysis of this period, see Philip Resnick, *The Land of Cain. Class and Nationalism in English Canada 1945-1975* (Vancouver, New Star Books), pp. 147-189.

53. Desmond Morton, *The New Democrats 1961-1986*.

54. Carrigan, *Canadian Party Platforms*, pp. 345, 347.

55. See Desmond Morton, *The New Democrats, 1961-1986*, pp. 91-7.

56. Philip Resnick,. *The Land of Cain*, p. 170 refers to this group as the "new petty bourgeoisie" and says they were comprised of salaried professionals including academics and those in training for such positions, that is to say students. He notes that 21 percent of the Waffle members were students, 10 percent were academics, and 19 percent were salaried professionals.

57. "Resolution 133 of the 1969 NDP Convention," (the Waffle Manifesto), cited in Godfrey and Watkins, *Gordon to Watkins to You*, p. 103.

58. Ibid., p. 111.

59. Desmond Morton, *The New Democrats, 1961-1986*, pp. 129-37.

60. Ibid., p. 185.

61. Canadian Institute of Public Opinion, *The Gallup Report*, March 28, 1970, "Canadians feel U.S. Domination is Increasing."

62. J. L. Granatstein and Robert Bothwell,_Pirouette, Pierre Trudeau and Canadian Foreign Policy* (Toronto: University of Toronto Press, 1990), especially Chapter 3.

63. Desmond Morton, *The New Democrats*, pp. 92-3.

64. Canada. *Report of the Royal Commission on Economic Union and Development*, Vol 1 (Ottawa; Supply and Services, 1985), pp. 299-300.

65. "U.S. Can't be Trusted says Lewis," *Edmonton Journal*, September 28, 1988, p. A16.

66. *Globe and Mail*, October 12, 1987, p. A7. See also Mel Watkins. "From the Heretic's Mouth. A Political Economist Exposes the Menace of Free Trade." *Canadian Forum*, August/September, 1985, pp. 7-10.

67. Mel Watkins, "Reservations Concerning a Free Trade Area Between Canada and the United States," in John Whalley and Roderick Hills, ed., *Canada-United States Free Trade* (Toronto: University of Toronto Press, 1985), pp. 85-90.

68. *Globe and Mail*, editorial, October 3, 1987, p. A6.

69. See letter to the editor by Jeff Rose, President of the Canadian Union of Public Employees, *Globe and Mail*, September 17, 1986, p. D17. .

70. Stephen Clarkson, *Canada and the Reagan Challenge* (Toronto: Lorimer, 1982).

71. *Globe and Mail*, October 21, 1987, p. A13.

7

Free Trade and Party Politics in Quebec

Pierre Martin

In 1991, the Canadian debate over North American free trade entered a new phase when the U.S. Congress authorized the President to initiate free-trade negotiations with Mexico. For the Canadian government, there was little choice but to participate in these negotiations, since a failure to do so would have exposed Canada to most of the anticipated costs, but few of the potential benefits, of a U.S.-Mexico free-trade arrangement.[1] In the turbulent context of Canadian and Quebec politics in the aftermath of the Meech Lake fiasco, the resumption of trade negotiations with the United States recast free trade as a central issue of contention between federal and provincial political parties across Canada. However, on this issue as for so many others, Quebec seems to be distinct.

Amidst the acrimonious debate over the constitutional future of Quebec, the messages emerging from Quebec's two major parties on the North American Free Trade Agreement (NAFTA) are remarkably convergent. Given the historical importance of trade in defining the cleavages between parties at the federal level,[2] this may be surprising. Nonetheless, both the Liberal Party of Quebec (PLQ), in power since 1985 under the leadership of Robert Bourassa, and the Parti Québécois (PQ), led by Jacques Parizeau, support continental trade liberalization. Perhaps surprisingly for outside observers, the central cleavage of Quebec politics, between the PQ's project of a sovereign Quebec and the Liberals' preference for a continuation of the federal structure, does not translate into major differences of opinion on the issue of free trade.

The agreement between the two main political parties on free trade reflects a bipartisan consensus at the elite level. Tensions within each party, however, have made trade a significant political issue in Quebec. Indeed, in the 1980s there were several flip-flops in party positions on free trade. In this chapter I first examine the roots of this underlying consensus on free trade between the two parties. In each party, support for free trade stems from a distinct view of Quebec nationalism and from particular societal pressures. Next I describe the changing politics of free trade in Quebec in the 1980s and the alignment of parties as the debate entered a new phase with the NAFTA negotiations. Cleavages within each party are identified as the main source of tension in the partisan confrontations over free trade. Finally I briefly elaborate on this survey of Quebec trade politics to speculate about the interaction between the free-trade issue and the future orientation of the Quebec party system.

Sources of Trade Consensus and Divergences

Regarding implementation of the U.S.-Canada Free Trade Agreement (FTA) and the NAFTA negotiations, there are sharp differences among Canadian federal parties. In contrast, as reflected in major policy statements on international economic policy produced by both parties in recent years, the two major Quebec parties agree on the fundamentals of free trade.[3] Elements explaining this consensus include the openness of the Quebec economy, the common roots of party elites who took part in major reforms in the 1960s, and the centrality of the institutions that emerged from this reformist period, known as the "Quiet Revolution." Most of all, just as free trade inflames Canadian nationalist passions, Quebec party attitudes toward North American free trade cannot be dissociated from the unavoidable issue of Quebec nationalism. Each party is in fact a coalition of interests that do not always converge on the free-trade issue. For that reason, Quebec political parties have not always been fully predictable on their support for free trade, although their leaders were united behind ratification of the FTA in 1988.

Quebec as a Small Open Economy: Structural Sources of Trade Policy Consensus

Two basic facts must be kept in mind when considering the politics of trade in Quebec. First, Quebec is a small and open economy which is dependent upon foreign markets for its exports and foreign capital for investment. Second, Quebec does not have constitutional authority over the main instruments of trade policy, namely, either the power to fix tariff levels or the power to negotiate trade agreements with other countries. Although the positions taken by Quebec politicians on the trade policies of the federal government may, to some extent, be symbolic, the effects of these policies on the Quebec economy are extremely significant. Symbols are important by themselves, but since Quebec politicians cannot always avoid blame for the consequences of the federal policies they support, their positions on trade policy cannot be considered purely symbolic.

The politics of trade in Quebec revolves around the high level of openness of the Quebec economy and its natural north-south orientation towards the North American market. In 1990, measured in Canadian dollars, Quebec's exports of goods outside Canada totalled $24.3 billion while its imports totalled $28.5 billion ($18.1 billion of exports to and $13.2 billion of imports from the United States); the share of exports in the province's GDP decreased from 20.6 percent in 1980 to 15.4 percent, the lowest since 1968. Increasingly, the lion's share of Quebec's exports are directed toward the United States (75 percent in 1990, 60 percent in 1980). For the same period, the United States accounted for about 50 percent of Quebec imports.

Foreign direct investment is also crucial for the Quebec economy, and even more so for its foreign trade, since intra-firm trade accounts for 40% of Quebec's exports. Although small and midsize firms are increasingly successful on export markets, the largest part of Quebec's exports are accounted by a small number of very large firms in wood products, transport and communications equipment, metals, and electronics. On the import side, vulnerable industries include textiles, clothing and furniture.[4] If we add the substantial proportion of Quebec's GDP represented by trade with the rest of Canada, the image of openness of the Quebec economy emerges even more fully.

The link between international economic openness and domestic political structures is the object of increasing interest in the comparative political economy literature. Trade openness has been found to affect the nature of policies adopted to deal with economic change, but also the dynamics of interest intermediation and the structure of party systems. Small states cannot use their power to force onto others the cost of adjusting to rapid economic change. As Peter Katzenstein and others have argued, elites in small states with open economies tend to let global markets determine the direction of economic adjustment, developing domestic political structures and policies to offset the social costs of rapid economic change.[5]

Economic openness is thus linked to a propensity for governments to support liberal trade policies while compensating for the uncertainties of global markets with effective social policies. Likewise important is the impact of economic openness on political institutions and political parties.

Exposure to international trade, as Ronald Rogowski has shown, tends to be associated with the centralization of political parties, both across nations and over time.[6] In short, trade openness in Quebec would tend to increase both policy convergence between parties and the capacity of their leaders to cope with internal dissent.

The relative sheltering of the Quebec economy behind the high Canadian tariff and the limited provincial control of economic policy instruments until the 1960s makes comparison with small northwestern European states problematic. But the rapid postwar liberalization of trade greatly reduced Canadian protective barriers, while the modernization of the Quebec state since 1960 gave the Quebec government control over important economic policy instruments. Increasingly, Quebec was led to formulate and implement economic policies in its expanding areas of effective policy competence with an eye on their external dimension.[7]

Conversely, external economic constraints (which means, practically, Quebec's trade and investment relations with the United States) have come to exert a key influence on modes of interest intermediation, on the content of economic policies and, by extension, on the relationship between economic policy and partisan politics. Indeed, the partial institutionalization of tripartite bargaining between labor, business and the state, initiated by the first PQ government in 1977, would tend to conform to the small open economy model discussed above.

Even if structural conditions conducive to the formation of a consensus behind free trade are present in Quebec, however, one should not draw hasty conclusions from them. For example, Ontario has a very comparable overall pattern of external trade[8] but its provincial parties were divided on free trade and its recent governments (Liberal in 1988 and New Democratic Party since 1990) have been adamantly opposed to both the FTA and NAFTA. Perhaps the different political dynamics of the free trade issue in Ontario can partly be explained by the fact that the province has traditionally been the center of Canada's protected capital-intensive industry. Still, mainstream economists note that Ontario may, in the long run, be the main beneficiary of free trade. For these observers, the widespread opposition to free trade in the province was a puzzle.[9]

This does not discredit the relevance of the consensus model discussed above, but it reinforces the need to look for internal political determinants to explain the agreement between Quebec parties on free trade. An essential element of this explanation is the widespread support among Quebec elites for the economic policies and institutions that emerged from the "Quiet Revolution." In the next section, I trace the common roots of these elites in this pivotal period of Quebec's political development.

Common Roots: The Quiet Revolution
and its Economic Legacy

If the openness of the Quebec economy conditions the choices made by politicians in favor of a liberal trade policy, the common experience of elites in both major parties in the political and socioeconomic reforms of the 1960s also explains the convergence of attitudes toward the broad orientations of economic policy. The "Quiet Revolution" of the 1960s was a defining moment in Quebec's social, economic and political history, following a long period of lagging social and economic development. Before 1960, francophones controlled only a small portion of economic activity and the role of the Quebec state was limited. The nationalism embodied in Maurice Duplessis's party, the Union Nationale, was essentially defensive and linked to the traditional idea of an agrarian French Canadian society.[10] The Quebec Liberal Party, elected in 1960, was determined to use the provincial government as a lever to allow Quebec to catch up with other western societies. As the Quebec government took on a more activist role, Quebec nationalism became associated with political modernization and progressive forces found in the emerging Quebec state an effective instrument of collective affirmation.[11]

This period of rapid reform led to a new dominant ideology in Quebec politics, allying nationalism and interventionism, but not *dirigisme*. This new ideology was characterized by a consensus on the role of state-owned enterprises, notably in the areas of energy (Hydro-Québec; Société québécoise d'initiatives pétrolières) and finance (Caisse de dépôts et de placements; Société générale de financement).[12] This economic dynamism of the Quebec state, in conjunction with the growing strength of a provincially regulated cooperative financial sector, fostered a sense of entrepreneurship among Quebecers and allowed the rapid development, after 1970, of francophone-controlled private enterprises. Although the two parties diverged in the 1970s, when the Liberals were closer to these new entrepreneurs, party attitudes became less differentiated in the 1980s. The present convergence of party positions on free trade reflects, in part, an underlying consensus among elites on the economic institutions created by the Quiet Revolution.

The major economic reforms and new policy instruments created a "new class" of state managerial elites in the 1960s, at first associated with the Quebec Liberal Party. It is important to note that the provincial and the federal Liberal parties had been, until the 1960s, part of the same organization. Before the 1960s, the Quebec Liberals and their federal counterparts were very closely tied, in much the same way that the national and state organizations of the two major U.S. parties are associated. Indeed, the leader of the PLQ through the period of the Quiet Revolution, Jean Lesage, had previously been a federal minister in the Liberal Cabinet of Louis Saint-Laurent.

However, as the Quebec government asserted its role in the early 1960s, the provincial wing of the party rapidly became isolated, and formally split from the federal party organization in 1964. Although the two parties have continued to share a significant part of the Quebec electorate and of their militant base, their respective organizations have drifted even further apart since the split.

Between 1964 and 1968, the expression of Quebec nationalism within the PLQ took two directions. René Lévesque, who had been a key minister of the Quiet Revolution, was forced out of the Liberal Party, in 1967, when a party congress rejected his proposal for "sovereignty-association." Lévesque's departure from the party was not a rejection of the Liberal agenda but was rather motivated by his conclusion that Quebec's social and economic development was constrained by its position in the Canadian federation. In 1968, Lévesque founded the Parti Québécois, soon attracting some of the top-level civil servants who had engineered the Quiet Revolution, including Jacques Parizeau. In short, the Parti Québécois was an outgrowth of the reformist Liberal Party of the 1960s, which contributes to explain the bipartisan agreement among elites on some of the fundamentals of economic policy.

In the late 1960s, the young Robert Bourassa, attracted at first to Lévesque's ideas, drew the opposite conclusion about the potential for reform within federalism. He ascended to the PLQ's leadership shortly before the April 1970 election that brought the Liberals back in power after four years of opposition. Reelected in 1973, Bourassa pursued an interventionist economic policy which left ample room for private-sector initiative. The development of the James Bay hydro-electric project was the centerpiece of Bourassa's economic strategy, along with other policies to foster the development of francophone business. The PLQ's pro-business stance and its hard-line approach to public-sector strikes in 1972 contributed to the consolidation of the PQ's support among public servants, labor groups and the left.[13] However, when the PQ was first elected in 1976, sending Bourassa into political exile, the implementation of its social-democratic platform was more modest than expected.[14]

When it took power, the Parti Québécois was torn between a commitment toward labor demands and a need to calm business fears caused by the PQ's radical image and by its sovereignist option. In response, the Lévesque government established institutions of tripartite concertation[15] and policies of government support to industry.[16] The decline of the left within the PQ was evident toward the end of the first mandate, as the more radical ministers and members of the National Assembly resigned in succession.[17] The transformation of the party's image was completed after the 1980 referendum defeat and the PQ victory in the 1981 election. As Gagnon and Montcalm point out, the 1980 referendum defeat "shifted the focus from *political* nationalism to *economic* nationalism: failure to achieve political independence, in other words, stimulated efforts by the PQ to achieve economic independence."[18]

In sum, while the PLQ and its federalist option have retained the favor of most of Quebec's business elites, the difference between the two parties' approaches to market-oriented development has narrowed since the 1970s. Overall, the institutions and ideas that evolved during the Quiet Revolution and its aftermath are not fundamentally contested by either party. In fact, the political generation that came of age during the Quiet Revolution and now forms the leadership of the two major parties has firm roots in this reformist period. Moreover, domestic and international economic policy are part of each party's nationalist objective to increase Quebec's autonomy vis-à-vis the rest of Canada. How can nationalism be associated with support for free trade?

Is Free-Trade Nationalism an Antinomy?

Nationalism is unavoidable in any analysis of Quebec politics. The puzzle, however, is that Quebec nationalism is *not* associated with protectionism but with free trade.[19] Although the outside observer may interpret nationalism strictly in terms of a conflict between federalists and sovereignists, this is not quite how it plays in Quebec, where both the Liberals and the PQ pose as "nationalists" opposed to the centralization of power in Ottawa. A sense of distinctiveness in a predominantly Anglo-Saxon continent makes almost every francophone Quebecer a nationalist. Yet, this feeling is characterized by ambiguity, as revealed by Quebec's support for the overtly anti-nationalist Pierre Trudeau from 1968 to 1979.[20] One thing is clear, however: no provincial party in Quebec can win anything by demanding less power for the Quebec government. Recently, the PLQ has demanded a radical decentralization of Canada's federalism which would leave only minimal functions to the central state,[21] while the PQ has returned to its original option of political sovereignty with an economic association, after a half-hearted post-referendum attempt at playing the federalist card.

Politically, for the proponents of sovereignty, free trade with the United States means a loosening of the constraints associated with economic ties with the rest of Canada. By making market access less contingent on the central government, free trade can potentially reduce Quebec's dependence upon the rest of Canada, thus also reducing the economic risks of sovereignty.[22]

A parallel to this rationale can be found in the support given by Scottish nationalists to the integration of the United Kingdom in the Common Market. The linkage between free trade and the reduction of Quebec's economic dependence upon Canada was not explicitly made by the PQ leadership in the party's early days, but it was articulated in 1970 by Rodrigue Tremblay, an economist who later briefly served in the first Lévesque cabinet.[23]

For the Liberal Party, the reasoning is similar, although less clear-cut. Greater economic openness such as that provided by continental free trade allows the Quebec government, even within federalism, to be less constrained by central government authority. The reduction of federal control on economic policy means a greater degree of relative autonomy to pursue Quebec's own economic interests in global markets. There is some parallel in the U.S. with the development of industrial policies at the state and local levels. Regional authorities in EC countries have also welcomed greater integration for similar reasons. It is useful to recall that, historically, Canadian nationalism has been associated with the maintenance of defenses against the powerful force of southward integration. It is thus not surprising that Quebec nationalism would define itself in opposition to this historical trend.[24]

After the 1980 referendum, the PQ shifted from political to economic nationalism, by adopting resolutely pro-business, market-oriented economic strategies. In Thomas Courchene's words, the PQ became "the most business-oriented or market-oriented government in Canada."[25] Notably by fostering the development of an efficient financial sector and of strong economic institutions, and by its support of free trade, Quebec has been able to effectively loosen its dependence on Canadian economic ties, thus improving its viability as a sovereign nation. Still, Courchene points out that there was little reason for the Liberal Party not to embrace the same economic program after its election in 1985. The PLQ, he argues, could easily "adhere to the position that a strong private sector controlled by Québécois can be a bulwark against independence." Quebec, he concludes, "is not so much 'opting out' of the Canadian federation as it is 'opting in' to the world economy."[26]

In sum, the two faces of Quebec nationalism represented by the leaderships of the two main provincial parties see opportunities in Quebec's integration into a continental and global economy, although for different reasons. But the dominant positions emerging from the two parties' parliamentary leaderships on free trade have never been shared unanimously by their electorates and rank-and-file memberships.

Two Coalitions of Divergent Trade Interests

The main reason why free trade has been an issue in Quebec politics since 1985 is not because the parties have fundamental disagreements on the matter, but rather because both parties are internally divided. In the Parti Québécois, and in the sovereignist movement, the leadership's free-trade stance finds a receptive audience in parts of business and in the general public. Although support for sovereignty is the exception among upper-level business leaders, there have been significant expressions of support for sovereignty since the rejection of the Meech Lake Accord in 1990.

For example, the *Mouvement Desjardins,* Quebec's financial giant built on grassroots credit unions, has been associated with the sovereignty option since an October 1990 poll of its 20,000 managers and volunteer administrators found a two-third level of support for a straightforward declaration of independence.[27] Desjardins' president, Claude Béland, has been one of the few top business leaders to take a highly visible stand for sovereignty. Most public-sector managers also tend to support sovereignty. The most prominent is Jean Campeau, former president of the *Caisse de dépôts et de placements* and copresident of the 1990-91 Commission on the Constitutional Future of Quebec, who later became chairman of the board of Domtar. In May 1992, he founded an association of pro-sovereignty business leaders, the *Regroupement Souveraineté-Québec Inc,* to counter the federalist *Regroupement Économie et Constitution.*

In contrast with the latter group, however, sovereignist business elites tend to be associated with small and midsize enterprises.[28] Frustration with Ottawa's economic policies has also led many small and midsize firms, through the voice of the Quebec Chamber of Commerce, to reveal their intention of leaning toward sovereignty if the process of constitutional revision does not lead to significant devolution of economic powers to Quebec. Indeed, a poll of business leaders published before the rejection of the Meech Lake Accord gave a 3 to 2 advantage to sovereignty within that group in the event that the Accord was rejected.[29]

Although the image of the PQ and that of its sovereignty option in the business community have made a quantum leap since the referendum, support for free trade among PQ and sovereignty sympathizers is far from unanimous. The PQ's social-democratic militant base is still there, and some of the most persistent supporters of sovereignty are found among labor unions, agricultural producers and other opponents of free trade.

In the rest of Canada, similar anti-free trade groups are typically associated with the New Democratic Party (NDP), but this party has never been effective in Quebec, largely because of its centralist image. Still, some of the NDP's arguments against free trade have been echoed in the Quebec left, notably in regards to NAFTA and its potential impact on social policy, wage levels and environmental standards. And although the viscerally nationalist dimension of opposition to free trade with the U.S. common among Canadian NDP supporters does not find a parallel in the Quebec left, the relationship between the PQ and organized labor is more complex than what is suggested by the harmony of their voices on the sovereignty issue. Indeed, this relationship soured considerably in the recessionary period after the 1980 referendum, when the PQ government rolled back salaries in the highly unionized public sector.[30] This paper's second section will show that opinions on free trade within the PQ varied considerably during the transition period between the departure of René Lévesque and the return of Jacques Parizeau. The party's program reflects this basic ambiguity by supporting trade liberalization, but with numerous conditions.

The Liberals' federalist stance brings them the support of a large part of the Quebec business community, generally wary of the economic risks of sovereignty. This is particularly true of top executives from some of the largest firms headquartered in Quebec, who formed the *Regroupement Économie et Constitution* in 1991 to counter the gains made by sovereignty in Quebec's public opinion. The leaders of this select group have been at the forefront of support for free trade: Laurent Beaudoin, president of the fast-growing transportation equipment manufacturer Bombardier (voted "most admired Quebec firm" in a 1990 poll of business people), Raymond Cyr, president of the communications giant Bell Canada Enterprises, and Guy Saint-Pierre, president of the world-class engineering firm SNC-Lavalin.[31] One should keep in mind, however, that these flagship firms of "Québec Inc." were among the prime beneficiaries of Quebec government policies, notably the Quebec Stock Saving Plan instituted by the PQ government when Jacques Parizeau was Minister of Finance.

Despite this strong core of support, the PLQ and, by extension, the federalist side in the constitutional debate, had two major weak spots on free trade in the 1980s, which should also play a role in the NAFTA debate.

First, Robert Bourassa has to take into account links between his party and the Liberal Party of Canada. Although the two organizations formally split in 1964, they still share an important part of the Quebec electorate, notably among English speakers in the Montréal region, whose first allegiance is to the federal party (as shown by their massive defection from the PLQ since 1988), but also among francophone voters across the province. I next show how this mattered in the free-trade debate, when tensions between provincial and federal Liberals in Quebec surfaced in the midst of a federal election.

Second, although the PLQ has close ties with the leaders of the "federalist wing" of Québec Inc., it also has long-standing ties with older, Canadian-based industries which are more vulnerable to free trade. Also, there are important electoral ties between the Liberals (at both levels) and the large immigrant labor force in low-wage import-sensitive industries such as textiles and clothing.

In sum, support for free trade by both the PQ and the PLQ can be interpreted as an expression of Quebec nationalism. This nationalist vision stems from the common experience of party elites in the socioeconomic reforms of the 1960s and their strong identification with the economic institutions that resulted from these reforms. Yet, the two parties are, to some extent, internally divided on free trade. If each party claims to offer the best recipe to favor the rapid growth of export-oriented industries, their programs and policies also keep a watchful eye on the interests of "soft" industries. In practice, the two parties realize that there is bound to be winners and losers as Quebec becomes further integrated into the global economy. They also recognize that high unemployment will be a major problem throughout the transition period to an integrated North American market, and perhaps even after.[32] To evaluate how the two parties will respond to further trade liberalization and economic integration, we turn to an examination of recent trade politics in Quebec.

Free Trade and Party Politics in Quebec Since 1980

During the 1970s, trade was overshadowed by investment as the key point of contention in Canadian-American economic relations. In fact, there was considerable bilateral trade liberalization in the 1970s but, because negotiations were held in the multilateral forum of GATT, this liberalization did not provoke as much partisan reaction as the restrictive investment policies of Pierre Trudeau's Liberal government. In Quebec, both the Liberal (1970-76) and PQ (1976-85) governments opposed federal investment policies because they infringed upon Quebec's own investment policy goals. However, implementation of investment policies by the Quebec government was similar to federal implementation[33] and public opinion toward U.S. investment in Quebec did not differ significantly from opinion in other provinces.[34]

The Parti Québécois and its U.S. Strategy, 1976-84

In the 1970s, the idea of closer economic ties with the United States as an antidote for Quebec's economic dependence upon Canada thus was entertained by analysts and politicians. In the PQ cabinet, besides Rodrigue Tremblay, who was not close to René Lévesque, the main economic ministers were strong proponents of closer economic ties with the United States. Jacques Parizeau and Bernard Landry, respectively Minister of Finance and Minister of State for Economic Development, saw free trade with the United States as an opportunity to allow Quebec's newly assertive entrepreneurs to conquer U.S. markets, while undercutting intrusions of the federal government in the definition of Quebec's economic development priorities.

Soon after the Parti Québécois took power, however, its leaders soon realized that the U.S. card would not let itself be played easily. When René Lévesque made his famous speech to the New York Economic Club in January 1977, the chilling reception of the financial community made it immediately clear that U.S. investors were not a neutral force in the PQ's struggle to gain acceptance for sovereignty.[35] The PQ government then invested considerable resources in building bridges with the United States. It succeeded moderately in shedding the PQ's radical image in the financial community, but failed to attract much U.S. sympathy for sovereignty. On the trade front, in 1983, PQ proposals for an eventual U.S.-Quebec FTA were flatly rebuffed by Washington.[36] It became clear that trade liberalization efforts with the U.S. would have to originate from Ottawa. Still, in the debate on Canada-U.S. free trade, the PQ was not about to stand idly by on the sidelines.

1985: Parti Québécois Enthusiasm, Liberal Reluctance

Near the end of the PQ mandate, following the defeat of the Lévesque government in its attempt to negotiate a constitutional compromise with the rest of Canada, the party underwent profound transformations. Between 1982 and 1984, the PQ was split on whether to put sovereignty on the back burner when it was to seek a third mandate in 1985. In November 1984, René Lévesque made it clear that the next election would not be fought on sovereignty, provoking the resignation of several ministers, including Jacques Parizeau. When Canada-U.S. free trade began to be seriously considered, after the Shamrock Summit of March 1985 in Quebec City, the PQ had already welcomed the Macdonald

Commission's proposal for free trade and was committed to a strategy of *rapprochement* with the new Conservative government of Brian Mulroney. Bernard Landry, then Minister of External Trade, enthusiastically supported a comprehensive approach to free trade.[37] René Lévesque himself, attending a conference of provincial premiers in the interim between his announced resignation and the election of his successor, was cautiously supportive.

At the same time, Robert Bourassa, reelected PLQ leader and back at the National Assembly since 1983, was reluctant to support a free trade agreement. Bourassa, who had spent part of his political exile studying Europe's Common Market, was favorable to trade liberalization in principle but initially opposed free trade, expressing concerns that an economic union would lead to a form of political union. For him, such integration was likely to compromise Canada's sovereignty in fiscal, monetary and social policies. Shortly after his election victory in December 1985, he declared in a *New York Times* interview that free trade would likely lead to the "assimilation" of Canada by the United States.[38]

Lévesque's successor at the helm of the Parti Québécois, Pierre-Marc Johnson, remained faithful to the party line on free trade in the few months before the December 1985 election. Johnson stood against Bourassa's attacks on the proposed FTA, although he had doubts about the potential consequences of free trade for Quebec's "soft" sectors and for its social policies.[39] Johnson's reservations reflected divisions within his party, which became more significant after the 1985 electoral defeat of the principal supporters of free trade in the PQ's parliamentary wing, including External Trade Minister Bernard Landry and the Minister of Industry and Commerce, Rodrigue Biron. Progressively, in 1986 and 1987, the PQ opposition members in the National Assembly became more critical of free trade. At the same time, the still very visible former PQ Minister of Finance, Jacques Parizeau, continued to actively promote the FTA idea.[40]

Throughout the 1985 electoral campaign, and in his first months in office as premier, Robert Bourassa was critical of free trade, but his position remained ambiguous. If Bourassa's skepticism toward free trade marked a shift from the previous government's policy, it was not the strongest contrast with the PQ in the trade area. Bourassa's clearest break from PQ policy in the trade area concerned the link between the political and economic dimensions of the Quebec government's international activities. For the PQ, the development of direct international political relations was intimately tied to its activities in external trade. In contrast, after 1985, the Bourassa government progressively changed the orientation of Quebec's external relations to depoliticize them and emphasize more exclusively their economic dimension.[41] Beyond the desire to retreat from the PQ's politically motivated ventures in external affairs, this trend in the Liberals' external policy also reflects the influence of francophone export-oriented businesses on the Liberal leadership. Given this bias toward export promotion, the reversal of the Liberal Party's position on free trade in 1987 and 1988 was not very surprising.

1986-87: *The Parti Québécois Retreats, Robert Bourassa Converts*

In 1986 and 1987, the two Quebec parties made 180-degree turns on their positions toward the FTA under negotiation between the U.S. and Canada. This change reflected a shift in the dominant voices within each party on the trade issue, but constitutional politics also played a role. The catalyst for Robert Bourassa's conversion to the free-trade credo was the belief that a free trade agreement would insure access to New England and New York markets for Quebec's hydro-electricity exports. Within the Parti Québécois, at the same time, the leadership increasingly adopted the tone of the social-democratic opponents to free trade.

The year 1986 opened with the leak of a report withheld by the outgoing PQ government, which claimed that free trade would cost more than 30,000 jobs in Quebec's "soft" industries. Throughout that year, Pierre-Marc Johnson's positions converged with the perception of the social-democratic elements of his party, confirming his earlier doubts about free trade. Whereas his pre-election criticism of the FTA was centered on federal infringement of Quebec's constitutional authority in the negotiations, his positions in 1986 and 1987 were similar to criticism by the NDP and organized labor in the rest of Canada: free trade would cost a large number of jobs, endanger agricultural producers and threaten social programs. As early as March 1987, the PQ leader called for a parliamentary commission to open a public debate on the issue.

When the commission met, in September 1987, the FTA negotiation was almost completed and the two Quebec parties had completely turned the tables on free trade. At this hearing, the most articulate voice against the FTA was a coalition formed by the three largest Quebec labor and agricultural producer unions.[42] In addition to unions and farm groups, opponents included representatives from declining manufacturing sectors and some fringe nationalist groups. Not unlike the English Canadian nationalist critics of the FTA, these groups claimed it would endanger the survival of Quebec's distinct culture and language by increasing exposure to U.S. cultural products.[43] However, this type of defensive nationalist discourse on free trade was not widely adopted within the PQ itself.

When the conclusion of a tentative agreement was announced in October 1987, Robert Bourassa welcomed it without reservation. Indeed, the Liberal premier embarked upon a crusade to defend the deal struck by his federal counterpart, the Conservative Brian Mulroney, despite a formal warning by the federal Liberal organization in Quebec that it would be vigorously opposing the deal.[44] One does not have to speculate very long to explain Bourassa's reversal in 1987 from a cautious critic of the FTA to its most ardent supporter. On April 30 of that year, at the retreat of the federal cabinet at Meech Lake, Mulroney, Bourassa and the nine other provincial premiers struck a deal that would allow Quebec to sign the recently patriated Canadian Constitution.[45] From that moment, Robert Bourassa had hitched his star to the success of his old friend Brian Mulroney.[46] In Bourassa's own cabinet, apart from embarrassment for ministers who had made a Quebec veto over portions of the FTA a *sine qua non* condition for supporting the FTA, pro-business ministers were generally pleased with their leader's conversion.

After having supported free trade in the 1985 election campaign, opposition leader Pierre-Marc Johnson and his parliamentary colleagues were now willing to go to any length to counter the FTA. Although the PQ National Assembly caucus was not opposed to trade liberalization *per se*, the lack of a guaranteed access to the U.S. market, the perceived threat to social programs, and the weakening of controls over foreign takeovers were central to their critique of the draft agreement.[47] At that time, however, Johnson's leadership was increasingly challenged within the PQ. Adding fuel to this contestation, Jacques Parizeau, who had never excluded a run at the party's leadership, sided with Bourassa and Mulroney on the FTA. Repeatedly intervening in the debate, Parizeau made clear that free trade would benefit Quebec's economy and improve the prospects for sovereignty.[48]

In November 1987, the death of PQ founder René Lévesque precipitated a leadership crisis in the Parti Québécois, leading to Johnson's resignation. Parizeau immediately announced his candidacy for the succession, and was unopposed at the PQ convention in March 1988. Between October and March, however, the parliamentary wing of the party continued to oppose the FTA in no uncertain terms. Such a position was not surprising on the part of the interim opposition leader, Guy Chevrette, who had risen through the ranks of Quebec's radical teachers' union prior to his political career. This line of opposition would be set aside by Parizeau, except for the PQ's greater emphasis on trade adjustment assistance measures.[49]

During the FTA negotiation, the leaderships of the two parties changed their basic approach to the issue. This flip-flop can be partly attributed to dissensions within each party, but also to the *de facto* strategic alliance that developed between Brian Mulroney and Robert Bourassa on the Meech Lake accord. In 1988, with Jacques Parizeau back at center stage and tensions developing between the PLQ and the federal Liberals, the issue would take on yet another partisan connotation.

1988: The Uneasy Consensus Behind the Mulroney-Reagan Agreement

The positions of the two Quebec parties on the FTA converged in 1988, but internal dissensions continued to be a key issue in the politics of free trade, which took center stage that fall. The Conservative government in Ottawa was forced to call an election on the issue after the Liberal-dominated Senate deadlocked the ratification of the bilateral agreement.

In contrast to the rest of Canada, opinion polls in Quebec showed a consistent pattern of support for free trade by a majority of Quebecers. In a December 1987 poll, as many as 73 percent identified free trade as an "important" or "very important" issue. After a decline in the spring and summer of 1988, the issue surfaced again in the fall and peaked in November, when a poll found 60 percent of respondents identifying free trade as their "principal preoccupation." In October, 62 percent said they would base their electoral choice on this issue, although a surprisingly large 73 percent considered that they lacked information on the subject. Still, not counting the undecided, the support for free trade in Quebec prior to the federal election was consistently superior to 50 percent.[50] The rest is history. On November 21, the Conservative Party received 43 percent of the national vote and 53 percent of the Quebec vote, sweeping 63 of the 75 electoral ridings in the province.

Interestingly, even if the organized opposition to free trade in Quebec included groups closely associated with the sovereignty option, the PQ remained impermeable to their pressures. In part because of its own Quebec nationalist leanings, the Quebec coalition against free trade could never really coordinate its actions with the nationalist "Pro-Canada Network" operating in the rest of Canada.[51] Much to the dismay of English Canadian nationalists,[52] the strong association made in the mind of the Quebec public between English Canadian nationalism and opposition to free trade may have contributed to mobilize the general public in Quebec even more in favor of the position shared by Mulroney, Bourassa and Parizeau.[53]

Indeed, when it became clear to francophone Quebecers that most of the opposition to free trade emanated from Ontario, the scare tactics of the Canadian-nationalist anti-FTA groups backfired. Lucien Bouchard, who was then one of the most popular Conservative Ministers in Quebec, effectively made the case that "opposition to free trade was basically a plot by the Ontario establishment to retain its wealth and privileges at the expense of the rest of the country, particularly Quebec."[54] It worked. From the point of view of Quebec nationalism, the Meech Lake Accord and free trade must be understood in tandem. The combination of the two gave Bourassa and his Quebec business supporters exactly what they wanted by turning the PQ formula of sovereignty-association "upside down." In the words of Graham Fraser,

> [Brian Mulroney] never made the connection overtly. But with the Free Trade Agreement, he was offering Quebec the ideal of economic independence; with Meech Lake, he was offering a political association with the rest of Canada. It was a powerful symbolic combination. . . marrying the traditional Quebec nationalists with the upwardly mobile middle class, enamored of the entrepreneurial spirit.[55]

Among business elites in Quebec, regardless of their provincial party affiliation, support for the ratification of the FTA (and by extension for the reelection of Mulroney's Conservatives and the success of the Meech Lake Accord) was dominant. In the weeks before the 1988 federal election, partisans of free trade in the business community mobilized to express their favorable views in no uncertain terms. Among those in the business community, supporters included the *Conseil du Patronat du Québec*, the *Mouvement Desjardins* and most of the assertive businesses collectively known as "Québec Inc."[56] Only two weeks before the election, some of the most prominent francophone business leaders in Quebec injected $300,000 for publicity to promote the passage of the FTA.[57]

Although the Quebec National Assembly had no formal say in the ratification of the bilateral deal, the federal election was a key test of cohesion on the free-trade issue for the two provincial parties. Before the election of Jacques Parizeau to the leadership of the Parti Québécois, it was not clear which direction the PQ would take on free trade.

For example, a probable contender for the leadership, former Agriculture Minister Jean Garon, was openly critical of the agreement. Garon, still closely associated with agricultural interests, was echoed in his criticism by those who had joined the PQ from the labor movement.[58] After Jacques Parizeau became leader, however, the party and its parliamentary representatives rallied behind his position, while articulating clear demands for adjustment assistance.[59] PQ members were not all wildly enthusiastic about the trade deal but their unity was made easier by the apparent disarray of the PLQ caucus on the eve of the federal election.

The Quebec Liberal leader, Robert Bourassa, had much to gain by supporting Mulroney and the FTA, but he faced difficulty in convincing members of his party caucus with strong ties to the federal Liberals. Bourassa himself invested considerable effort in campaigning for the FTA, which included a tour of western Canada "glorifying" the agreement.[60] Although the Quebec premier denied that he was also campaigning for the survival of Mulroney and Meech Lake, the connection was not too difficult to make.   At the same time, the PLQ leader was severely criticized by his own troops for abandoning the federal Liberals in Quebec.

The crucial test came shortly before the election, as the Parti Québécois tried to force Bourassa's hand by demanding a National Assembly vote on a non-binding resolution to approve ratification of the FTA. But even if he claimed he had the full support of his caucus, Bourassa was not able to create a consensus large enough to risk putting the matter to a vote in the National Assembly.[61]

With the Conservative victory, no further obstacles stood in the way of the FTA, but Bourassa and Mulroney would not be so fortunate with the Meech Lake Accord. After Bourassa's reelection in September 1989, the Accord failed to gain the approval of all provinces before the deadline of June 1990, and Canada was plunged anew into constitutional crisis. English Canada's rejection of Meech Lake provoked a massive revival of public support for sovereignty in Quebec.[62] In spite of the constitutional crisis and the recession, however, support for free trade has not lost much ground in Quebec public opinion and group attitudes, in contrast with the situation in the rest of Canada.[63] Even union leaders have reluctantly recognized the necessity to adapt their demands to the realities of continental and global economic integration.[64] The Bélanger-Campeau Commission on the Constitutional Future of Quebec confirmed that, regardless of the decision reached on the issue of sovereignty, Quebec's economic strategy would necessarily have to be structured around the creation of a continental market.

In sum, during the period 1985-1990, free trade with the United States was a central issue of debate in Quebec, but the important societal cleavages surrounding this issue did not translate into lasting inter-partisan divergences. Even if the recession has made many Quebecers skeptical of the rosy promises of free trade enthusiasts, current debates on trade policy in Quebec are no longer centered on the principle of integration in the continental and global economies. Rather, the two political parties, labor and business groups tend to concentrate on the modalities of this integration, notably adjustment policies. These issues surfaced in the context of recent debates on the extension of the North American free trade zone to include Mexico.

Quebec Party Politics and NAFTA

In September 1990, the Canadian government announced that it was considering participation in trade talks involving the U.S. and Mexico. In sharp contrast with Ontario's NDP government, Quebec supported Canadian participation in the NAFTA talks.[65]

The Bourassa government invoked political and economic reasons. Politically, the government made clear that it intended to follow the path traced since its enthusiastic support of the FTA; Canadian participation in NAFTA talks would also protect the gains of the FTA. Economically, there was some interest in enhanced access to the Mexican market, but the main issue was to avoid the risk of investment diversion that might result from Canada's exclusion from a U.S.-Mexico deal.

In Quebec, most industries were only marginally affected by an eventual NAFTA and their representative associations remained relatively indifferent to Canada's participation. In the early phase, opponents included plastic products, footwear, furniture, and the very large clothing industry. Several industries openly supported the extension of the FTA, but their motivations were primarily defensive, reflecting a concern for the protection of gains made in the FTA.[66]

As was the case during the negotiation of the FTA, public opinion in Quebec has generally been more favorable to NAFTA than in the rest of Canada. A June 1990 Gallup poll showed a dramatic difference between support for NAFTA in Quebec (57 percent in favor) and in Ontario (27 percent in favor), while support in other provinces hovered around 40 percent.[67] As they had been for the FTA, the pro-sovereignty *Mouvement Desjardins* and the federalist *Conseil du Patronat*, the largest employer association in Quebec, have been supportive of NAFTA, despite recent problems linked with the perceived increase in protectionism in the U.S.[68]

As was the case in the FTA negotiation, opposition to NAFTA has centered on the coalition of unions and agricultural producers. The key concerns of labor has been the potential effect of the extension of the FTA to Mexico on wage levels and safety standards in industry. The coalition has also been joined by organizations preoccupied with development and environmental issues, which are concerned by the social and ecological consequences of free trade for Mexico and Quebec. Still, opposition to this new round of trade talks has not had a wide effect on Quebec public opinion.[69]

The recent positions of the two Quebec parties on NAFTA tend to be relatively similar, with some differences of emphasis. The position of the Liberal Party itself on the new round of trade talks is reflected in the government positions stated above. A PLQ discussion paper on external trade for the 1991 Liberal Party Congress clearly emphasized the pro-export and pro-free orientation of the party. The PLQ working group was headed by Claude Lemay, the president of a computer company exporting to 46 countries, Guy Saint-Pierre, of SNC-Lavalin, and Pierre McDonald, a former PLQ minister close to business interests. Although the report did not elaborate on NAFTA, its conclusions were revealing of the impact of exporters on the direction of the PLQ's external trade policies.[70]

The two Parti Québécois tenors of free trade, party president Jacques Parizeau and vice-president Bernard Landry, have taken the same position in the NAFTA debate as they did on the FTA. However, the revival of protectionism in the U.S., the depth of the recession, and the persistence unemployment in Quebec have made free trade increasingly hard to sell to critics within the Parti Québécois. Although these critics have not directly challenged their leader's position on NAFTA, they have increasingly questioned the benefits of free trade for Quebec. Former Agriculture Minister Jean Garon echoed the concerns of the farm-labor coalition against free trade when he claimed that none of the advantages of the FTA had really materialized.[71]

To accommodate some of these criticisms and to confront the Liberal government on a more concrete ground, the PQ leader has recently reoriented his discourse on free trade to emphasize the need for effective provincial-level adjustment policies. Parizeau's condemnation of the Liberal "inertia" in its adaptation to trade liberalization, notably in the area of professional formation, has struck a sensitive chord with Quebec's recession-hit manufacturers.[72]

In sum, although the bipartisan concern for improved adjustment policies responds to labor demands, the anti-NAFTA coalition had not yet been successful in defining the terms of public debate on the issue. As was the case in 1988, there was still very little coordination between opposition groups in Quebec and in the rest of Canada.

In contrast with 1988, however, there was no sense of urgency in the debate. Whereas the 1988 FTA wrangle overshadowed the constitutional debate, the reverse has certainly been true since the rejection of the Meech Lake Accord by English Canada. Even if the constitutional debate contributed in making the trade talks less salient, the federal Conservative government was hurt in public opinion by its own secretive attitude toward the NAFTA negotiations. It was extremely unlikely that the federal Conservatives could benefit from a bipartisan consensus between Quebec parties on free trade like they did in 1988. In brief, the key to the acceptance of the agreement on North American free trade was certainly not in Quebec.

Conclusions

This survey of the partisan politics surrounding the free-trade debate in Quebec has addressed two distinct questions. First, why is there apparently so little disagreement between the parties over trade issues? Second, if trade is not a very contentious issue between the two parties, then why has it remained an important issue in Quebec partisan politics over the last 10 years? The first section identified some of the main structural sources of trade consensus in the high degree of interdependence of the Quebec economy. The convergence of elite opinion and, to some extent, of public opinion on the principle of trade openness is consistent with the pattern of trade-policy consensus typical to other small open economies.

However, as a brief comparison with Ontario suggested, this structural factor is far from sufficient to explain the long-term convergence of party positions on free trade. What is also crucial is the role of nationalism in orienting the free-trade debate. But economic nationalism in Quebec does not translate into protectionism. Free trade has been embraced both by provincial autonomists within the Liberal Party and by partisans of sovereignty associated with the Parti Québécois. The two faces of Quebec nationalism perceive the advantages of an open trade strategy in reducing the relative control of the Canadian government on the Quebec economy. For the sovereignists, in particular, closer economic ties with the United States and the global economy reduce the economic risks inherent in the severance of political links with the Canadian federation. This chapter also emphasized the common origins of party elites in the reformist period of the 1960s, and the relative consensus that evolved since then concerning Quebec economic institutions and the relationship between the state and markets.

Despite the relative bipartisan consensus which occurred at a crucial moment in 1988 and is still apparent now, free trade with the United States (and beyond) has nonetheless remained an important issue in Quebec politics in the last decade. The fact that both parties are internally divided on the free-trade issue accounts for much of the instability in party positions since 1985. Why is this important if ratifying the FTA was strictly a federal responsibility? The results of the federal election of November 1988 tell the story directly. The Conservatives won with an overall majority of 169 seats to the Liberals' 83 seats and the NDP's 43 seats; in Quebec, the Conservatives swept 63 of the 75 seats, assuring the ratification of the FTA. It is doubtful that the Parti Québécois would have supported the FTA so overtly if its leadership had been more closely tied to labor unions or agricultural producers. Similarly, Robert Bourassa might have taken quite a different position on free trade in 1988 if he had been less tied to Brian Mulroney's constitutional agenda or if he had been more sensitive to demands by federal Liberals. The consensus between Quebec parties on free trade was instrumental in helping the Conservatives ratify the FTA in 1988. But that consensus is unlikely to have the same impact on an eventual electoral ratification of NAFTA because of widespread dissatisfaction with free trade and the Conservative government in English Canada, and because the sovereignist Bloc Québécois won a significant share of Quebec's 75 seats in the federal election, becoming the official opposition party at the federal level, and helping to reduce the Conservatives to a mere two seats.

This chapter has shown that orientation toward free trade has not been a determinant factor in shaping the Quebec party system for the last 25 years, mainly because of the centrality of the cleavage between federalists and sovereignists but also because of the openness of the Quebec economy, which creates strong forces in the direction of trade liberalization. In a sovereign Quebec, however, the present cleavage between parties would necessarily be replaced by other issues. What would then be the place of trade in determining the new shape of Quebec partisan politics? Would the cleavage of the Quebec party system develop along the very salient dimension of protectionism *versus* free trade? These are important questions to which this chapter can only suggest a partial and tentative answer.

The analysis of the partisan politics of free trade in the last decade shows that the two main Quebec parties have certainly not been monolithic on this issue. It is also generally assumed in Quebec that the coalitions of disparate economic interests that are presently grouped under the banners of the Parti Québécois and of the Quebec Liberal Party would be unlikely to hold together forever after sovereignty. Nevertheless, as indicated in this chapter's first section, protectionism has generally not been a viable option in small states with open economies. Such states, as typified by several small northern European countries, have tended to develop partisan consensus around open trade strategies, and to foster mechanisms of concertation between socioeconomic interests. Quebec, for its part, has begun to experience such mechanisms over the past fifteen years and, even if success has been mixed, concertation has largely replaced partisan confrontation as the first resort of socioeconomic groups with conflicting interests.

Another key part of this equation, however, is the strength of liberal international economic institutions, both at the global and regional levels. Indeed, the small European economies have been able to maintain their cohesive trade policies in the postwar period in large part because of the strength of the trade regime itself. Although neither the GATT nor the emerging North American trade regime are absolutely insured against a protectionist backlash, it is hardly in the interest of Quebec (whether sovereign or not) to precipitate this breakdown. Constrained by an international structure that restricts the scope of realistic trade-policy options, political parties in a sovereign Quebec would certainly have different views on the modalities of trade liberalization, but they would be unlikely to polarize on this specific issue.[73] In Quebec since 1985, participants in the free trade debate have often taken divergent positions, but the two main parties have been able to reinforce the widely held notion that it is no longer possible to turn the clock back on global or continental economic integration.

Notes

For comments and suggestions on this chapter, I am grateful to André Blais, Antonia Maioni, Yves Martin and Alain Noël. The editors of this volume, Charles Doran and Gregory Marchildon, also provided useful advice. Of course, responsibility for errors or omissions remains my own.

1. Ronald Wonnacott, *U.S. Hub-and-Spoke Bilaterals and the Multilateral Trading System*, C. D. Howe Institute Commentary 23, Toronto, C. D. Howe Institute, October 1990, discusses the nature of the structural constraints behind Canada's decision to join the negotiation.

2. See the chapter by Duncan McDowall in this volume. For an analysis of the changing place of free trade in federal elections, see Richard Johnston, André Blais, Henry Brady and Jean Crête, "Free Trade in Canadian Elections: Issue Evolution in the Long and Short Run," in *Agenda Formation*, ed. William Riker (Ann Arbor: University of Michigan Press, forthcoming 1992).

3. For the Parti Québécois, see *Le Québec dans le monde ou le défi de l'interdépendance: énoncé de politique de relations internationales*, (Québec: Ministère des Relations internationales, 1985); for the Liberal Party, see *Le Québec et l'interdépendance, le monde pour horizon: éléments d'une politique d'affaires internationales*, (Québec: Ministère des Affaires internationales, 1991).

4. Source of data for this paragraph: *Le Québec et l'interdépendance*, pp. 40-51 and statistical annexes; all figures, Canadian dollars. For a series showing export data from 1968 to 1987, see Simon Langlois, *La société québécoise en tendances, 1960-1990* (Québec: Institut québécois de recherche sur la culture, 1990), p. 53.

5. For an application of this argument to small northern European countries, see Peter Katzenstein, *Small States in World Markets: Industrial Policy in Europe* (Ithaca: Cornell University Press, 1985). The argument equating trade openness with higher degrees of cohesiveness between the state, labor and business is also presented by David R. Cameron, "The Expansion of the Public Economy: A

Comparative Analysis," American Political Science Review, Vol. 72, December 1978, pp. 1243-61.

6. Ronald Rogowski, "Trade and the Variety of Democratic Institutions," International Organization, Vol. 41, Spring 1987, pp. 203-23. For a more general analysis of the links between trade and domestic political development, see Ronald Rogowski Commerce and Coalition: How Trade Affects Domestic Political Alignments (Princeton: Princeton University Press, 1989).

7. For an analysis of Quebec's foreign economic policy which places a particular emphasis upon state-owned enterprises as the instruments of its implementation, seeLuc Bernier, "The Foreign Economic Policy of a Subnational State: The Case of Quebec," in Perforated Sovereignties and International Relations: Trans-Sovereign Contacts of Subnational Governments, Ivo D. Duchacek, Daniel Latouche, and Garth Stevenson, eds. (New York: Greenwood Press), pp. 125-39.

8. John N. McDougall, "North American Integration and Canadian Disunity," Canadian Public Policy, Vol. 17, December 1991, p. 398.

9. Thomas J. Courchene, What Does Ontario Want? (Toronto: Robarts Centre for Canadian Studies, York University, 1989), p. 43.

10. Marcel Rioux and Yves Martin, French-Canadian Society (Toronto: Macmillan and Stewart, 1964); Louis Balthazar, Bilan du nationalisme au Québec (Montréal: L'Hexagone, 1986).

11. Edmond Orban, La modernisation politique du Québec (Sillery: Boréal Express, 1976); Alain G. Gagnon and Mary Beth Montcalm, Quebec Beyond the Quiet Revolution (Scarborough, Ont.: Nelson, 1990); Kenneth McRoberts, Quebec: Social Change and Political Crisis, Third Edition (Toronto: McClelland & Stewart, 1988).

12. On the political culture of Quebec's state-owned enterprises, see Luc Bernier, Soldiers of Fortune: State-Owned Enterprises as Instruments of Public Policy, Unpublished Ph.D. dissertation, Northwestern University, 1989.

13. Employment in the public sector and membership in a labor union are two strong correlates of vote for the Parti Québécois in the 1981 election and for sovereignty in the 1980 referendum among French-speaking Quebecers. André Blais and Richard Nadeau, "L'appui au Parti québécois: évolution de la clientèle de 1970 à 1981," and "La clientèle du OUI," in Comportement électoral au Québec, ed. Jean Crête (Chicoutimi: Gaëtan Morin éditeur, 1984), pp. 279-318 and 321-34.

14. Kenneth McRoberts, Quebec: Social Change and Political Crisis; Graham Fraser, René Lévesque and the Parti Québécois in Power (Toronto: Macmillan Canada, 1984).

15. On the significance of economic summits established by the PQ government, see Pierre Jalbert, La concertation comme mode de gestion étatique des rapports sociaux, Unpublished Ph.D. dissertation, Université de Montréal, 1990; A. Brian Tanguay, "Concerted Action in Quebec, 1976-1983: A Dialogue of the Deaf," in Quebec: State and Society, ed. Alain-G. Gagnon (Toronto: Methuen, 1984), pp. 365-85.

16. See the comprehensive economic policy plan elaborated by Bernard Landry, Minister of State for Economic Development in the first PQ government: Government of Québec, Bâtir le Québec (Québec: Éditeur officiel du Québec, 1979). On relations between labor, business and the state since the first PQ government,

see A. Brian Tanguay, "Business, labor, and the State in the 'New' Quebec," *The American Review of Canadian Studies,* Vol. 17, Winter 1987-88, pp. 395-408.

17. Kenneth McRoberts, *Quebec: Social Change and Political Crisis,* p. 380.

18. Gagnon and Montcalm, *Quebec: Beyond the Quiet Revolution,* p. 65.

19. On the association between economic nationalism and protectionism, see Robert Gilpin, *The Political Economy of International Relations* (Princeton: Princeton University Press, 1987).

20. Stéphane Dion, "Explaining Quebec Nationalism," in *The Collapse of Canada,* ed. R. Kent Weaver, (Washington, D.C.: Brookings Institution, 1992), pp. 77-121.

21. The PLQ has adopted this approach of radical decentralization in its 1991 Congress. The party's position, somewhat diluted in subsequent declaration by Robert Bourassa, was defined in what has become known as the "Allaire Report": Jean Allaire, *Un Québec libre de ses choix: Rapport du Comité constitutionnel du Parti libéral du Québec* (Montréal: Parti libéral du Québec, March 1991). However, PLQ leader Robert Bourassa soon made it clear that he did not consider himself tied by this platform, and he would use it primarily as a negotiation tool.

22. For a rational-choice analysis of Quebec nationalism emphasizing this dimension of the reduction of economic risk, see Hudson Meadwell, "The Politics of Québécois Nationalism," Unpublished paper, McGill University, 1992.

23. Rodrigue Tremblay, *Indépendance et marché commun Québec-États-Unis* (Montréal: Éditions du Jour, 1970).

24. See Jacques Parizeau, "Préface," in Bernard Landry, *Commerce sans frontières: le sens du libre-échange* (Montréal: Québec/Amérique, 1987), pp. 9-18.

25. Thomas J. Courchene, "Market Nationalism," *Policy Options,* Vol. 7, October 1986, pp. 7-12, p. 7.

26. Courchene, "Market Nationalism," p. 11 and p. 12.

27. "Consultation des dirigeants du Réseau Desjardins sur l'avenir politique et constitutionnel du Québec," annex 2 of the brief presented by the Mouvement des caisses Desjardins to the Commission on Quebec's Political and Constitutional Future, November 1990, p. 7.

28. Denis Lessard, "Jean Campeau met sur pied un regroupement de gens d'affaires souverainistes," *La Presse,* May 20, 1992.

29. See the brief submitted by the Chamber of Commerce to the Commission on the Constitutional Future of Québec: Chambre de Commerce du Québec, "L'avenir politique et constitutionnel du Québec: sa dimension économique" (mimeo, November 1, 1990), p. 2; the results of the poll of the leaders of the 500 largest industrial enterprises in Québec were published in the business weekly *Les Affaires,* Vol. 62, May 12-18, 1990.

30. On this episode and its impact for PQ support among public employees, see André Blais and Jean Crête, "Can a Party Punish its Faithful Clientele? The Parti Québécois and Public Sector Employees in Quebec," *Canadian Public Administration,* Vol. 32, September 1990, pp. 623-32.

31. Jean-Paul Lejeune, "Grands patrons -- Souveraineté: pas question," *Revue Commerce,* October 1991, pp. 76-87. The poll cited was published by the same magazine in December 1990.

32. On the political consequences of lasting high unemployment in Quebec's

economy, see Alain Noël, "Politics in a High Unemployment Society," in *Quebec: State and Society,* Second Edition, ed. Alain-G. Gagnon (Toronto: Nelson Canada, Forthcoming 1992).

33. Bernard Bonin, "U.S.-Quebec Economic Relations: Some Interactions Between Trade and Investment," in *Problems and Opportunities in U.S.-Quebec Relations,* eds. Alfred O. Hero and Marcel Daneau (Boulder: Westview Press, 1985), pp. 17-38; p. 34.

34. J. Alex Murray and Lawrence LeDuc, "Changing Attitudes Toward Foreign Investment in Canada," in *Host National Attitudes Toward Multinational Corporations,* ed. John Fayerweather (New York: Praeger, 1982), pp. 216-35.

35. See Jean-François Lisée, *In the Eye of the Eagle* (Toronto: Harper Collins, 1990), chapters 9-10, on this important episode in U.S.-Quebec economic relations.

36. Jean-François Lisée, *In the Eye of the Eagle,* chap. 18.

37. Lise Bissonette, "Landry souhaite le libre-échange le plus complet," *Le Devoir,* March 2, 1985, p. 1.

38. Pierre O'Neil, "Mise en garde de Bourassa à la conférence des premiers ministres: Attention aux écueils du libre-échange," *La Presse,* August 21, 1985, p. 1. *New York Times,* December 6, 1985.

39. Rudy Le Cours, "Libre-échange: Prochain sujet d'affrontement entre Johnson et Bourassa," *La Presse,* October 7, 1985.

40. Pierre O'Neil, "Parizeau favorise le libre-échange avec les USA," *Le Devoir,* February 26, 1986, p. 1; Jacques Parizeau "Le libre-échange avec les États-Unis," text of a conference delivered June 6, 1986, at a meeting of the Montreal Chamber of Commerce.

41. On this depoliticization of Quebec's external relations policies, see Panayotis Soldatos, "Les relations internationales du Québec: la marque d'un déterminisme économique," in *L'année politique au Québec, 1987-1988,* ed. Denis Monière (Montreal: Éditions Québec/Amérique, 1989), pp. 109-123; Yves Martin, "Des «Relations» aux «Affaires» internationales," *Le Devoir,* March 19, 1988, p. 11.

42. This coalition's study of the projected effects of the FTA in eight sectors predicted massive job losses and very limited benefits from enhanced exports; Coalition québécoise d'opposition au libre-échange CEQ-CSN-FTQ-UPA, "Mémoire concernant les négotiations sur le libre-échange entre le Canada et les États-Unis," Brief submitted to the Commission de l'Économie et du Travail, Québec, September 15, 1987.

43. See, for example, Mouvement Québec Français, "Mémoire présenté à la Commission de l'Économie et du Travail de l'Assemblée Nationale du Québec," September 12, 1987. This group's concerns about the preservation of Quebec's distinct language and culture in a free-trade context were not shared by a majority of Quebecers.

44. Pierre O'Neil, "L'entente sur le libre-échange: Le Québec sera plus attrayant pour les investisseurs--Bourassa," *Le Devoir,* October 6, 1987; Bernard Descôteaux, "Bourassa part en croisade pour le libre-échange," *Le Devoir,* October 8, 1987.

45. For a summary of the issues involved in the Meech Lake Accords, see François Rocher and Gérard Boismenu, "New Constitutional Signposts: Distinct Society, Linguistic Duality, and Institutional Changes," in *Canadian Politics: An*

Introduction to the Discipline, eds. Alain-G. Gagnon and James P. Bickerton (Toronto: Broadview Press, 1990), pp. 222-45.

46. For a perceptive account of this tacit alliance between the two leaders, see Daniel Latouche, "Politics and the Mulroney/Bourassa Alliance," *The New Federation,* Vol. 1, May 1989, pp. 20-2.

47. The PQ's trade spokesman articulated these criticisms in a short article. See Jean-Guy Parent "Le libre-échange: Un accord inacceptable," *Le Devoir,* October 24, 1987.

48. Bernard Descôteaux, "Libre-échange: Parizeau se range du côté de Bourassa," *Le Devoir,* October 9, 1987. Jacques Parizeau, "Interview," in *Canadian-American Free Trade: Historical, Political and Economic Dimensions,* eds. A.R. Riggs and T. Velk (Montreal: IRPP, 1987).

49. "L'accord de libre-échange: les conditions posées par le Québec ne sont pas respectées," and "Libre-échange: l'opposition exige des mesures d'assistance pour les travailleurs et les entreprises," Parti Québécois press releases, Quebec National Assembly, December 16, 1987. The PQ insistence upon the implementation of adjustment policies was reiterated in November 1988 as a condition for support of the FTA package; Gilles Lesage, "La motion unanime sur le libre-échange: Parizeau met des conditions," *Le Devoir,* November 5, 1988, p. 1.

50. For summary reports of all available polls on the free trade issue in Quebec for the whole period under consideration, from which the results in this paragraph were obtained, see Édouard Cloutier, "Les tendances de l'opinion publique," in *L'année politique au Québec, 1987-1988,* pp. 167-74; and in *L'année politique au Québec, 1988-1989,* ed. Denis Monière (Montréal: Éditions Québec/Amérique, 1989), pp.181-91.

51. Joyce Napier, "La coalition québécoise contre le libre-échange rame seule," *La Presse,* October 13, 1988.

52. For a representative perspective of the shockwave felt by the English-Canadian nationalist after the massive support in Quebec for Mulroney's Conservative Party, free trade and Meech Lake, see Philip Resnick, *Letters to a Québécois Friend* (Montréal and Kingston: McGill-Queen's University Press, 1990).

53. A variant of this hypothesis is presented by Daniel Latouche, who argues that support for free trade in Quebec was in part a reaction to the contempt for Quebec exhibited by the "right-thinking members of the progressive English Canadian left." Such contempt, Latouche claims, "practically forced Quebecers to vote for the Conservatives." Daniel Latouche, *Le Bazar: des anciens Canadiens aux nouveaux Québécois* (Montréal: Boréal, 1990), p. 141.

54. Graham Fraser, *Playing for Keeps: The Making of the Prime Minister, 1988* (Toronto: McClelland & Stewart Inc., 1989), pp. 367-8.

55. Graham Fraser, *Playing for Keeps,* p. 354.

56. See Conseil du Patronat du Québec, "La libéralisation des échanges commerciaux avec les États-Unis: à nouveau un oui prudent, mais sans équivoque," Brief presented to the Consultative Committee on Trade Liberalization (Warren Committee), September 1986. For the position of the Mouvement Desjardins, see: "Libre-échange: Pourquoi les caisses populaires disent oui," *La Presse,* November 14, 1988.

57. Heading this effort under the banner of the *Regroupement québécois pour le libre-échange* were the presidents of Bombardier, Power Corporation and Canam-Manac; Michel van de Walle, "Des Québécois lancent une campagne de $300 000 en faveur du libre-échange," *La Presse*, November 9, 1988. Quebec business supporters were not alone in funding the pro-FTA advertising campaign. Across Canada, Liberal Party estimates of pro-free trade advertising money pumped into the 1988 campaign above the regulated Conservative Party expenses was between $2 and $3 million; labor groups estimates hovered around $10 million, and other estimates ran even much higher; see Graham Fraser, *Playing for Keeps*, p. 325.

58. Suzanne Dansereau, "Le libre-échange ne fait pas l'unanimité au sein du Parti québécois," *La Presse*, March 7, 1988. The agricultural producers' objections to the FTA are detailed in Union des Producteurs Agricoles, "Libre-échange canado-américain et agriculture québécoise," Brief presented to the Quebec Parliamentary Commission on Free Trade, September 1987.

59. Also rallying behind Parizeau's position was the former leader Pierre-Marc Johnson. In a November interview, he defended the PQ's support of free trade but justified his earlier reluctance to support the FTA by the fact that U.S. negotiators had vowed to put "everything on the table," early in the negotiation, including federal and provincial social programs. Gilbert Lavoie, "P.M. Johnson se porte à la défense du libre-échange," *La Presse*, November 7, 1988, p. 1.

60. "Bourassa glorifie le libre-échange," *Le Devoir*, November 2, 1988, p. 1.

61. Gilles Lesage, "Bourassa affirme que la solidarité ministérielle est totale et intacte," *Le Devoir*, November 18, 1988.

62. Édouard Cloutier, Jean-H. Guay and Daniel Latouche, *Le virage: L'évolution de l'opinion publique au Québec depuis 1960, ou comment le Québec est devenu souverainiste* (Montréal: Québec/Amérique, 1992).

63. An analysis of Canadian public opinion supporting this view is Harold D. Clarke and Allan Kornberg, "Support for the Canadian Federal Progressive Conservative Party Since 1988: The Impact of Economic Evaluations and Economic Issues," *Canadian Journal of Political Science*, Vol. 25, March 1992, pp. 29-53.

64. Seeking to mend fences after the conclusion of the FTA debate, the president of the FTQ (Federation of Quebec Workers), Louis Laberge, declared to an audience of employers, that his organization had been "against the free-trade pact. But we cannot be against free trade itself." Paule des Rivières, "Libre-échange: Laberge range son fusil," *Le Devoir*, December 1, 1988.

65. Chantal Hébert, "Le Québec adhère au libre-échange trilatéral: L'Ontario s'y oppose," *Le Devoir*, February 12, 1991, p. 1. For an official statement of the Quebec government's position on NAFTA, see *La libéralisation des échanges commerciaux entre le Canada, les États-Unis et le Mexique* (Québec: Ministère des Affaires internationales, Direction générale de la politique commerciale, 1992).

66. Information for this paragraph was taken from a report on the sectoral impact of NAFTA in Quebec. *Impact sur les secteurs manufacturiers relevant de la compétence du ministère de l'Industrie, du Commerce et de la Technologie d'un accord de libre-échange Canada-États-Unis-Mexique*, (Québec: Ministère de l'Industrie, du Commerce et de la Technologie, Direction générale de l'analyse économique, 1990).

67. "Gallup: les Québécois sont d'accord pour élargir le libre-échange au Mexique," *La Presse*, June 18, 1990.

68. See Yves St-Maurice, *Libre-échange Canada-États-Unis-Mexique* (Lévis: Confédération des Caisses populaires et d'économie Desjardins, Direction Analyse économique, May 1991); Gilles Lajoie, "Libre-échange: la confiance du milieu des affaires commence à s'effriter," *Les Affaires*, March 21, 1992.

69. Rollande Parent, "Une coalition syndicale veut avoir son mot à dire sur le libre-échange à trois," *Le Devoir*, April 5, 1991; Paul Cauchon, "La Coalition québécoise dénonce le processus de négociation du libre-échange," *Le Devoir*, March 9, 1992; Ingrid Peritz, "The Human Cost of Free Trade," (series of 3 articles), *The Gazette*, March 16-18, 1992.

70. "Document de réflexion: Commerce extérieur," mimeo (Montréal: Parti libéral du Québec, March 1991).

71. "Jean Garon: «Où sont passés nos experts du libre-échange?»," *Le Soleil*, March 3, 1992, p. A8.

72. Robert Dutrisac, "Parizeau réclame des mesures d'adaptation pour le libre-échange," *Le Devoir*, April 10, 1992, p. 5.

73. A similar argument is made by Daniel Latouche, "Le Québec est bien petit et le monde, bien grand," in *Répliques aux détracteurs de la souveraineté du Québec*, eds. Alain-G. Gagnon and François Rocher (Montréal: VLB Éditeur, 1992), pp. 345-72.

8

Trade Policy and Economic Development in Twentieth Century Mexico

Dale Story

In January of 1990, Carlos Salinas arrived in Europe expecting to be warmly received and with considerable attention from both public and private sector groups that favored his program of economic and political reform. He was hoping to buttress his economic recovery program with enhanced trade and investment from Europe and to promote a policy of trade diversification. Apparently, he was sadly disappointed to find that Europe had little interest in Mexico and was focusing on its own economic integration. Salinas returned from Europe, not with a host of promises of new investment and trade opportunities from across the Atlantic, but with a new Mexican commitment to establish a North American Free Trade Agreement (NAFTA) to compete with the evolving trade arenas of Europe and Asia.

The news that Mexico was negotiating a Free Trade Agreement with its northern neighbors (first leaked in March of 1990) surprised many long-time Mexico watchers. Even as late as 1980 Mexican President José López Portillo had made a very nationalistic and well-publicized decision not to join the General Agreement on Tariffs and Trade (GATT). Periodic U.S. suggestions to consider a North American Common Market were vehemently rejected in Mexico throughout the 1970s and 1980s. Of course, postwar Mexican economic policy had a significant tradition of protectionism for "new and necessary industries."

Thus, the announcement that Salinas was pursuing a Free Trade Agreement with the "Colossus of the North" seemed to be contradicting decades of nationalist economic ideology by his own ruling party (the Party of the Institutionalized Revolution, or the PRI). The traditional

Party and State apparatus had strongly favored protectionist policies, and Salinas seemed to be challenging an entrenched political establishment. However, his own technocratic elite soon proved to be a more dominant (and even more popular) force than the old coalition of party *políticos*, labor bosses, and a nationalistic private sector. Partly as a result of his own political acumen, Salinas seemed to have reversed decades of protectionist tradition. However, the successful transition from a protectionist to a free trade position was not simply a master stroke of an astute politician (Carlos Salinas), but can also be viewed as the culmination of a shift in economic stages of development.

In the development of Latin American countries, three different stages of industrialization can usually be delineated: (1) export-oriented industrialization, concentrating on the processing of primary (not manufacturing) export products; (2) horizontal import-substituting industrialization (ISI), stressing the substitution of nondurable consumer goods (generally light or traditional industries); and (3) vertical ISI, stressing the substitution of intermediate and capital goods (generally heavy or dynamic industries, also termed "backward-linking" ISI) and the movement into exporting manufacturing goods.[1] The industrialization process thus returns to the export sector; however, the initial stage is devoted to exporting primary products while in the final stage the emphasis is on the exportation of finished goods.

These industrial stages can often be linked with specific periods of political regimes and public policies. In terms of regime types, the export-oriented stage is associated with traditional oligarchies (such as the administration of Porfirio Díaz in Mexico); horizontal ISI with populism (best epitomized by Lazaro Cárdenas in Mexico); and vertical ISI with "bureaucratic-authoritarianism" (most readily equated with the military regimes in Argentina and Brazil beginning in the 1960s).[2]

Finally, in terms of trade policies, three periods in the evolution of protectionist policies can typically be identified: (1) a period when such policies are intended either as temporary responses to balance-of-payments crises or as revenue measures: (2) a period when such policies are specifically designed to encourage industrialization (most industrial promotion policies, such as subsidies and tax exemptions, are also instituted during this phase of protectionism); and (3) a period when protectionism is deemphasized in favor of efficiency.[3] The revenue generating phase of protectionist policies will be found primarily in the latter stages of export-oriented growth. The second stage of promotion and protection of domestic industries (when government economic policies are most deliberately employed to aid industrial growth) comes in the phase of horizontal ISI; while vertical ISI usually leads to the third stage of trade policies, when trade liberalization predominates.

TABLE 8.1 Linkages Among Stages of Growth, Political Regimes, and Trade Policies

Economic Growth	Political Regimes	Trade Policies
Export-Oriented	Traditional Oligarchy	Revenue Measures
Horizontal ISI	Populism	Protectionism
Vertical ISI	Bureaucratic-Authoritarianism	Liberalization

Source: Compiled by the author.

These linkages among stages of economic development, political regime types, and trade policies are summarized in Table 8.1. Mexico experienced export-led growth throughout the second half of the nineteenth century and up to the Revolution of 1910. The next two decades were so chaotic that any economic progress or evolution was stymied, and horizontal ISI did not begin in earnest until the 1930s and 1940s. Finally, at some point in the late-1950s and 1960s, Mexico entered the phase of vertical import substitution. The initiation of NAFTA can be seen as a much delayed outcome of this phase of economic development in Mexico.

The era of Porfirio Díaz (1876-1910) was the apex of export-oriented growth. Economic policies favored the primary export sectors by encouraging foreign investment and land concentration and by providing for the integration of the market through improved internal transportation and communication facilities. Growth in the export sector was astounding, as the value of exports rose 600 percent in thirty-five years. Exports also became diversified, since gold and silver were declining while industrial minerals such as lead and copper were increasing in importance and new agricultural exports were being introduced, including coffee, cattle, cotton, and sugar.[4]

Some tariffs were granted to the incipient industrial sector in the nineteenth century. In fact, these tariffs, which primarily applied to textiles, provided 60 percent of all federal government revenues in 1868.[5]

But tariffs did not become relevant to other industrial branches until 1916, when a new tariff was granted to jute and malt manufacturers.[6] By this time the first phase of industrialization policies was in full swing. The state had begun selectively to consult with interested private parties over tariff revisions, but had not adopted a policy of encouraging industry in general through higher tariffs.

Exports of primary products dominated the economy, but they also stimulated the emergence of modern industry. The export boom required greater industrial inputs and, by creating a larger domestic market, led to increased consumption of manufactured goods. Other factors favoring industrial growth included improved domestic transportation, the abolition of taxes on internal transactions (*alcabalas*), peso depreciation from 1876 to 1905, and stability in the prices of imported goods and the costs of labor.[7]

The leading industries established in the Porfiriato were primarily in areas related either to exports or to agricultural production (cotton and wool mills, jute factories, paper mills, sugar refineries, breweries, cigarette factories), and many of these have remained the most important enterprises in their respective areas.[8] Yet in Mexico, industrialization was less linked to the export sector than in many other Latin American countries. For example, all leather products were exported without tanning, and many fibers (most notably henequen) left the country without elaboration.

The first industrial promotion policies were initiated in the 1920s. The government announced tax relief for certain new industrial ventures in 1920 and decreed additional tax exemptions for some industries in 1927 and 1932. Yet these had little effect until they were extended considerably around 1940. Credit policies acquired some importance in the 1930s with the expansion of public credit institutions and the financing of public works that were beneficial to industry. Nacional Financiera (NAFINSA, the National Development Bank) was created in December 1933 to engage in a wide variety of financial operations, including industrial loans. Also, in 1937 the Industrial Development Bank (Banco Nacional Obrera y de Fomento Industrial) was established. Still, these credit policies benefitted industry only in a minor way.

Export-led industrialization was clearly over by 1929, when the creation of the National Revolutionary Party (Partido Nacional Revolucionario, PNR, the forerunner of the PRI) ended the era of "*caudillismo*" in Mexican politics and the Depression diminished Mexico's foreign trade by half.[9] Of course, the Revolution had begun the dismantling of the traditional export economy, as the old coalition of foreign interests and the agro-export elite was defeated by an alliance of previously dispossessed groups. Certainly, one component of the Revolution was the populist struggle of the rural peasantry and urban labor for agrarian reform, labor rights, etc. However, the fight against Porfirion Díaz was actually led by a new political and economic elite committed to democratic reform, economic restructuring, and a more modern and industrial development. Thus, in some ways, the Revolution pitted an incipient industrial sector against the entrenched elite of the agricultural and mineral interests.[10]   The 1917 Constitution at least symbolized the emerging nationalism of the new regime in its Article 27, which allowed the state to expropriate private property (directed specifically at the old agricultural elites) and recognized state subsoil rights. Industrial entrepreneurs were also emerging as important actors, as the Revolutionary President Venustiano Carranza and his Minister of Industry, Commerce, and Labor in November, 1917 helped organize the Confederation of Industrial Chambers, which was given semi-official status within the new revolutionary coalition.

The Mexican post-revolutionary regime was clearly being created as a single party system with a strong orientation toward nationalism, industrial development, and state intervention in the economy. From its creation, the PNR (and later the PRI) was envisioned as a dominant, governing party. In the words of Portes Gil (a provisional president of the nation as well as president of the party), "the PNR is a government party."[11] The administration of Lázaro Cárdenas in the 1930s solidified the organization nature of the state as well as the emerging dominance of the industrial sector. The traditional agricultural elite was dealt a crippling blow with massive agrarian reform under Cárdenas, who redistributed more land to the peasantry than the six presidents before him combined. He was the first president to attack directly the semifeudal *hacienda* landholding system, and by the end of his term he had effectively destroyed the economic and political power of the traditional *hacendados*. The other major accomplishment of Cárdenas was to implement the nationalization promises of Article 27 of the 1917 Constitution. In 1937 he nationalized the railroads, and in 1937 he expropriated the foreign-owned oil companies. The political events initiated in 1929, which continued under Cárdenas in the 1930s, marked the crucial turning point from export domination to domestic industrialization and import substitution. The precursor to the modern PRI was established with a definite protectionist agenda.

Cárdenas' successor in the Mexican presidency, Manuel Avila Camacho, institutionalized the policy changes of the 1930s while stabilizing the political system, which had experienced a dizzying rate of change over the last 30 years.   With his reassurances to the entrepreneurial sector, Avila Camacho set the stage for the postwar Mexican "economic miracle." Though he attempted to placate some of the alienated foreign companies by settling claims of expropriated owners, he continued to favor nationalist and statist objectives. As will be seen later, he strengthened NAFINSA and initiated the first major programs designed to promote and protect private Mexican industries.

Avila Camacho also produced the last major reorganization of the ruling party. The party officially became the PRI, incorporating three juridical branches: organized labor, rural peasants, and the "popular" sector (essentially the middle-class). Thus, at the stage of initiating the process of import substitution and protectionist policies, the major institution of state dominance (the PRI) had already accomplished the task of incorporating the lower classes. The PRI had now created an alliance with the national industrial class and a bureaucratic umbrella for controlling the lower classes. These accomplishments enabled the Party to pursue its policies of industrial promotion.

Horizontal ISI in Mexico became evident between 1930 and 1955. The data in Table 8.2 show that imports of traditional industrial goods as a proportion of total supply dropped from 26.8 percent to 14.2 percent in this period. The only time ISI in these goods was not achieved was from 1939 to 1944. Rapid growth in all industrial sectors in the early forties was not due to import substitution but rather to vastly increased domestic demand. In the war years, both domestic production and imports of manufactured goods increased.

The 1930 tariff law was the basis for all future tariff legislation, and it placed the highest levies (ranging from 40 to 100 percent) on textiles. However, in the 1930s most tariffs were still levied primarily for revenue purposes. In 1930, trade duties and tariffs represented 37 percent of total federal revenues, while in 1940 the share was 23 percent. There were some tariffs that were high enough to be considered protective in the 1930s (mostly for textile and food products), but in general even the tariff increases were implemented to raise revenues. The average tariff was only 16 percent *ad valorem*, which hardly constitutes protectionism. The fact that the tariff was assigned according to weight or volume (a specific tariff) also undermined protectionist purposes, since the effect of the tariff decreased as the price of imported goods increased. Finally, in December, 1942 the United States and Mexico signed a trade agreement in which both countries agreed not to increase certain tariff rates. This further inhibited any attempts to increase the protectionist nature of Mexican tariffs. Thus, the Great Depression did not lead to major qualitative changes in economic policies in Mexico, partly because of the continued preoccupation with consolidating political power after the Revolution.

The second phase of industrialization policies, in which economic policies are deliberately used to protect and promote industry, began in the 1940s. Promotion of industry through tax exemptions and credit policies became especially significant between 1939 and 1941, and foreign trade policies became overtly protectionist in the four-year period from 1944 to 1947. The progress in both horizontal and later vertical ISI was clearly boosted by specific policy decisions of the Mexican elite. The import-substitution strategy adopted in postwar Mexico aimed at aiding

TABLE 8.2 Import Coefficients, Mexican Industry, 1929-1981 (percentages)

| | *Import Coefficient* | | | | *Import Coefficient* | |
	Traditional	*Dynamic*			*Traditional*	*Dynamic*
1929	26.8	73.6		1955	14.2	40.4
1934	23.5	70.2		1960	9.7	46.4
1939	20.4	51.5		1965	10.4	39.2
1944	21.6	53.9		1970	10.8	38.5
1950	17.1	51.0		1981	10.0	38.5

Source: Trade data are from Direccion General de Estadistica, *Anuario estadístico del comercio exterior, Annuario estadístico, Compendio estadística,* and Instituto Mexicano de Comercio Exterior, *Boletín Mensual.* Industrialization data prior to 1981 are from the results of various industrial censuses published by the United Nations, Department of Economic and Social Affairs, Statistical Office, *Growth of World Industry.* Industrial data for 1981 are from Banco de Mexico, *Actividad industrial, cuaderno 1975-1982, Vol. 2, producto interno bruto,* 1982.

industrial development with selective economic policies while protecting domestic production from external competition (imports). Protectionist policies included foreign-exchange regulations, tariff rates, and import licenses, whereas promotion policies primarily embodied credit manipulation and tax exemptions.

Tax exemptions have been an important part of industrial promotion law in Mexico. A 1939 decree and the 1941 Law of Manufacturing Industries granted five-year exemptions from virtually all federal taxes to "new and necessary" industries. The law defined necessary industries as those "devoted to the manufacture or preparation of goods not produced in the country in sufficient quantity to meet the needs of domestic consumption."[12] The 1946 Law for the Development of Manufacturing Industries extended exemptions to more industries and granted exemptions for up to ten years, though eligibility requirements became more precise and fewer taxes were covered. Due to changes in the administration of this law in 1948, even fewer taxes were included in the exemption program, and restrictions were applied to the qualifying firms, such as requiring a certain amount of inputs to be bought in Mexico and fixing price ceilings. The Law for the Development of New and Necessary Industries in 1955 codified these restrictions. Though the number of qualified firms and the amount of the exemptions were being reduced, the government was furthering its effort to promote import substitution by aiding industries with the potential to replace imports.[13]

Public credit became a significant factor in industrial development in December 1940, when a new charter reorganized NAFINSA to concentrate on industrial development.[14] From then until 1946, NAFINSA's principal assets were in iron and steel, electrical appliances, sugar, paper, and fertilizers. One of its most notable accomplishments was the Altos Hornos de México iron and steel plant at Monclova in the northern state of Coahuila. This project was initiated by private capital during the Second World War, but NAFINSA had become the majority stockholder by 1947, since private investment proved inadequate. After 1947 NAFINSA's promotional efforts became particularly concentrated in infrastructure and heavy industry. Throughout most of the postwar period it reflected Mexico's commitment to import substitution, since a major criterion for assistance was the potential for import replacement. Most recently its emphasis has been on the capital-goods industry. By 1981 the NAFINSA industrial group included eighty-one enterprises of which nineteen were created in the 1977-1981 period. These included firms to manufacture steam turbines, heavy steel castings, petrochemicals, electrical equipment, tractors, and the like.[15]

Protectionist policies have been more important in achieving industrial growth in Mexico than the credit or tax-exemption policies, and the quantitative control of imports through a licensing system as well as *ad valorem* tariffs have been the mainstays of this protectionist system since 1947. Before 1947 the only instrument for protecting domestic industries from foreign competition was the specific tariff, and this was used mostly for purposes of revenue. The protectionist era in Mexico's trade policy was ushered in by two dramatic decrees in July 1947: the creation of import controls, and a change in the tariff system.[16] The officially declared purpose of these measures was to correct the balance of payments deficits incurred after World War II, but the actual intent (as demonstrated in the size of the tariff increases and the types of goods subjected to controls) was to protect many Mexican industries from foreign competition. The tariff decree increased a number of duties, and in November 1947 the method of levying duties was changed from specific to compound (a combination of specific and *ad valorem* methods), which halted the erosion of the effectiveness of the specific rate. Most of the items selected for the tariff increases, which were as much as 100 to 200 percent, were essential consumer goods, thus strongly suggesting a protectionist purpose behind the new tariffs.

The import control system had actually been created in 1944 under an emergency war powers act, but it was not applied until 1947. The type of goods subjected to import licensing under the 1944 decree suggests that an underlying purpose was protectionism for import-substitution industries. Up to the summer of 1947 the government had one general list and several minor lists of goods requiring permits, and the majority of these goods were semimanufactured or finished products that were competing with domestic output. The controls were not applied, however, until July 1947, when a group of luxury goods representing some 18 percent of total imports in 1946 were prevented from entering Mexico in order to correct the balance of payments deficit. Yet even this ban on luxury goods was adopted with an eye to protectionism. For instance, the ban on automobiles was accompanied by annual quotas on imports of assembly parts, so that between 1946 and 1948 the number of automobiles assembled in Mexico increased from 10,460 to 21,597.

Thus, the 1944 decree and the 1947 application of import controls, along with the 1947 changes in the tariff system, set up the framework for the protectionist system of postwar Mexico. The import controls were eased in 1951, but reimposed and extended in 1954, when a number of consumer goods were added to the list of controlled imports. Beginning in 1959, industrial integration (or "backward-linking" industrialization) was emphasized as a major objective of protectionist policies. Manufacturers were encouraged by substantial domestic inputs, especially in electronics and automotives.

The role of the PRI in initiating these policy changes is undeniable. Besides creating new legislation to favor so-called "infant industries," the PRI has been charged with establishing "captive groups" of industrial associations to promote and benefit from the new industrialization policies. Specifically, the National Chamber of Manufacturing Industries (CANACINTRA) has been viewed by some as an organization controlled by the PRI to suit the Party's purposes.[17] Though these arguments are certainly overstated, CANACINTRA and the PRI did share an ideological affinity and mutual alliance regarding the promotion and protectionist policies established in the 1940s. CANACINTRA was formed in November 1941, less than three months after a new Chambers Law (governing all trade associations) had been promulgated. The new law's most important provision was the required separation of all commercial and industrial chambers and confederations. The impetus for forming CANACINTRA no doubt came from this new Chambers Law. The original ninety-three member firms in CANACINTRA (for the most part recently established industries needing protection from foreign imports) supported and benefitted from the PRI's new commitment to promote import-substituting industrialization. Yet, CANACINTRA did maintain a degree of independence from the state. As one example, the industrial chamber opposed the 1942 Trade Agreement with the United States. More recently, CANACINTRA was a vocal opponent of the economic policies of President Echeverría in the 1970s and, continuing its protectionist tradition, was the principal opponent against Mexican entry to the GATT in 1980.

Of course, import substitution was first completed in finished consumer goods (those that are imported as final, complete products as opposed to those that must be assembled). Data show that by 1939 imports of these goods were only a negligible part (2.7 percent) of total expenditures for consumption. Then, by 1945 imports were less than 10 percent of all consumer goods, and most of these imports were in durable consumer goods. The import share of total supply of consumer goods increased from 1946 to 1947 and again from 1950 to 1953 to 13 to 14 percent, but devaluations in the 1948-1949 period and in 1954, plus other industrialization policies, apparently contributed to lowering this proportion below 10 percent each time. The greatest decreases were in consumer durables.[18] By 1960, data on individual categories show that only in automobiles (24.8 percent) did imports provide more than 10 percent of domestic consumption of finished consumer goods, and most of these automobile imports went only into the United States border areas of Mexico.

The early development of heavy industry in Mexico achieved some unusual progress in vertical ISI in the late 1930s. Imports as a percentage of total supply in the dynamic industries fell from 70.2 percent in 1934 to 51.5 percent in 1939, which represents the largest drop in any five-year period. Average annual growth rates in capital goods also reached their peak between 1935 and 1940 (22.9 percent annually). Though vertical ISI slowed significantly in the 1940s, it picked up again after 1950. And since 1960 import substitution has concentrated exclusively on dynamic industries. Yet, progress had been slow in the substitution of consumer durable, intermediate, and capital goods. As of 1966, over 55 percent of all investment in machinery and equipment was spent on imports, and in 1970 over one-third of the total supply of goods in dynamic industries was still being imported. The late 1970s actually saw increases in the import coefficients of some critical industries, and by 1980 around half the total supply in a number of heavy industries was being imported: basic chemicals (62.3 percent), machinery (59.5 percent), automobile (47.9 percent), and electrical appliances (47.6 percent).[19] Even so, one economist says that "Mexico appears to have import-substituted more effectively than many other developing countries of similar size and wealth"[20]

During the 1960s the promotion of industrial integration continued to be a major goal of trade policies, though some emphasis was being placed on more efficient production of domestic goods and on the exportation of manufactured goods. No major revisions were made in tariffs, but the proportion of items in the tariff code subject to import controls was increasing, from 44 percent in 1962 to 60 percent in 1966. And the greatest protection was afforded those items with the largest degree of product elaboration in the internal market.   President Echeverría then reinforced the system of protectionism in the first half of the 1970s through a general tariff rise and the extension of controls to all imports.

Trade liberalization received its first impetus during López Portillo's administration, when the petroleum boom improved the balance of payments picture for Mexico and the demand for imports escalated. López Portillo began to replace import licenses with tariffs and to lower tariff levels gradually.   In 1979 he initiated a policy of figuring import duties according to the "normal value" of the imported good rather than the "official price."   This change was an attempt to produce "economically rational" duties that in most cases would be lower then previous duties. These measures had the greatest effect on increasing the imports of durable consumer and capital goods.

The process of trade liberalization has not been a steady one, however. With the deficit in the external sector growing in 1981, new measures were taken in the summer to stem the flow of imports.   Tariffs were raised substantially on some three hundred "luxury" goods, and import controls were reestablished on almost all items. Of course, the imposition of foreign exchange controls and the general lack of foreign exchange in mid-1982 greatly reduced the level of imports.   The scarcity of foreign currency continued in 1983, but the new government of Miguel de la Madrid did revive the goal of trade liberalization.   The average level of tariffs began to fall substantially from a level exceeding 20 percent, and the policy of granting prior permits on imports was eased.[21]   The Secretary of Commerce and Industrial Development, speaking before the National Association of Importers and Exporters, summarized the trade policy of the de la Madrid team when he criticized the "permanent protection" of previous governments and emphasized the goal of making Mexican industries more competitive in international markets.[22]

Beginning in the summer of 1985, de la Madrid seriously deepened the Mexican commitment to trade liberalization.   By the following summer, the percent of domestic production covered by import licenses had fallen to below 50 percent and to below 20 percent by 1990 (see Table 8.3). Maximum tariffs in the latter-1980s were reduced from 100 percent to 20 percent, and average tariffs declined by half to 12.5 percent in 1990.

Exchange rate policies in the 1970s were not an instrument of government aid to industry, but rather were more of a burden on the industrial sector. Throughout the postwar period Mexico had maintained a remarkably stable exchange rate system. But by the 1970s the peso was

TABLE 8.3 Mexican Trade Reforms (percentages)

	June 1985	June 1986	June 1987	June 1988	June 1989	June 1990
Import Licenses[a]	92.2	46.9	35.8	23.2	22.1	19.9
Maximum Tariff	100.0	45.0	40.0	20.0	20.0	20.0
Average Tariff	23.5	24.0	22.7	11.0	12.6	12.5

[a]Percent of domestic production covered by import licenses.

Source: Gary Clyde Hufbauer and Jeffrey J. Schott, *North American Free Trade: Issues and Recommendations* (Washington, D.C.: Institute for International Economics, 1992), pp. 12-15.

becoming increasingly overvalued. The overvalued peso generally was a deterrent to more rapid industrial growth in that it discouraged Mexican exports (especially manufactured products that were characterized by price elasticity in demand) while encouraging imports. Of course, demand for imports was still being dampened by tariffs and licensing requirements. Though Presidents Echeverría and López Portillo devalued the peso in 1976 and 1982, respectively, these actions were too late and too little. Figuring an equilibrium exchange rate according to a theory of "purchasing power parity," the Mexican peso remained overvalued, in spite of the devaluations. This overvalued peso in turn dampened industrial expansion by increasing the relative prices of manufactured exports and decreasing the relative prices of competing imports. Only with the establishment of a "free" rate of exchange by de la Madrid in December 1982 did Mexican manufactured exports finally become price competitive. But even then, exporters complained that they were forced to exchange their foreign currency at a "controlled" rate, some 33 percent lower than the "free" rate.

The peso was devalued again in 1984 and 1985, when trade liberalization was beginning to take effect.[23] This depreciated peso delayed the impact of liberalization and continued to protect Mexican industry from more competitive imports. However, the structural adjustments were forced upon the industrial sector by 1986 and 1987. The peso appreciated considerably while trade liberalization continued to progress. Imports became very affordable and more readily available. In 1988 merchandise imports rose by over 50 percent, and by 1989 Mexico was experiencing its first trade deficit since the economic crisis began in the early-1980s.[24]

The deficit in merchandise trade in 1989 was solely due to the increased demand for imports. Merchandise exports had generally been expanding in the 1980s. The energy glut of the mid-1980s caused a temporary decline in Mexican exports, but manufactured exports made a remarkable recovery in the latter half of the 1980s. In fact the real value of Mexican exports of manufactured goods had almost tripled in the 1980s. In 1980, energy provided 64 percent of all merchandise exports, and manufactures were only 25 percent. By 1989, manufactured goods had become 55 percent of all merchandise exports, while energy had dropped to 37 percent.[25] The move into industrialization based on exportation of finished goods (or export substitution) had clearly begun.

As Mexico entered the phase of trade liberalization, membership in the General Agreement on Trade and Tariffs (GATT) became a key issue.[26] Entering the 1980s, Mexico was one of the few countries not a signatory to GATT. Several objective conditions had made Mexico's entry to the GATT a relevant issue in the late 1970s. First, the General Agreement had become more sympathetic to the demands of developing nations. The original GATT (created in 1948) included few Third World and only three Latin American nations (Brazil, Cuba, and Chile). By 1979 the eighty three contracting parties to the international body contained fifty two developing nations (eleven from Latin America). The major change benefiting the less-developed countries (LDCs) occurred in the mid-1960s, as Part IV, "Trade and Development," was added to the original General Agreement. This section allowed for nonreciprocity on the part of LDCs and for the reduction of trade barriers in developed countries to the export products of the Third World. The GATT was gradually becoming more attractive to LDCs, and more Third World nations began to join. By 1981 the body included eighty three nations as contracting parties (of which 52 were Third World nations, including American additions of Argentina, Jamaica, and Trinidad and Tobago). Several Latin American nations that were considerably less developed than Mexico had joined the GATT, and among the larger and more advanced Latin American nations only Mexico and Venezuela had not acceded to the General Agreement.

In the 1970s a number of provisions of the Tokyo Round of multilateral trade negotiations were formulated specifically for the LDCs. The developed nations agreed to extend "special and differential" treatment to the developing countries in regard to the various non-tariff codes, and the principle of non-reciprocity envisioned in Part IV of the GATT was given a firmer legal standing.

Even though Mexico did not sign the final document, it did actively participate in the Tokyo Round and did reach bilateral trade agreements,

under the auspices of the Tokyo Round, with the United States and eight
other developed countries or groups of countries. These bilateral agreements appeared to be quite favorable to Mexico, and may in fact have
been signed by the developed nations as an enticement to Mexico to there
the GATT. In the bilateral negotiations, Mexico offered concessions on
328 products totaling $503 million in 1976 and representing 4.4 percent
of the total import items in that year and 8.5 percent of the total import
value. The concessions involved setting tariff limits in some cases and
eliminating import permits in other cases. Yet these concessions were no
threat to domestic industries fearful of foreign competition. Only 21
items were going to have actual tariff reductions over the transition
period, and only 34 would have their import licenses removed.[27] So
Mexico's concessions were not a very significant move in the direction of
freer trade. On the other hand, the developed nations offered Mexico
substantial tariff concessions on 248 items, totaling $612 million in 1976.

Thus, the Mexican consideration of GATT membership came after a
period in which the international organization had attempted to address
the concerns of LDCs and had grown from the twenty three original
states in 1948 under U.S. and British domination to 111 nations currently,
with broad Third World participation. Mexico chose to participate
actively in the Tokyo Round from 1973 to 1979, and these talks resulted
in the negotiation of bilateral agreements favorable to Mexico. The
process of Mexican accession to the GATT, then, began as the Tokyo
Round came to a close.

Mexico's decision to negotiate entry to the GATT in 1979 can be
attributed to the confluence of two factors: a seemingly new orientation
on foreign trade policies under López Portillo and the level of
development attained by Mexico. López Portillo began to revise
protectionist policies in 1977 by starting to replace the burdensome
system of import licenses (requiring prior permits) with import tariffs.
By the summer of 1980, over 70 percent of Mexico's imported items had
been free from the requirement of import licensing. In another move
toward liberalization and rationalization of trade policies, López Portillo
in 1979 established a new method for valuing imported products for
customs purposes. The previous, somewhat arbitrary, system of "official
prices" was replaced by a more equitable valuation based on the "normal
value" of the goods. Though both these policy initiatives preceded the
GATT discussions with Mexico over entry, they were wholly congruent
with GATT principles. The Mexican president seemed to be preparing
the nation for eventual adhesion to the GATT.

GATT entry became important to the López Portillo administration
largely due to the perception of an overdue need to reduce Mexican
protectionism. Since the creation of import controls in 1947 Mexico has

had one of the highest levels of effective protection in Latin America, even though some efforts were made in the mid 1960s to emphasize manufactured exports and efficient production.[28] The López Portillo administration felt some liberalization was necessary and, along with the new trade policies, viewed GATT membership as beneficial to Mexico. In particular, the rewards of GATT entry were said to include increasing the competitiveness and efficiency of Mexican industries, gaining better access to foreign markets, and thereby improving Mexico's balance of trade (especially in boosting nonpetroleum exports). In a broader sense, the GATT negotiations begun in 1979 were part of the conservative reaction under López Portillo to the leftist policies of his predecessor, Luis Echeverría (1970-76). Whereas Echeverría alienated the private sector, especially large industrialists, López Portillo strove to renew the confidence of big business in Mexico. GATT adherence was to be another aspect of this new development strategy.

Various objective economic conditions in the late 1970s were making GATT membership more appropriate for Mexico. By a number of macro-economic indicators Mexico had achieved the second highest levels of economic development in the region. In terms of gross domestic product, domestic investment, total trade, and value added in manufacturing, Mexico had been second only to Brazil and the next most advanced nation, Argentina, had lagged significantly behind Mexico. These aggregate levels of development in Mexico by 1980 had been due to continuous economic growth in the postwar period. After a brief economic lull in the mid 1970s, the economy regained its robust rates of expansion in the late seventies. From 1977 to 1979 the economy averaged 7.5 percent annual growth, with 9.8 percent annual growth in the industrial sector.[29]

The level of development achieved by Mexico and the previous policy initiatives of López Portillo in the trade area provide the context in which Mexico began in January 1979 to negotiate entry to the GATT. In October the Group produced the Protocol of Accession.[30] Mexico had until 31 May 1980 to decide whether to accept the negotiated protocol. Most observers within and outside Mexico stated that the terms were unusually flexible.[31] However, despite the flexibility of the terms and contrary to all predictions, López Portillo made his announcement in March 1980 "to postpone our participation in GATT," which effectively ended the possibility of Mexican adherence to the treaty for the time-being. Essentially, an alliance of protectionist industrial groups (particularly CANACINTRA), leftist intellectuals and opposition parties, and the Ministry of Industry within the government swayed López Portillo from his initial support for the GATT. The President determined that a positive decision on GATT membership for Mexico would have alienated too many important political actors (and pleased surprisingly few) and that the political costs of entry clearly outweighed any potential political and economic benefits, at least at that juncture in Mexican development.

U.S. policy-makers were obviously disappointed and pointed out that the decision would result in the cancellation of bilateral agreements favorable to Mexico that had been negotiated during the Tokyo Round of trade talks from 1973 to 1979, that countervailing duties on Mexican exports could be more readily applied, and that Mexico would lose other benefits of the multilateral GATT umbrella.

The GATT decision reflected the prevailing PRI view at the time that a bilateral approach to trade negotiations with the developed nations (rather than the multilateralism of the GATT) was in Mexico's best interests.[32] Specifically, Mexican officials argued that Mexico should link its petroleum sales to purchases of Mexican manufactured goods abroad and should pursue a generalized system of preference concessions with individual countries. The new variable of enormous petroleum reserves provided Mexico, it was argued, with the political opportunity to gain trade and other economic advantages through bilateral negotiations. On a multilateral level, this leverage, it was said, would be diminished. Certainly, at the time of the GATT decision in 1980 the power of Mexico's oil wealth was an attractive and probably reasonably effective tool in bilateral relations.

Even before the 1980 GATT decision, and as a precursor to the North American Free Trade Agreement, the idea of a North American Common Market first surfaced during the U.S. administration of Jimmy Carter.[33] The chief advocates of a regional economic integration scheme linking the United States, Canada, and Mexico were U.S. businessmen, but the Carter administration embraced the idea at least initially. But in the late-1970s and early-1980s, Mexico's preference for bilateralism in its relations with industrial countries was evident in its strong and persistent rejection of the Common Market idea. López Portillo and other Mexican government and Party officials objected that such a scheme would reduce Mexican sovereignty and was only a U.S. subterfuge for acquiring a steadily increasing supply of Mexican oil and for ensuring Mexican markets for U.S. industrial products. Indeed, Mexican critics argued that economic integration schemes historically have created "poles of development" in the advanced nations to the detriment of the lower income nations, and no plan has ever envisaged a common market between such disparate economies as the United States and Mexico without compensating mechanisms. Realizing the Mexican resistance to such a concept, the Carter administration quickly disassociated itself from the idea and blamed it on individuals outside the government.[34] U.S. policymakers were showing some sensitivity to Mexican concerns about national autonomy at this point. As was the case with the 1980 GATT decision, the Mexican government manifested its preference for international economic negotiations with industrial nations through bilateral channels that provided it some leverage rather than through multilateral institutions that were perceived to favor the developed countries.

As mentioned, the administration of President Miguel de la Madrid initiated a number of important changes in Mexican trade policy. Of course, de la Madrid renewed the trade liberalization policies that were begun but then dropped by President López Portillo. In addition, the administration resurrected the notion of GATT membership. Commerce Secretary Héctor Hernández Cervantes, who was the leading advocate of the GATT under López Portillo, began pushing Mexican entry into the GATT again in the summer of 1985. Citing that López Portillo had only "postponed" the decision about GATT, members of the de la Madrid administration made clear their desire to examine seriously any possible advantages in GATT membership. In December 1985, the government of Mexico announced its intention to negotiate Mexican entrance into the GATT, and Mexico formally acceded to the GATT in 1986.

In April of 1985, in another area of trade policy change, representatives of Mexico and the United States signed an "Understanding on Subsidies and Compensatory [Countervailing] Duties."[35] For its part, the United States recognized that subsidies can be an "integral part of economic development programs," after years of complaining about Mexican export and other subsidies. In turn, Mexico promised not to apply any subsidies that would adversely affect the interests of the United States. Mexico would dismantle the program of *Cedis* (tax exemptions for export products) and not engage in preferential pricing practices that affected exports. Mexico also agreed to eliminate gradually all export financing with a maturity of two years or less. Finally, Mexico promised not to include any export subsidies in future development programs and to avoid any nonexport subsidies if they caused or threatened to cause damage to a U.S. industry.

The United Stated conceded to use the injury test provision (*prueba de daño*) in applying countervailing duties, even before Mexico had become a GATT member. Before applying a compensatory duty, adverse effects on U.S. industries "must be demonstrated through positive proof utilizing formal proceedings and investigations prescribed in U.S. law applicable for determining the economic impact of Mexican exports on a productive sector in the U.S." The agreement concluded by stating that the two nations would begin consultations with the goal of reaching a more comprehensive means for dealing with bilateral trade relations.[36] These bilateral talks moved from the 1985 specific issues of subsidies and countervailing duties to sectoral talks under a bilateral framework in 1987 and 1989. The 1987 Framework of Principles and Procedures for Consultation Regarding Trade and Investment Relations provided dispute mechanisms for trade problems and an "immediate action agenda" for negotiations on bilateral issues in goods and services sectors, resulting in sectoral accords on steel and textiles. The 1989 Understanding Regarding Trade and Investment Facilitation Talks started a new round of bilateral negotiations on a wide variety of issues, including intellectual property controversies.[37] Finally, the two countries agreed to pursue a Free Trade Agreement in 1990. In the second half of 1990, Canada decided to join the negotiations for a regional pact, and in February of 1991 President Bush announced that the three countries of Canada, Mexico, and the United States would initiate negotiations on the NAFTA.

Conclusion

Table 8.4 summarizes the major initiatives in terms of the three principal phases of Mexican industrialization policies, concentrating on trade issues. Export-oriented growth in primary products dominated at least until the Mexican Revolution, and policies emphasized either industrialization linked to the primary sector or tariffs principally as revenue-generating measures. The newly established ruling party (initially the PNR, but renamed the PRI years later) began the transition to horizontal ISI in the 1930s and solidified the move with various tax exemptions, new tariffs, and import controls in the 1940s. A reciprocal relation was evolving between economic development and public policy change. As one phase of development became exhausted, policy initiatives would respond to assist the transition to a new stage of industrial growth. The Mexican ruling party, in alliance with a burgeoning but youthful industrial sector and its political associations (such as CANACINTRA), helped initiate import substitution in the 1940s. Then, as import substitution in the traditional and consumer goods industries became exhausted, the PRI again responded to pressures to promote another stage of industrial development. However, since this third phase of trade liberalization runs counter to the entrenched ideology of Mexican nationalism, the policy changes have moved slowly and erratically. López Portillo began the process with the easing of import restrictions and new tariff rules in the late-1970s, but he countered with rejecting GATT membership and reestablishing import controls in the early-1980s. De la Madrid returned to the trade liberalization agenda in 1983 and brought Mexico into GATT in 1986. Salinas thus essentially has

TABLE 8.4 Major Industrialization Policies, Mexico

Date	Policy

Phase I: Revenue Measures

1868	Tariff on textiles
	60 percent of revenues from tariffs
1930	Tariff law
	40-100 percent duties
	37 percent of revenues from tariffs
1933-38	NAFINSA (public credit)
	Public works
	Industrial Development Bank (credit expansion)

Phase II: Protectionism

1939	Tax exemptions
1940	NAFINSA reorganized (public credit)
1941	Law of Manufacturing Industries
	Tax exemptions for "new and necessary industries
1944	Emergency war powers act creates import controls
1946	Law for the Development of Manufacturing Industries
	Tax exemptions extended
1947	Import controls codified: ban on luxury imports
	Tariff increases and *ad valorem* tariff
1951	Import controls reimposed and extended
1954	Import controls extended
1955	Law for the Development of New and Necessary Industries
	Tax exemptions for specific import-substituting industries
1959	Import controls for industrial integration
1964	Emphasis on more efficient production
1970-75	Tariff increases and extension of import controls

Phase III: Liberalization

1976	Some import controls replaced by tariffs
1979	"Normal" valuation for import duties
1980	GATT membership "proposed"
1981	Import controls reestablished
1983-88	Tariff reductions and substantial easing of controls
1986	Mexico enters GATT
1990	NAFTA negotiations commence

Source: Compiled by the author.

completed the transition, and NAFTA is really the culmination of a process of transition from an inward-looking policy of import substitution to an outward-oriented approach of export substitution--not reliance on the exports of primary products, but emphasis on competing globally in a whole range of export products.

Though this chapter has argued that Mexican participation in NAFTA is to a considerable extent the result of the exhaustion of the import substitution phase of industrial growth, one should appreciate the political obstacles that Carlos Salinas has overcome. He has led the bureaucratic state and his dominant party, the PRI, into a new era of economic policy in Mexico. His greatest challenge has not been to overcome the opposition of the other political parties, but rather to convince skeptics within the PRI of the utility of economic reform.

Though Mexico can claim to exhibit a multi-party system, the non-PRI parties have never mounted serious alternatives at the national level (except, some would say, during the 1988 presidential election). The most significant opposition party in the postwar period has been the right-wing National Action Party (PAN). The national vote total for the PAN, however, has never exceeded 20 percent. Besides, in terms of Salinas' economic agenda and NAFTA, the PAN has not presented an appreciable difference from the PRI. In fact, the PAN in many ways has become the most important ally of the Salinas forces. As the PRI has been split among *tecnicos* (the Salinas wing of technocratic leaders committed to economic restructuring) and *políticos* (more traditional forces centered in the labor sector and opposed to the economic reform program), the *Panistas* have been an important source of support for the Salinas initiatives.

At the other end of the political spectrum, the political left has usually been splintered among various, minor parties, whose total national vote has not gone beyond 10 percent. The left did coalesce in 1988 under the banner of Cuauhtémoc Cárdenas, who had split with the PRI over issues of internal democratization and economic policy. Cárdenas represented the strongest electoral threat ever to the PRI, but after garnering over 30 percent of the 1988 vote (according to official results) his party has steadily lost electoral strength in more recent regional elections. The *Cardenista* forces do pose a legitimate alternative to Salinas' economic reform program and NAFTA negotiations, but they have been overwhelmed by the political acumen of President Salinas. Some commentators have equated the left's opposition to NAFTA in Mexico to trying to stop a locomotive with a full head of steam.

Other than the opposition parties, the remaining segments to be countered in terms of NAFTA are nationalists in both the private sector and organized labor. As mentioned, CANACINTRA led the charge against GATT membership in 1980, but the industrial chamber has been noticeably silent regarding NAFTA. Undoubtedly, the private sector has accepted the inevitability (at least from the Mexican perspective) of the Free Trade Agreement. Many of the older and less competitive industrial establishments either have already adjusted to a new world of international competition or have gone out of business. Organized labor in Mexico has never been a strong, independent force within the PRI. Salinas particularly demonstrated his administration's dominance of the labor sector when he arrested the notoriously corrupt leader of the largest and most powerful Mexican union, the oil-workers' union, in one of his first acts as President in 1989. Thus, labor is in no position to veto Mexico's participation in NAFTA. Carlos Salinas then has marshalled the necessary political support and essentially mollified any potential opposition to the Free Trade Agreement. The combination of Salinas' political skills and determination along with the exhaustion of the import substitution model have made approval of NAFTA a more certain fact in Mexico than in her northern neighbors.

Notes

1. This is termed "backward-linking" ISI because it stresses the production of goods that are the inputs to the production of consumer nondurables. Thus, ISI is the continually moving "backward" through the production process.

2. See Guillermo O'Donnell, *Modernization and Bureaucratic-Authoritarianism: Studies in South American Politics*, Politics of Modernization Series, no. 9 (Berkeley: Institute of International Studies, University of California, Berkeley, 1973).

3. Dale Story, *Industry, the State, and Public Policy in Mexico* (Austin: University of Texas Press, 1986).

4. Timothy King, *Mexico: Industrialization and Trade Policies Since 1940* (London: Oxford University Press, 1970), p. 4; and Roger D. Hansen, *Mexican Economic Development: The Roots of Rapid Growth*, Studies in Development Progress, no. 2 (Washington, D.C.: National Planning Association, 1971), pp. 13-14.

5. Moisés T. De la Peña, "La industrialización de México y la política arancelaria," *El Trimestre Económico*, Vol. 12, No. 2, July-September, 1945, p. 190.

6. On this and other industrialization policies of the 1920s and 1930s, see Sanford A. Mosk, *Industrial Revolution in Mexico* (Berkeley: University of California Press, 1950); William P. Glade, "Revolution and Economic Development: A Mexican Reprise," in William P. Glade and Charles W. Anderson, eds. *The Political Economy of Mexico* (Madison: University of Wisconsin Press, 1963), pp. 19-20, 45, 85; Stanford G. Ross and John B. Christensen , *Tax Incentives for Industry in Mexico* (Cambridge, Mass.: Law School, Harvard University, 1959) pp. 29-31, 42-43, 187-189; Raymond A. Vernon, *The Dilemma of Mexico's Development* (Cambridge, Mass.: Harvard University Press, 1963); Clark

Reynolds, *The Mexican Economy: Twentieth-Century Structure and Growth*, (New Haven, Conn.: Yale Univ. Press, 1970), pp. 216-218; Roger D. Hansen, *The Politics of Mexican Development* (Baltimore: The Johns Hopkins University Press, 1974); and Adriaan Ten Kate et al., *La política de protección en el desarrollo económico de México* (Mexico City: Fondo de Cultura Económica, 1979), pp. 30-31.

7. Fernando Rosenzweig, "La industria", in Daniel Cosío Villegas, ed., *Historia Moderna de México*, Vol. 7, pt. 1, *El Porfiriato, La Vida Económica* (Mexico City: Editorial Hermes, 1965), pp. 318, 326-327.

8. George Wythe, *Industry in Latin America* (New York: Columbia University Press, 1949), pp. 275-276.

9. Ricardo Cinta G., "Burguesía nacional y desarrollo," in Jorge Martínez Ríos, ed., *El perfil de México en 1980, Vol. 3* (Mexico City: Siglo Veintiuno Editores, 1972), pp. 169-182; and René Villarreal, "The Policy of Import-Substituting Industrialization, 1929-1975," in José Luis Reyna and Richard S. Weinert, eds. *Authoritarianism in Mexico* (Philadelphia: Institute for the Study of Human Issues, 1977), pp. 67-70.

10. Dale Story, *Sectoral Clash and Industrialization in Latin America* (Syracuse, New York: Maxwell School of Citizenship and Public Affairs, 1981), pp. 23-27.

11. Octavio Rodríguez Araujo, *La reforma política y los partidos en México* (Mexico: Siglo Veintiuno Editores, 1983), pp. 29-30.

12. See Julián Bernal-Molina, *A Statement of the Laws of Mexico in Matters Affecting Business in Its Various Aspects and Activities* (Washington, D.C.: Inter-American Development Commission, 1948), p. 81.

13. For more detail on the 1939 decree and the 1941, 1946, and 1955 laws, see Julián Bernal-Molina, *A Statement on the Laws of Mexico in Matters Affecting Business in Its Various Aspects and Activities*, Second Edition (Washington, D.C.: Pan American Union, General Legal Division, Department of Legal Affairs, 1956), pp. 93-95; and W. Paul Strassman, *Technological Change and Economic Development: The Manufacturing Experience in Mexico and Puerto Rico* (Ithaca, N.Y.: Cornell University Press, 1968), pp. 297-298.

14. On the history, purpose and effect of NAFINSA, see Charles W. Anderson, "Bankers as Revolutionaries: Politics and Development Banking in Mexico," in William P. Glade and Charles W. Anderson, *The Political Economy of Mexico* (Madison: University of Wisconsin Press, 1963), pp. 124-125; Calvin P. Blair, "Nacional Financiera: Entrepreneurship in a Mixed Economy," in Raymond Vernon, ed., *Public Policy and Private Enterprise in Mexico* (Cambridge, Mass.: Harvard University Press, 1964); Frank R. Brandenburg, *The Development of Latin American Private Enterprise* (Washington, D.C.: National Planning Association, 1964), pp. 71-72; Robert T. Aubey, *Nacional Financiera and Mexican Industry: A Study of the Financial Relationship between the Government and the Private Sector of Mexico* (Los Angeles: UCLA Latin American Center, 1966), pp. 38-52; and Joseph S. LaCascia, *Capital Formation and Economic Development in Mexico* (New York: Praeger, 1969), pp. 39-42.

15. Nacional Financiera, *1981 Annual Report*, pp. 6, 47-52.

16. See Rafael Izquierdo, "Protectionism in Mexico," in Raymond Vernon, ed., *Public Policy and Private Enterprise in Mexico* (Cambridge, Mass.: Harvard

University Press, 1964), pp. 263-266; and Gerardo M. Bueno, "The Structure of Protection in Mexico," in Bela Balassa, ed., *The Structure of Protection in Developing Countries* (Baltimore: The Johns Hopkins University Press, 1971), pp. 180-182.

17. See Robert Jones Shafer, *Mexican Business Organizations: History and Analysis* (Syracuse, N.Y.: Syracuse University Press, 1973), pp. 54-58, 67-70, 107-112; and John F. H. Purcell and Susan Kaufman Purcell, "Mexican Business and Public Policy," in James M. Malloy, ed., *Authoritarianism and Corporatism in Latin America* (Pittsburgh: University of Pittsburgh Press, 1977), pp. 194-195. Several of the more conservative business leaders in Mexico also told this author that they believed CANACINTRA was a tool of the Mexican State. And even the leftist magazine *Proceso* (21 February 1983) described CANACINTRA as "unofficially official."

18. See United Nations Economic Commission for Latin America, *External Disequilibrium in the Economic Development of Latin America: The Case of Mexico, pt. II, 1957.*

19. Claudia Schatán, "Efectos de la liberalización del comercio exterior en México, *Economía Mexicana*, No. 3, 1981, pp. 86-87; and José I. Casar, "Ciclos económicos en la industria y sustitución de importaciones: 1950-1980," *Economía Mexicana*, No. 4, 1982, p. 94.

20. Reynolds, *The Mexican Economy*, p. 212.

21. *Razones*, 24 January-6 February 1983; and *Unomásuno*, 16 February and 9 May 1983.

22. *Excélsior*, 1 January 1983.

23. With an index of 1980=100, the rates were 1981=87.2, 1982=122.0, 1983=138.9, 1984=119.0, 1985=114.9. Inter-American Development Bank, *Economic and Social Progress in Latin America, 1990 Report* (Baltimore: The Johns Hopkins University Press, 1990), p. 147.

24. Ibid. Again with 1980=100, the exchange rates were 1986=163.9, 1987=178.6, 1988=144.9, and 1989=129.9

25. Gary Clyde Hufbauer and Jeffrey J. Schott, *North American Free Trade: Issues and Recommendations* (Washington, D.C.: Institute for International Economics, 1992), p. 49.

26. Dale Story, "Trade Politics in the Third World: A Case Study of the Mexican GATT Decision," in *International Organization*, Vol. 36, No. 4, Autumn 1982, pp. 767-794.

27. William P. Glade, "Mexico and GATT: An Evolving Relationship," Paper presented at Seminar for Instituto Mexicano de Ejecutivos de Finanzas (Saltillo, Mexico, 28 February 1980), pp. 19-20.

28. Gerardo Bueno, "The Structure of Protection in Mexico," in Bela Balassa, ed., *The Structure of Protection in Developing Countries* (Baltimore: Johns Hopkins University Press, 1971); and Adriaan ten Kate, et al, *La política de protección en el desarrollo económico de México* (Mexico, Fondo de Cultura Económica, 1979).

29. Inter-American Development Bank, *Economic and Social Progress in Latin America, 1979 Report* (Washington, D.C.).

30. The documents were published in all major Mexican daily newspapers on 5 November 1979. They appear in Spanish in GATT document #L/4849.

31. *Wall Street Journal,* 19 November 1979.

32. Gary Clyde Hufbauer, W.N. Harrell Smith IV, and Frank G. Vukmanic. 1981. "Bilateral Trade Relations," in Susan Kaufman Purcell, ed., *Mexico-United States Relations* (New York: Academy of Political Science).

33. Dale Story, "Mexican-U.S. Trade Relations," in Robert E. Biles, ed., *Inter-American Relations: The Latin American Perspective* (Boulder, Colorado: Lynne Rienner Publishers, 1981), pp. 165-178.

34. Address by Ambassador Nava at the annual meeting of the American Chamber of Commerce of Mexico, (Mexico City: International Communication Agency, U.S. Embassy, June 5, 1980).

35. *Comercio Exterior,* 1985, 35, No. 6, pp. 609-611.

36. *Diario Oficial,* 1985, May 15.

37. Hufbauer and Schott, *North American Free Trade,* p. 4.

9

The Free Trade Policy
"Revolution"
and Party Politics in Mexico

Gustavo Vega-Canovas

This chapter analyzes the economic and political determinants of Mexico's dramatic shifts in trade policy towards liberalization and the search for a free trade agreement with the United States and Canada. Its main line of argument is that the reorientation in trade policy is best understood as the result of a combination of external and internal factors, the most important of which is the ideological commitment of both President Miguel De la Madrid and his successor Carlos Salinas and both of their economic cabinets to neoliberal economic policies and to export promotion. For over forty years, Mexico's development strategy had emphasized growth based on import substitution and expansion of the internal market. But the weakness of the world oil market and the scarcity of external funds following Mexico's debt crisis caused the Mexican government to break with tradition and to promote growth through exports. I will argue that the Mexican state, and by this I mean the Partido Revolucionario Institutional (PRI), despite moves towards liberalization, is not attempting to relinquish its position as director of national development. Opening the economy and searching for a free trade agreement has been justified as an inevitable step towards the "ongoing Mexican Revolution's development goals."

In the first section of this chapter, I discuss the evolution of Mexican trade policy and Mexican-U.S. trade relations in the post war period until 1990. In a second section, I discuss the domestic politics of trade liberalization in Mexico. A final section reviews the views and positions of the main political parties in Mexico towards the North American Free Trade Agreement (NAFTA).

Evolution of Mexican-U.S. Trade Relations

Any important negotiation between two governments is significantly shaped by their overall political relationship. That relationship is, in turn, a function at least in part of the broader foreign policies the two governments are pursuing. And such policies are strongly influenced by the way leaders in each country perceive the world situation and how their nation can best cope with that situation. To the degree that there is a consensus on such fundamentals within a nation's leadership, such predominant conceptions of national interest, what Morton Halperin calls "shared images," set limits to the range of debate within the nation, and even more to the range of policy actions receiving a serious hearing within the government.[1] They can be a powerful force in the overall policies a nation pursues, but how strong a constraint they prove to be is a function of how "shared" they are. The impact of such predominant national interest conceptions on a bilateral relationship depends not only on how important they are within each nation, however. It depends also on their content.

If views of the world in Washington and Mexico City are similar or at least compatible, if the preferred means for coping with that world are consistent or mutually reinforcing, then there exists a strong basis for cooperation. If, however, world views are mutually inconsistent or if the ways leaders in one country seek to cope with the world are threatening to the other, the prospect for conflict is heightened. During the nineteenth century and the decades between the two World Wars in the present century, for example, Mexican and U.S. political leaders saw the world in very different ways and frequent tension and conflicts characterized the climate of relations between both governments.

During this period there were many reasons for Mexicans to lament their proximity to the "Colossus of the North" besides the war of 1847 and the loss of half of Mexican territory. In 1914, President Wilson invaded and occupied the port city of Veracruz in order to teach Mexicans to elect honest men. And in 1916, Black Jack Pershing scoured the northern countryside searching in vain for the elusive Mexican hero Pancho Villa. The source of the trouble in this period was evident. American investors trying to protect their property, and American officials concerned with international laws regarding foreign investment, clashed with triumphant Mexican revolutionaries trying to assert authority over their country's economy.[2]

The modern Mexican state emerged after two decades of revolution, civil war and military revolts (1910-29). A group of triumphant Mexican generals from the state of Sonora created an elite-centered consensus which permitted regional strongmen to dominate their areas in return for peace in national politics. Under the presidency of Lázaro Cárdenas (1934-40), this elite coalition was broadened to include labor and peasants. In addition, the representation of business and industry was formalized through mandatory membership in peak associations. This coalition was constructed on the basis of material and ideological interests; and according to a number of political analysts, the ideological principles of the Mexican Revolution, chief among them social justice and national sovereignty, have been fundamental to the longevity of the coalition.

The period of tension and conflict between American investors and Mexican nationalists was brought to a head in March 1938, when the Mexican government expropriated the properties of major American and British oil corporations.[3] The labor dispute of 1936 that eventually led to the expropriation occurred at a time when Mexican-U.S. relations were already troubled by an agrarian reform program in Mexico and by controversies over debts and claims. From March 1938 through the spring of 1940, the U.S. government tried several tactics to effect a change in Mexican policy, but without success. Eventually, the growing threat of war, and the desire of U.S. officials to secure Mexican cooperation in hemisphere defense plans led to a settlement in November 1941.

For reasons that are still hotly debated among Mexican historians, the climate of relations between Mexico and the United States changed dramatically during the war. The change had to do with the arrival into power of the Avila Camacho administration in 1940 whose policy preferences were noticeable different from those of the Cárdenas government. During the Avila Camacho administration (1940-1946) there developed in Mexico a new official concept of the state's role and a new goal for the government. President Lázaro Cárdenas (1934-1940) had described the state as an arbiter among competing class interests and offered as a fitting objective for government the quest for social justice. Avila Camacho, and most later presidents, said the state was more of an economic regulator in a unified society pursuing its true goal, rapid economic growth.[4] "By the time Avila Camacho left office in 1946," wrote Raymond Vernon in the 1960s, "the Cardenas image of Mexico based upon a contented, semi-industrialized, semi-commercialized peasantry had been obscured by a new image of Mexico, an image of the modern industrial state".[5]

Perhaps the most important aspect of Mexican-U.S. relations after World War II, apart from the common border, is the consolidation of power in Mexico by a regime whose first commitments after political stability were to rapid industrial growth through import-substituting industrialization (ISI) and to the quest for national sovereignty (i.e., autonomous development).[6] These two commitments are mutually reinforcing. The Mexican Revolution of 1910 embodied a xenophobic reaction to centuries of foreign domination and installed the search for national self-determination as an integral part of the national psyche. The constants in Mexican foreign policy embodied in terms such as self-determination, nonintervention, juridical equality of states, and peaceful settlements of disputes reveal a never ending Mexican desire for obtaining formal recognition as an equal actor in the international system, with complete legal jurisdiction over Mexican soil and territorial waters. It is in this context that we must remember one of the attractions of ISI: it promised to insulate the domestic economy from much of the international fluctuations to which developing countries were especially vulnerable. In practice, ISI merely transferred the vulnerability of the domestic economy from the export to the import side. However, its initial successes led policy makers to peceive autonomous national development as a goal not only desirable but also, with the correct state policies, attainable.

These commitments to ISI and national sovereignty meant that, with the brief exception of a 1942 bilateral agreement under the Reciprocal Trade Agreements Program, Mexico avoided any economic diplomatic entanglements with the United States. It stood largely apart from the developments leading to the postwar multilateral trade and payments system. It did not join the GATT. Rather it accepted the proposition that infant industries are best nurtured behind protective walls.[7] While Mexico and the United States extended MFN treatment to each other, there was no treaty basis for this nor did it matter much: throughout most of the postwar years, foreign trade constituted less than ten percent of Mexico's GDP.[8]

The ISI policy had some important initial successes. Development from within did foster the establishment of an industrial structure in Mexico. Because of its sheltered nature, however, Mexican production was noncompetitive on world markets. The entire system had a relatively short life because it depended almost entirely on the limited domestic market in Mexico.

From the 1950s through the early 1970s, a period which in Mexican history is referred to as the Era of Stabilizing Development, the Mexican government, backed by the private sector and the unions, brought about high levels of growth with low levels of inflation. Thus, from 1940 through 1970, Mexico's economy grew at an average rate of 6.8 percent, while its population grew at an average rate of 3.2 percent, a net gain of 3.5 percent per annum on average. Unfortunately, however, the policy of protecting industry against foreign imports, which had allowed for economic growth, had introduced all sorts of distortions. The protected markets had allowed the prices of industrial output to rise beyond the world average for the same products and, in some sectors, had promoted wage increases that surpassed increases in productivity. Then when the foremost exporting sector, agriculture, began decreasing its total exportable output after 1965, the flow of foreign exchange to finance imports was reduced. The decrease in output had two causes: protectionism, which squeezed the agricultural sector through excessively high prices and low quality for its inputs, and a policy of setting prices for agricultural products that were all too often erratic and insufficient.[9]

Moreover, one should not forget that ISI also became highly dependent on foreign investment. Thus, although the initial wartime and postwar growth of manufacturing was the work mostly of Mexican entrepreneurs, in the mid- and late 1940s, American firms that had been selling in the Mexican market began to establish assembly and final processing plants in order to avoid the rising Mexican tariffs and to benefit from the expanding Mexican economy. In the 1950s, the Mexican government's call for foreign investment became explicit, and despite ambiguity in the Mexican welcome, the quantity and strategic importance of U.S. direct private investment in Mexico continued to grow. In 1938, U.S. capital accounted for 61.6 percent of total direct foreign (U.S. and non-U.S.) investment in Mexico; two decades later the percentage was 74.4, and by 1972 it had grown almost to 80 percent. More important, the postwar U.S. investment was, and is, located in manufacturing, the economy's most dynamic sector. In 1940, manufacturing claimed only 2.7 percent of total U.S. investment in Mexico; by 1957, it accounted for 45.3 percent, and by 1972 it attracted 69 percent.[10]

The effects of the ISI strategy on the Mexican economy are reflected in productivity gains among the different activities that comprise the industrial sector.[11] During the period 1974-1981, productivity gains were absent or negative in 16 of 35 industries. For 22 of the same 35 industries, productivity gains were lower during the period 1977-81 than they were in the previous four years. Even if several factors may in principle account for the low or negative advances in productivity in many industrial activities, there is no doubt that the limited exposure of the Mexican industrial sector to foreign competition played an important role in that respect. That policy was enforced through a regime of import permits, which were rarely granted when the imported good was produced domestically. Thus, the degree of protection conferred to domestic firms was absolute.

Import-substituting industrialization had run its course by the early 1970's, indeed earlier. It was kept alive during the 1970's and first two years of the 1980s, however, because the administrations of Luis Echeverria Alvarez (1971-1976) and José López Portillo (1977-1982) were able to obtain foreign exchange for its necessary imports from sources other than the exports of manufactured goods, mostly from oil and external debt. It was the collapse of both these sources that forced a change in the development model in 1983.

The costs of protection were noted by economists during the Echeverria electoral campaign. But the inefficient industrial policy was "saved" by the rise in the terms of trade and by the abundance of world credit that resulted from the international oil shock. In addition, Echeverria foreign policy sought to pressure the industrialized countries into agreement on a New International Economic Order (NIEO) because the NIEO implied greater access to lucrative markets at higher prices through political, not economic, mechanisms. The failure of the NIEO meant the failure of this line of attack. Under López Portillo, there was an apparent serious attempt to support the import requirements of ISI through an orthodox strategy of export stimulation based upon increasing the international competitiveness of the national economy and negotiating political access to export markets. Accession to GATT was to be one of the main vehicles of Mexico's more open orientation. Mexico participated in the Tokyo Round of GATT negotiations and gained significant tariff concessions from other participants. In 1979, it negotiated a protocol of accession to GATT. In March 1980, however, President López Portillo changed his mind Petroleum exports, highly valued in 1979-81, were to be tied to purchase of nonpetroleum exports and investment in the Mexican economy. In this sense, Portillo returned to Echeverria's strategy of making international actors pay for Mexican exports, but this time with an apparently stronger bargaining chip than NIEO, petroleum.[12]

The administration of Miguel de la Madrid (1983-1988) not only had to weather a drastic fall in oil prices, but also a world wide depression. Mexico found itself saddled with a debt load that it could not service, a manufacturing sector that could not compete, a bloated public sector that sucked up much needed investment capital and a business sector that had lost confidence in Mexico's ability to recover. Billions of dollars of private capital fled to safer havens (mostly in the U.S.). The value of the peso plummeted and inflation soared. The standard of living for most ordinary Mexican citizens was cut in half.

Three economic tasks presented themselves to the new administration: finding a solution to the foreign debt, stabilizing the crashing economy, and undertaking structural change to permit a growth free from addiction to foreign debt. The Mexican government decided to adjust the economy and maintain debt servicing while improving the terms of existing debt obligations. The IMF program signed toward the end of 1982 guaranteed new bank financing for both 1983 and 1984.[13] Hence, from the outset, the government was certain that the country's future would be threatened if it tinkered with debt payments. The latter, however, did not hinder opposition parties, primarily from the intellectual left, from criticizing the government's economic program, its decision to service debt and the austerity that followed. The left's position was essentially that the people should not be punished with austerity programs, unemployment, and declining living standards, in order to service a debt from which it did not benefit. Taking a critical stance but never recommending anything specific except stopping debt repayment and servicing, if not repudiation, the left managed from 1982 to 1986 to gain more and more listeners.

At first, however, few voices advocated an outright default (negotiated or not). But by 1985, when it became clear that the country's plight was so severe that an internal adjustment would not be sufficient to restore economic growth (no matter what was done), many more people began to raise the possibility of default. In 1985, in the midst of the renewal of the dramatic decline in oil prices which cost Mexico US $6-7 billion in 1986, a fissure began to appear in the strong consensus on taking the orthodox route to recovery, when Finance Minister Jesus Silva Herzog, who had negotiated the previous packages with the IMF and transnational banks, began to advocate a harder line toward international creditors. The likelihood that the only Latin American showcase for orthodox stabilization was on the verge of defecting (Argentina, Brazil, Venezuela, Colombia, and Peru had all rejected IMF guidance, while Chile's military government was an embarrassment to the U.S.) probably forced the U.S. government's hand. The Federal Reserve Board Chairman, Paul Volker, visited Mexico and promised to help Mexico obtain a better deal from the international banks, a deal which finally came through after months of strenuous negotiations in 1986.

But the most dramatic shift in opinion pre-1985 and post-1985 was not on the default issue. Before 1985, most Mexicans believed that there would be some years of austerity, as in López Portillo's Presidency, after which growth would be restored and the crisis would end. In 1985 it became obvious that what was required was not only a financial adjustment, but a restructuring of the functioning of the key markets of the economy. Though the latter was obviously necessary, what began to emerge in 1985 was a growing recognition of the seriousness of the country's plight, of the lack of easy solutions, and of the need to make basic structural changes. And this is precisely what Mexico set out to do.

By mid-1985, it had become apparent that without fundamental change in the economy, high rates of economic growth would not be forthcoming. Policy makers were concerned that continued protection was constraining the growth of non-oil exports. In 1985 manufactured exports dropped 12 percent in value from 1984. This was in sharp contrast to the growth that had been attained in 1983 and 1984 when manufactured exports increased 51 percent and 24 percent, respectively. Thus, on July 25, 1985, an executive decree introduced major trade reforms that were aimed at rationalizing import policy in an effort to stimulate economic adjustment in the industrial sector and increase non-oil exports.[14] The first significant step was the removal of import license requirements from over 2000 categories on Mexico's tariff schedule.

In a second stage in November 1985, Mexico announced that it would reapply for entry into GATT in 1986, thus promising further liberalization in its trade regime. GATT accession added momentum to trade reforms already underway in Mexico, particularly in the areas of removing import license requirements, reducing tariffs, and phasing out official import reference prices. Finally, the Economic Solidarity Plan launched at the close of 1987 as a form of shock treatment to control inflation (consumer prices were rising at an annual rate of 160 percent) and bring about a return to rapid output growth, also contained trade reforms.[15] The exchange rate was depreciated by 22 percent and was later frozen. Wages and many prices were controlled, and fiscal and credit policy were tightened. It was at this moment that the maximum import tariff rate was reduced from 40 to 20 percent and most import taxes and import permits were eliminated. As a result the inflationary process showed a marked deceleration during the next four years. Inflation measured by the CPI fell to an annual rate of 43 percent in 1988, was below 20 percent in 1989, and then rose only slightly to 24 percent in 1990.

As a result of these measures, in the last five years Mexico has become one of the most open economies in the developing world (Table 9.1). The Mexican economy moved from an extremely restrictive import regime in which almost every item was subject to an import permit, granted only at the will of foreign trade officials and not at all in the case of some products, to a regime in which quantitative restrictions apply only to a few selected sectors of the economy: agriculture, oil and derivatives, motor vehicles, pharmaceutical products, footwear and electronic equipment. One observes a similar trend regarding the abolition of official prices, which had been used quite often as a protective device, fixed many times above their international counterparts and then used as a reference to determine ad valorem import taxes. Finally, import tariffs have reached reasonably low levels, having been reduced from a 0 to 100 percent range at the beginning of the process to a 0 to 20 percent range as of December 1987.[16]

During the same period, Mexico has taken additional measures of liberalization pertaining to foreign investment, technology transfer and intellectual property rights which have complemented a policy of deregulation and privatization that is contributing to increased efficiency and productivity of Mexican industry. For instance, in May 1989, Mexico

TABLE 9.1 Recent Trade Reforms in Mexico, 1985-1989 (in percentages)

	1985		1986		1987		1988	1989
	June	Dec.	June	Dec.	June	Dec.	June	Mar.[c]
Import Permit[a]	92.2	47.1	46.9	39.8	35.8	25.4	23.2	22.3
Reference Price[a]	18.7	25.4	19.6	18.7	13.4	00.6	00.0	00.0
Maximum Tariff	100.0	100.0	45.0	45.0	40.0	20.0	20.0	20.0
Average Tariff Rate[b]	23.5	28.5	24.0	24.5	22.7	11.8	11.0	12.6

[a]With respect to tradable output.
[b]Trade-weighted average tariff.
[c]Preliminary figures.

Source: SECOFI (Mexico's Ministry of Commerce and Industrial Development), USITC Publication No. 2275.

made sweeping reforms to its rules governing foreign investment which broadened the range of economic sectors expressly open to wholly foreign ownership. Foreign investment of up to 100 percent is allowed in unclassified activities which account for 72.5 percent of the 754 economic activities that comprise the Mexican economy. Included are certain industries such as glass, cement, iron, steel and cellulose for which foreign participation was previously restricted. Of the remaining 207 classified activities, 40 more are open to 100 percent foreign investment with prior approval. The implications in several areas of the new regulations are especially noteworthy. For example, telecommunications is now considered a classified activity in which foreign investment is allowed up to 49 percent; it previously had been prohibited. Similarly, Mexican law and enforcement of intellectual property protection has undergone significant change over these past few years. For instance, Mexicohas announced plans to strengthen process and product patent protection and improve the enforcement of trademarks and trade secrets. As a result, Mexico has been removed from the U.S. special 301 "Priority Watch List."[17]

The reforms paid dramatic and favorable results reflected in a number of indicators. A report of the Banco Nacional de México (Banamex) phrased the objective of the restructuring as follows: "The recent years of adjustment, recession and instability have meant a transition toward a new development model, one promoting exports. The exports referred to were products other than petroleum, particularly manufactured goods. That objective without doubt was achieved."[18] From 1985, the year that marks the implementation of the first strong reforms of the trade regime, to 1987, non-oil exports almost doubled and thereby helped to absorb the impact of decreased domestic demand that resulted mainly from the declining world oil prices. Real per capita consumption showed a 6.4 percent increase followed by a 25.3 percent increase in 1988, after an average yearly decline of 2 percent the previous five years. Real GDP, after stagnating and then decreasing, rose 1.5 percent in 1987, 1.1 percent in 1988, and 3 percent in 1989. Official and private foreign debt reduced from US $107.4 billion in 1987 to US $96.3 billion by the middle of 1989. Labor productivity, after decreasing steadily in the first half of the 1980s, rose 8.4 percent in 1989 and 34.9 percent in 1988. And new foreign investment rose from US $4.6 billion in 1982-1985 to almost US $12 billion in 1986-1989. Most important of all, Mexicans again showed confidence in their own economy; in 1989 alone, Mexicans brought home and invested US $2.5 billion.[19]

Of course, all these changes have not been popular in all segments of society. The remarkably effective presidential campaign of Cuauhtémoc Cárdenas, son of Lázaro Cárdenas and the candidate of a coalition of parties called the Frente Democratico Nacional (FDN), was based in part on the need to reinvigorate the internal market in Mexico to reduce excessive reliance on export-led growth. Because they are no longer assured of a protected domestic market, many small industrialists supported Cárdenas in the hope that the import liberalization would be reversed.[20] On the other hand, none of those factors traditionally highlighted as the major evils of an import liberalization program, such as widespread closures of domestic firms and massive purchases of imported durable goods, have so far been observed in the Mexican economy.

It would be wrong, however, to attribute the extraordinary performance of Mexico's non-oil exports only to the import liberalization program. As mentioned above, there was a sharp reduction in domestic aggregate demand as a result of the negative (from the Mexican point of view) oil price shock of 1986. Thus, foreign markets turned into a shelter for products that could not clear the domestic market. Also, a large reduction in domestic real wages (during August 1988 the real wage rate for unskilled was 50 percent below its previous peak) provided a strong competitive edge for domestic firms. Finally, from 1983 until 1989, there was also an undervalued exchange rate and aggressive export financing. In other words, the reduction in aggregate demand, the undervalued exchange rate, and the resulting domestic real wages were important elements in providing a competitive edge to domestic firms. These attributes, especially the undervalued exchange rate, may not endure. However, the fact that more fundamental changes are gradually taking place at the level of training and investment decisions by domestic economic agents, as well as in the institutional framework, points to the ability of Mexico's productive apparatus to compete internationally in a wide range of products on a long-term basis. Consider, for example, that more than one-third of Mexico's top 100 items exported to the United States in 1987 were not exported in 1984.

Table 9.2 disaggregates Mexico's merchandise exports into four main sectors for selected years between 1976 and 1991. The recent decline of oil exports relative to the rise of manufacturing exports since the 1980-85 high point of oil exports is pronounced. In absolute terms, Mexico's manufactured exports have grown from $9.7 billion (U.S.) in 1987 to $16.0 billion in 1991, whereas oil exports have declined from $8.6 billion to $8.2 billion over the same period.[21]

As Sidney Weintraub has already pointed out, these export data reveal two lessons. First, export earnings from primary commodities such as oil are highly cyclical and therefore unstable. Second, the assumption of export pessimism underlying Mexico's old policy of import substitution industrialization is faulty, if the rapid growth of Mexican manufactured goods under an increasingly neoliberal economic regime is any indication.

TABLE 9.2 Commodity Distribution of Mexican Exports (in percentages*)

Commodity	1976	1980	1985	1987	1989	1991
Manufacturing	47	18	23	48	55	59
Oil	15	69	68	42	34	30
Agric./Fishing	32	10	07	08	08	09
Mining	06	03	02	03	03	02

*Figures may not add to 100 due to rounding.

Source: Adapted from Sidney Weintraub, *Mexican Trade Policy and the North American Community*, p. 13; *Indicadores Económicos*, Banco de México, Nov. 1992.

Mexico's switch to these policies during the late 1980s and the resulting growth of manufactured exports (at the same time that oil exports declined) suggests that "producers and exporters responded as mainstream economic theory predicted they would."[22]

Mexico is now firmly on the road toward becoming a market-oriented, open economy with a disciplined public sector and solid prospects for growth. It is trying to imitate the successful policies pursued earlier by the Asian NICs and the Southern tier of Europe in developing a modern mixed economy. The public sector is no longer seen as the primary vehicle for economic development, and government policy is encouraging more productive use of foreign and domestic private capital. The public share of gross fixed investment declined from a high of 46.5 percent in 1982 to 29.6 percent by the end of 1988.[23]

The final lesson these trends offer is that if Mexico is to have steady economic growth in the future without the booms and busts associated with excessive reliance on a single primary commodity, there is no alternative to a solid export position in manufactures. A healthy manufacturing sector and exports are now considered critical for Mexico's economic well-being. One indication of the role of manufacturing is that while the index for GDP as a whole in 1988 was 101 (1980=100), the index was 109 for manufacturing and 355 for manufactured exports. In terms of output per worker, manufacturing is far more productive than services and agriculture. Indeed, output per worker in manufacturing is greater than in all sectors other than petroleum, electricity generation and finance and real estate, all of which contribute only modestly to employment. Notwithstanding the beneficial elements of the reforms that have been undertaken, there is still an urgent need to create even more jobs in Mexico. The evidence is that in the 1980s, there was a net loss of jobs; employment in the largest industrial companies of Mexico declined by 11 percent in the period 1982-1986 due to economic stagnation in the de la Madris "*sexenio.*" That is why the most important task of the Salinas government has been the restoration of growth.[24]

This imperative for a solid export position in manufactures is what makes the role of the United States so crucial in Mexico's trade future. The United States now takes upward of 60 percent of Mexico's total exports. But new problems arose. As Mexican companies penetrated the American market with new zeal, they found themselves caught in U.S. contingent protectionism: antidumping and countervailing duties multiplied. Between 1980-1985, Mexico was caught in 26 countervailing duty investigations, seventeen resulting in an affirmative International Trade Administration (ITA) preliminary finding and four resulting in a suspension agreement. Access to other markets proved similarly unreliable. For Mexican manufacturers, priorities had changed, making concern about access real for the first time. Exports, rather than the domestic market, were now to provide the engine for growth. And more than anything else, the American market, as the only realistic market in the short to medium term, became the main focus of attention.[25]

In order to improve access to Mexico's most important market, negotiations were initiated with the United States to satisfy some of the more egregious American complaints about Mexican practices and to gain more secure access in return. The results included a 1985 agreement on subsidies which entitled Mexican products to the injury test under U.S countervailing duties procedures; a 1987 framework agreement involving a work program leading to possible further concessions by both sides; and a 1989 Understanding Regarding Trade and Investment Talks, further expanding a work program aimed at more extensive agreements. These bilateral discussions built mutual confidence and provided each side with valuable negotiating experience while scoring small but important successes. For instance, Mexico has agreed to continue to restrain exports of steel and textiles but in return has gained larger quotas than might otherwise have been imposed.[26] But the thorny issue of contingent protectionism (antidumping and countervailing duties and safeguards) has remained impermeable to negotiations and thus maintained Mexican anxiety about the security of its access to the United States market.

To consolidate its reforms, Mexico agreed to bind its new trade regime in the GATT. Unlike the 1979 report which suggested a militantly defiant Mexico insisting on special and differential treatment as a developing country, the report of the 1986 GATT working party shows a determined Mexican government prepared to accept the necessary pain to bring the regime into compliance with GATT obligations. This is how two Mexican economists explained the Mexican position:

> Mexico entered the GATT in 1986 under less favorable conditions than those observed in 1979, and in contrast to 1979 there was little public debate. The entry into GATT was seen as part of the government's general economic policy that sought the structural adjustment of the productive sector toward an export-oriented strategy. It is interesting to note that the terms of the debate in 1986 were mainly technical as the only skepticism regarding the decision concerned whether it was necessary to enter the GATT in order to implement a policy of structural adjustment.[27]

A business-like Working Party made short work of the Protocol of Accession and on August 24, 1986 the Contracting Parties welcomed Mexico as its 92nd member. Mexico agreed to bind its tariffs at 50 percent and to continue its program of reform. It agreed to join the GATT Antidumping, Licensing, Standards and Valuation Agreements and bring its regime into line with these codes. To underscore that it had become a full member of the club, however, Mexico emphasized that future reforms would require some reciprocity. Its political capacity for unilateralism was nearing exhaustion. Additionally, it stressed that its protocol of accession would require similar provisions to the original protocol of 1947, i.e., it would not be able to bring all of its laws into conformity with GATT but would strive to make gradual reforms.[28]

But Mexico is also discovering that GATT participation has its limits. While it will gain some improvements in access to the markets of the United States, the EC and Japan, these will in no way match the extent to which Mexico has opened its markets to U.S., EC and Japanese goods. Mexico's voice is but one of many. The brave ideas discussed early in the Round are being modified in the light of negotiating realities as the Round draws to a conclusion. Issues of greatest importance to Mexico are no longer at the top of the priority list. Joining the GATT in 1986 was a major step involving significant political risk. It is successfully under-writing domestic economic reform. But to consolidate that reform, many Mexicans will expect it to pay dividends in terms of improved access to foreign markets and improved rules for the conduct of trade.

To maintain the moment of domestic reform, therefore, Mexicans are considering whether GATT negotiations are enough. The critical factor in this equation will be the extent to which the Uruguay Round of multilateral trade negotiations addresses the issues of greatest concern to Mexico, like in services trade, agriculture, and opens up the American, Japanese and European markets and contains contingent protectionism in the United States and Europe. The Mexican private sector had concluded by late 1989 that the Uruguay Round would not be enough to achieve this objective; Mexican politicians and officials agreed by mid 1990.

An important factor that influenced Mexican thinking regarding a possible bilateral agreement with the United States, was the successful conclusion of the Canada-U.S. FTA in 1987. Even though the U.S. and Canadian governments defended their agreement on the basis of its trade creating effects, Mexico realized that there would be disadvantages for Mexico on those products where Mexico and Canada compete directly in the U.S. market. Moreover, it so happened that the sectors in which Mexico would have increased competitive disadvantages in the U.S. market as the provisions of the U.S.-Canada Free Trade Agreement were increasingly phased in, are those areas where Mexico has gained an important presence in the U.S. market, such as the automotive, petrochemical, steel, paper, textile and machinery sectors.[29] In the following two years, Mexican business and government leaders and well respected academics studied the issue and finally concluded that they had to achieve access to the U.S. equivalent to that gained by Canada.[30]

The combined effect of a changing domestic economy, the need for greater and more secure access to its principal foreign market, the United States, realization of the inability of the GATT directly and immediately to address Mexican trade policy concerns, and increasing contingent protectionism in the United States thus fueled the debate in Mexico about the future direction of its trade policy and relations with the United States. The bilateral or regional option took on an urgency that no one would have foreseen a few years before. Originally confined to academics and other specialists, it gradually expanded to business leaders and then to politicians and government officials. The next step will be to determine whether an agreement responsive to Mexican interests is negotiable.

The Politics of Trade Liberalization in Mexico

A number of observers and analysts in Mexico have emphasized in detail the role of external forces and particularly of international organizations like the International Monetary Fund (IMF) and the World Bank in this process. According to this perspective, with the rapid and prolonged plunge in oil prices commencing in 1981, Mexico was forced to rely extensively upon funds which were controlled either by the IMF, or by governments and institutions which were strongly influenced by the willingness (apparent or real) of President de la Madrid's government to follow policy recommendations of the FMI. The Fund's long-standing enthusiasm for export-promotion policies are renowned. Undoubtedly, the Fund was a considerable factor in the policy shift which occurred in the early 1980s. So, too, was the World Bank whose largely unnoted role in Mexico's policies of modernization has been as important as that played by the Fund.[31]

Nevertheless, this approach does not account for the timing and pace of the shift in policy. We must remember that initially the new shift toward a heightened emphasis on export promotion appeared to be measured. It was not until 1986 that the consolidation of the project of "all-out export promotion" was achieved. Whence came de la Madrid's renewed enthusiasm for export promotion from 1986 onward? In my view the deepening economic crisis of 1985-1986 forced a showdown between high-level policy-makers who sought to adhere to Mexico's past commitment to nationalistic and populist growth policies and those who believed that Mexico could and should opt for a bold new path of "all-out export promotion." In my interpretation of the de la Madris "sexenio," 1986 should be seen as a threshold year for several reasons. First, in

1986, the fragile economic recovery which commenced in 1984 was cut short as the GNP declined 3.8 percent. The commitment to gradualism, which had seemed so much an integral component of the de la Madrid style, was now cast aside. Quickly Mexico joined the GATT. The peso was also devalued. Perhaps most indicative of a fundamental change in the past, but not the trajectory, of policy change was a massive debt restructuring program which brought in approximately $19 billion (US) in new loans from the multilateral agencies and the private banks. In addition, the terms of repayment were changed in 44 billion of public debt and 9.5 billion of private sector debt repayment. Since the precipitous fall in oil prices was overwhelmingly the underlying cause of the downturn of 1986, the Mexican government now sought a rapid reordering of its policy priorities best signified by new programs designed to stimulate exports.

Policy-makers who were in favor of pursuing the nationalist path, even if they were willing to make major concessions in the direction of more laissez-faire policies than they had in the past, were defeated and forced to either leave the government (e.g. former Secretary of the Treasury Silva Herzog) or quietly adapt to the new power alignment. Divisions within the PRI between the *tecnicos* (technocrats) and the *politicos* (those who pay their dues in the political arena) had existed for some time. The last three presidents, López Portillo, De la Madrid, and Salinas, have been *tecnicos*, and the top governmental posts have gone to *tecnicos*. The predominance of the *tecnicos* within the PRI is what partly explains the separation of an important group of politics from the party to form the so-called "democratic current" under the leadership of Cuauhtémoc Cárdenas who later became the main opponent of Carlos Salinas in the election of 1988.

The champions of all-out laissez-faire and export promotion now occupied the apex of the policy-making pyramid. Whatever ambivalence the government expressed toward a major shift in policy in the 1982-1985 period was gone. The growing ideological commitment of President de la Madrid's economic cabinet to neoliberal economic policies was reinforced by the entry into power of President Salinas de Gortari. (As one well-known economist employed by President Salinas stated: "Somos más Banco Mundial que el propio Banco Mundial" [We are more oriented toward the idea of export promotion than even the World Bank]). It would be a fruitless exercise to attempt to determine if the shift toward export-promotion was primarily determined by *internal* or *external* forces. Both forces were determinant at this crucial historical juncture; for better or for worse, Mexico had no other option than export-promotion.

Should this decision be read merely as an economic imperative or can we also find a political rationality behind it?

In this chapter we have tried to show that over the last two decades a series of major economic shocks during the 1970s and 1980s led to a deepening political debate and to a rapid growth of political consciousness about the nature of the economic crisis of the 1980s and about the possible solutions to it. In the 1970s when an attempt at reform was made, vested interests threatened not to go any further. This reaction was interpreted by President Echeverria as a potential for instability, and he abandoned all attempts to introduce profound reforms. Echeverria could afford not to reform simply because the economy kept on growing at about 6 percent, fueled largely by increasing foreign borrowing after the oil shock of 1973. When in 1985 the economic reform was finally introduced, Mexico was in the midst of a profound depression with very high and growing levels of inflation. This time, however, the country could not ride the wave of growth as in the previous decade and thus the liberalization of the economy, the ongoing deregulation process and other policies that appear to be solely of an economic nature should also be seen as the result of a political imperative: the need to recover the path of economic growth even at the cost of affecting major vested interests and power strongholds in the PRI. Thus, the decision to initiate a profound economic reform in 1985 was not a technical or technocratic action, but the result of a careful political calculation of the need (and the appropriate means for maintaining the political stability of the country.

The calculation was very risky if one judges from the results of the 1988 election which many people believe was won by the FDN led by Cuauhtémoc Cárdenas. These results clearly showed that the reforms, at least at the point of inception were not the result of a social consensus, but of government initiative. However, though these changes have had a profound bearing on Mexican society and directly affected the traditional privileges of the PRI bureaucracy and bosses, they are being driven by a government that has recognized the challenge posed by both Mexico's backwardness and stagnation as well as by changes that have taken place in the rest of the world over the last decade and a half. The reform, it should be recognized, has been gaining support as it begins to deliver an incipient economic recovery. Furthermore, the government has established the Solidarity Program through which it is channeling important financial resources to large segments of the population that otherwise would not have perceived any benefits from the reform. The Solidarity Program has diminished the potential for instability in the poorest areas of the country and thus become the single most important component that explains the impressive popularity of the Salinas government.[32] This Program can also be seen as an attempt to create a new constituency not only for the government carrying out the reforms but for the reforms themselves.

Despite these positive signs, it is important to recognize that after decades of misgovernment Mexicans have profound suspicions about any new government policy. It is in this context that the NAFTA negotiations have more than economic significance. At the heart of the search for a free trade agreement lies the aim to consolidate the domestic economic reform and to search the stage for a transformation of the political system. The ongoing NAFTA negotiations thus have an enormous political significance for the three nations. NAFTA will be crucial in the long term consolidation of Mexico's reform.

Political Opposition to the
Trilateral Free Trade Agreement

Despite the tremendous importance that the Mexican government gives to reaching a Free Trade Area in North America, NAFTA has been attacked by the two main opposition parties, namely, the National Action Party (PAN) and the Party of the Democratic Revolution (PRD). Although the PRI still has an overwhelmingly consolidated position as the party in power, especially after the mid-term elections of 1991, since the 1988 elections the road to political pluralism in Mexico is slowly being constructed. The opposition has gained a new prominence, although it has in no way been able to match the momentum gained in the last presidential elections.

Of the two most important opposition parties, the senior one is the PAN which was founded in 1939 with the main purpose of promoting citizen participation in the country's political life in order to pressure the government towards the common good. In 1972 there was a division in the party among those who believed that it should take a more practical approach to politics by encouraging a more active role in elections. A decade and a half later, this current of thought won out partly due to growing discontent among many people because of the economic crisis. The PAN elected as its presidential candidate in the 1988 elections, Manuel Clouthier, a highly charismatic businessman from the North of Mexico. The PAN which is a conservative party has its strongest base in the industrialized north, the maquiladora region par excellence.

As far as the NAFTA is concerned, there is no apparent consensus within the party. On the one hand, the PAN's leader, Jesus H. Alvarez declared in October of 1991 that it was very important for all Mexicans to present a unified front at the moment that the negotiations for the NAFTA were becoming a concrete reality. He did point out however that his party was worried about the haste with which the government seemed to want to sign the agreement and the secrecy of the negotiations. In January of this year the PAN asked that the national debate regarding the NAFTA be reopened. Additionally, the PAN has presented a bill proposing a reform of the Mexican Constitution to make sure that all international agreements would be submitted to a referendum.

Some members of the PAN frankly oppose an agreement as they are very concerned that a NAFTA would place Mexico in a position similar to that of Puerto Rico vis a vis the United States. The principal worry is that of the limitation of sovereignty that would result from such an agreement, a high price to pay for what they perceive as limited economic benefits. Another point against the NAFTA is that it would be an obstacle towards Latin American integration.

Felipe Calderón Herrera, a PAN member of Congress in January of this year mentioned four elements that might be included in NAFTA due to pressure from the American Democratic Party which would hurt Mexico's interests: (1) more restrictive provisions on Mexican labor and more stringent regulation on environment; (2) the creation of a supranational tribunal with widespread jurisdiction in dispute settlement; (3) a provision imposing a tax on Mexican export goods to create an unemployment fund for Americans who might lose their jobs because of the NAFTA; and (4) a provision assuring the U.S. secure energy supplies in the event of a shortage.

The PRD which was formed after the 1988 elections represents a nationalist position which leans towards the left. The PRD considers that in trade negotiations with the United States it is unavoidable not to take into account the troubled past between Mexico and the United States and the fact that we will be dealing with the world's largest market and the most powerful economy. The PRD therefore proposes that Mexico needs strong safeguards to protect Mexico's sovereignty and national identity.

The PRD has also argued that trade liberalization has not had a beneficial effect on Mexican political life, to the contrary all it has done is to strengthen the authoritarianism of the government. According to party officials this has been most aptly illustrated by the fact that foreign investment has not increased in the productive sectors of the economy, but in the speculative sectors where the wealth of the country is concentrated among few people who are close to the government. The PRD rejects the whole maquiladora project as being denigrating to Mexico as a country and to Mexicans as a people. It sees a process of economic integration where Mexico has an increasingly subordinate role. What this party fears most is that Mexico should end up as a modern day colony whose main attractions are cheap labor, primary resources, energy, government deregulation, tax shelters, and political stability. Under this perspective, a NAFTA would have absolutely nothing to offer Mexico as a country. This does not mean however that the PRD is in favor of extreme protectionism.

The PRD's leader, Cuauhtémoc Cárdenas on several occasions in the United States has proposed an alternative to a North American free trade area. He favors a wide reaching continental agreement embracing the North American region and the rest of the Western Hemisphere. This agreement would achieve free trade among Mexico, Canada and the United States, but it would recognize the different level of development of Mexico as well, and not affect negatively the environmental, labor and social standards of the United States and Canada. To achieve these goals, the continental agreement would include five provisions: (1) elimination of tariff and non-tariff barriers; (2) the adoption and harmonization of rules in the following areas: investment, antitrust legislation, intellectual property and a social charter; (3) income transfers for Mexico; (4) the negotiation of effective dispute settlement mechanisms; and (5) free movement of labor.

Although not opposed to the principle of a free trade agreement with our northern neighbors, Cárdenas has pointed out that he would reject outright an agreement that would simply trilateralize the existing Canada-U.S. agreement. In general, the Canada-U.S. agreement is perceived by the PRD to have been detrimental to Canadian interests. Therefore, the PRD has voiced its support of the Canadian New Democratic Party's efforts to rescind the 1988 agreement. Both the PRD and the PAN are strongly opposed to the inclusion of energy and basic grains in any agreement.

In conclusion, Mexico has undertaken a major revolution in her trade policies. For more than forty years Mexico followed an import substitution industrialization based in the internal market. But the weakness of the world oil market and the scarcity of external funds following Mexico's debt crisis caused the Mexican government to break with tradition and to promote growth through exports. In the last five years, Mexico has adopted liberalization policies that have made its economy one of the most open in the developing world. Thus, Mexico became a member of the General Agreement on Tariffs and Trade (GATT) in 1986, and the maximum Mexican tariff fell from a level of 100 per cent to 20 per cent between 1985 and 1990. The country has also significantly liberalized its policies in such areas as foreign investment and intellectual property rights.

For instance, in May 1989, Mexico made sweeping reforms in its rules governing foreign investment which allow foreign ownership of up to 100 percent in 72.5 percent of the 754 activities that comprise the Mexican economy and may be prepared to go even further. Likewise, in June

1991, Mexico passed a new law of intellectual property and transfer of technology which includes: (1) increasing the patent term to 20 years, a term similar to that used by a number of developed countries, (2) offering product patent protection for products and processes not previously subject to patent protection, and (3) strengthening its trade secrets law. Mexico, in short, has now a law that meets many of the international standards sought by countries that export intellectual property goods and services.

Mexico is therefore serious about looking for new ways to integrate more efficiently into the global economy. Its active participation in the Uruguay Round of GATT and its interest in a free trade agreement (FTA) with the United States and Canada form part of that strategy. Since the Mexican government has already instituted a considerable amount of liberalization, the measures required to decrease protectionism in an NAFTA would have a less traumatic effect on the Mexican economy.

Notes

1. Morton H. Halperin, *Bureaucratic Politics and Foreign Policy* (Washington, D.C.: The Brookings Institution, 1974), pp. 11 ff.

2. See Gabriel A. Almond and Sidney Verba, *The Civic Culture* (Boston: Little Brown, 1965); also, David R. Mares *Penetrating International Markets: Theoretical Considerations and a Mexican Agriculture Case* (New York: Columbia University Press, 1987).

3. An account of this conflict and its outcome can be found in E. David Cronon, *Josephus Danields in Mexico* (Madison: University of Wisconsin Press, 1960); Lorenzo Meyer, *México y los Estados Unidos en el Conflicto Petrolero, 1917-1942*, 2nd ed. (México: El Colegio de México, 1972); and Bryce Wood, *The Making of the Good Neighbor Policy* (New York: W.W. Norton, 1961).

4. Mario Ojeda, *Alcances y Límites de la Política Exterior de México* (México: El Colegio de México, 1976); also, Olga Pellicer, "Mexico in the 1970's and its Relations with the United States," in R. Fagen and J. Cotler, *Latin America and the United States: The Changing Political Realities* (Stanford, Cal., 1974), pp. 315-318; Rafael Segovia, "El Nacionalismo Mexicano: Los Programas Politicos Revolucionarios, 1929-1964," *Foro Internacional*, Vol. 8, No. 4 (1968), p. 356.

5. Blanca Torres, *México y los Estados Unidos Durante la Segunda Guerra Mundial* (México: El Colegio de México, 1978), especially chapters 3 and 4. Raymond Vernon, *The Dilemma of Mexico's Development: The Roles of the Private and Public Sectors* (Cambridge: Harvard University Press, 1963), pp. 94-95.

6. The history of foreign domination is strong in Mexico: three centuries of Spanish colonialism ended only after a thirteen year struggle (1810-1823); French troops occupied the country in support of the emperor Maximilian in the mid-19th century; and the United States invaded Mexico three times (1846, 1914,

and 1916), seizing half of its territory after the initial incursion. See David Mares, *Penetrating International Markets*, and Albert O. Hirschman, "The Turn to Authoritarianism in Latin America and the search for Its Economic Determinants," in David Collier, ed., *The New Authoritarianism in Latin America* (Princeton: Princeton University Press, 1979), pp. 65-68.

7. Mexico was not a member of the preparatory committee charged with developing a charter for an International Trade Organization (ITO) and which, concurrently, negotiated the GATT as an interim agreement in 1947. Mexico, nevertheless, was an active participant at the Havana Conference which sought to establish the ITO but was dissatisfied with the result and consequently declined to join the GATT. Instead it choose to follow the policies most closely associated with the name of Raúl Prebisch and the institution he then directed, the economic Commission for Latin America (ECLA). Prebisch and the ECLA concluded that the path to development was through the establishment of a manufacturing base. Political elites in Mexico believed that only in this way could Mexico eliminate the unequal exchange that results from the deterioration in the terms of trade of a country that exports mostly primary products and imports manufactured goods. See Joseph L. Love, "Raúl Prebisch and the Origins of the doctrine of Unequal exchange," *Latin American Research Review* 15, No. 3 (1980), pp. 45-72, for a through discussion of Prebisch's thinking about core-periphery trade. On the discussion in Mexico about joining the ITO and the GATT, see Blanca Torres, *Hacia la Utopía Industrial* (México: El Colegio de México, 1984).

8. Mexico's ratio of combined exports and imports to GDP rose from under 10 percent in 1970 to almost 40 percent in 1987. See, Bilateral Commission on the Future of United States-Mexico Relations, *The Challenge of Interdependence: Mexico and the United States* (New York: University Press of America, 1989), p. 59.

9. See Luis Rubio and Francisco Gil Díaz, *A Mexican Response* (New York: Twentieth Century Fund, 1987). Also, David R. Mares, "Explaining Choices of Development Strategies. Suggestions from Mexico 1970-1982," *International Organization*, Autumn 1985.

10. See Mario Ojeda, *Alcances y Límites*, Chapter 3; Raymond Vernon, *The Dilemma*, p. 102.; Olga Pellicer, "El Llamado a las Inversiones Extranjeras, 1953-1958," in Bernardo Sepulveda Amor, et al., *Las Empresas Transnacionales en México* (México: El Colegio de México, 1974) pp. 75-104.; Herbert K. May, *The Impact of Foreign Investment in Mexico* (New York: Council of the Americas, 1973) p. 23; and Richard S. Newfarmer and Willard T. Mueller, *Multinational Corporations in Brazil and Mexico: Structural Sources of Economic and Noneconomic Power*, A Report to the Subcommittee on Multinational Corporations of the Committee of Foreign relations, U.S. Senate, 94th Cong., 1st sess. (Washington: Government Printing Office, 1975), p. 62.

11. The figures on productivity gains can be seen in Ricardo Samaniego, "The Evolution of Total Factor Productivity in the Manufacturing Sector in Mexico, 1972-1982," in *Documentos de Investigacion*, (México: El Colegio de México, 1985).

12. Mexico's 1979 protocol of accession to GATT can be found in GATT, *Basic Instruments and Selected Documents*, Vol. 26 (Geneva, 1981) p. 238. A similar

interpretation of Echeverria's and López Portillo policies is offered by David R. Mares "Explaining Choice of Development Strategies."

13. Mexico was able to reach the agreement with the IMF due to the quick U.S. government intervention with enough money to give Mexico time to reach the agreement.

14. Jaime Zabludovsky, "Trade Liberalization and Macroeconomic Adjustment in Mexico, 1983-1988," draft, May 1989, p. 17. Zabludovsky is now the second most important government official in the team responsible for negotiating the FTA with the United States.

15. See United States International Trade Commission, *Review of Trade and Investment Liberalization Measures by Mexico and Prospects for Future United States-Mexican Relations* (Washington, D.C.: USITC Publication 2275), Chapter 1.

16. See United States International Trade Commission, *Review of Trade and Liberalization Measures by Mexico and Prospects for Future United States Mexican Relations* (Washington D.C.: USITC Publication 2275), April 1990.

17. Ibid.

18. Banamex, *Review of the Economic Situation of Mexico*, Vol. LXIV, No. 752 (July 1988), p. 307. Banamex is not the central bank, which is Banco de México (Banxico, for short).

19. The data was extracted from *Review of Trade and Investment Liberalization Measures by Mexico*.

20. According to official figures Cardenas won 31.1 percent of the national vote in the 1988 presidential campaign. But according to numerous people he really won the election.

21. Data compiled from *Indicadores Económicos*, Banco de México, November 1992; Sidney Weintraub, *Mexican Trade Policy and the North American Community* (Washington, D.C.: Center for Strategic and International Studies, 1988), p. 12.

22. Weintraub, *Mexican Trade Policy*, p. 15.

23. These are Banco de Mexico's (Mexico's Central Bank) figures reproduced in a handbook prepared by SECOFI (Ministry of Commerce and Industrial Development).

24. For a breakdown of production changes in the different branches of manufacturing during the 1980s, total output, employment and output per worker in various sectors, including manufacturing during the 1980s, see Sidney Weintraub, *Transforming the Mexican Economy. The Salinas "sexenio"* (Washington, D.C.: National Planning Association, 1990); for data on employment figures during the first seven years of the 1980s, see Saúl Trejo Reyes, *El Futuro de la Política Industrial en México* (México: El Colegio de México, 1987).

25. See Sidney Weintraub, "The North American Free Trade Debate," paper prepared for the International Forum: "Mexico's Trade Options in the Changing International Economy," Universidad Tecnológica de México, Mexico City, June 11-15, 1990, p 2; Spanish translation in Gustavo Vega C. (coord.), *México ante el Libre Comercio con América del Norte*, pp. 145-165. See also Luis Rubio, "The Changing Role of the Private Sector," in Susan Kaufman Purcell, *Mexico in Transition: Implications for U.S. Policy* (New York: Council of Foreign Relations, 1988), pp. 31-42.

26. Jeffrey Schott in "A strategy for Mexican Trade Policy in the 1990s," paper

prepared for the International Forum: Mexico's Trade Options in the Changing International Economy, Universidad Tecnológica de México, Mexico City, June 11-15, 1990, p. 4; also in Gustavo Vega (coord.), *México ante el Libre Comercio*, pp. 95-109.

27. Nisso Bucay and Eduardo Pérez Motta, "Trade Negotiation Strategy for Mexico," in John Whalley, ed., *The Small Among the Big* (London: Ontario Center for the Study of International Economic Relations, 1988).

28. The report of the Working Party can be found in GATT, *Basic Instruments and Selected Documents*, Vol. 33 (Geneva, 1987), p. 56. The GATT Protocol of Provisional Accession was the vehicle used in 1947 to bring the General Agreement into effect until the more comprehensive negotiations on the Havana Charter concluded. The Protocol required that parts I and III of the GATT be brought into force fully and part II, containing many of the key articles, only insofar as it was not inconsistent with existing legislation. In this way, the U.S. administration was able to bring the GATT into effect without congressional approval and without overstepping its negotiating authority.

29. The likely discriminatory impact on Mexico of the Canada-US FTA was predicted in Gustavo Vega C., "El Acuerdo de Libre Comercio entre Canadá y Estados Unidos: Implicaciones para México y los Países en Desarrollo," in *Comercio Exterior*, Vol. 38, No. 3, March 1988; also Sidney Weintraub, "The Impact of the Agreement on Mexico," in Peter Morici, ed., *Making Free Trade Work: The Canada-U.S. Agreement* (New York: Council of Foreign Relations, 1990, pp. 102-123). More precise quantitative estimates were undertaken by the Government of Mexico showing that the Canada-U. S. Free Trade Agreement has had some trade diversion consequences for Mexico. In terms of 1988 trade flows, the gross trade diversion was $662 million, of which $421 million was in the automotive sector and $102 million was in consumer electronics. Offsetting the diversion was $257 million of trade creation, of which the largest component was $123 million for knitting mills. See Staff of Economic advisors to the Minister of Industry and Trade, *Tariff Elimination between the United States and Canada: Effects on Mexico's Trade Flows*, unpublished report, Mexico City, 1990, abstract.

30. Gerardo Bueno, a former head of the National Council of Science and Technology and former Mexican Ambassador to the EEC and a leading exponent of a North American Free Trade Agreement, argued as early as 1987 that Canada and the United States should be prepared to contemplate Mexican Accession to their FTA. See his "A Mexican View," in William Diebold, Jr., ed., *Bilateralism, Multilateralism and Canada in U.S. Trade Policy* (New York: Council on Foreign Relations, 1988). I made the same recommendation in my article quoted above. Similar views were expressed by businessmen for example at the November 1989 Meeting in Monterrey of CONACEX (Consejo Nacional de Comercio Exterior) the main organization of Mexican export companies where talk of the need for U.S.-Mexico free trade agreement dominated the discussions. See *Excelsior*, November 20, 1989 pp. 1 and 28; *Financiero*, November 20, 1989, pp. 1, 8, 28. Likewise in the national hearings undertaken by the Mexican Senate to study Mexico's Trade Options in the World Economy in March and April 1990, one can find extensive support from the Mexican private sector to a possible negotiation of a free trade agreement with the United States. See Senado de la República,

Consulta Pública sobre las Opciones Comerciales de México con el Mundo, Vol 3, *Relaciones comerciales con Estados Unidos y Canada* pp. 7-8; 15-17; 25-27; 49-51; 68-71; 97-101; 123-125; 157-160.

31. See Miguel Angel Olea, "Las Negociaciones Comerciales Internacionales de México en los Años Ochenta," in Gerardo Bueno and René Villarreal, eds., *México: Política Comercial y Negociaciones Comerciales Internacionales* (México: Limusa, forthcoming); James Cypher, "Strings Attached: World Bank Tightens Control of Third World Economies," *Dollars and Sense*, No. 152 (December 1989), pp. 9-19. Leticia Campos, "Algunos Rasgos de la Política Económica del Nuevo Gobierno," *Momento Económico*, No. 44 (March-April 1989).

32. Most analysts believe that the tremendous victory of the PRI candidates in the Mid-term elections of 1991 is a clear result of the Solidarity Program.

10

Trade and Party: Flip-Flops and Causal Linkages

Charles F. Doran

An overriding query shapes this study. The major political parties in the United States, Canada, and Mexico have profoundly altered their historical positions on foreign trade. In fact, they have exchanged positions. Why did each political party change its orienation towards free trade? What were the causes, and what were the consequences, for the choice of regional versus universal trade liberalization? How have political institutions in each country contributed to these political party flip-flops on free trade? What factors or processes explain how a political party adopts a position on trade, and how governments actually take a stand? This chapter draws on the prior chapters to build a theoretical model attempting to explain the long-term relationship in North America between trade and political party.

Trade Liberalization: What Causes It?

Traditional theory in international political economy explains a nation's propensity for free trade or protectionism as the effect of hegemonic dominance or domestic interest groups. The former is external (international systemic) and structural, whereas the latter is internal to the state and common to all democratic polities. Neither effect need be considered exclusive, or sufficient, though each is arguably necessary as explanation.

"Openness," according to Stephen Krasner, "is most likely to occur during periods when a hegemonic state is in its ascendancy."[1] Robert Gilpin places the explanation in terms of the costs and benefits to the hegemon of maintaining an open trading regime.[2] Confirming the thesis, Robert Baldwin asserts that the United States fared well in its hegemonic role of promoting openness in trade in terms of both added growth and resource-use efficiency, thus extending the period of its dominance.[3] Robert Keohane analyses the post-hegemonic period, seeking the origins of trade liberalization in a regime without a single dominant state where the reputation of governments and their interdependence would replace the hegemonic inducements to cooperation.[4]

E. E. Schattsneider offered the classic treatment of the interpretation that interest groups explain trade outcomes through their power to shape votes in Congress. In so-called weak states, policies determine politics and interest groups shape policy.[5] In the framework of the Stolper-Samuelson Theorem of neo-classical economics, this argument receives additional theoretical support.[6] The abundant factor of production benefits from free trade and thus lobbies for openness. But when that factor becomes relatively more scarce, it begins to favor tariffs. For example, when the steel industry in the United States was considered capital intensive in a country where capital was the abundant factor, it sought trade liberalization; when the industry became relatively less capital intensive and more labor intensive, partly through its own miscalculations, it became one of the largest proponents of protectionism.

In the contemporary political setting, G. K. Helleiner argues, trade policy is "determined" by two main groups.[7] Organized labor presses for the maintenance or increase of protectionism, especially for the industries in which its representation is largest, the labor-intensive, older, "rust belt" industries. The multinational corporations press for reductions of trade barriers for classifications in which they trade. They show little interest in comparatively labor-intensive industries in which they are not directly involved. Thus emerges a kind of mixture of policy that contains both protectionist and liberalization overtones, with the power of the firm predominating and liberalization therefore getting the political edge.

The "institutionalist" literature on international political economy broadens and deepens the explanations provided by the hegemonic and interest group interpretations. To some extent, the assumptions as to cause are different as well. According to Peter Katzenstein, most writing on public policy has assumed that the "political logic of the problem is more important than the political logic of the country."[8] He believes these writers have got the situation backwards. It is the "institutional organization of power" which is more important than the "imperatives for action" within the "policy problems" themselves. This takes international political economy in a somewhat different direction.

David Lake supports this institutional emphasis by arguing that even though interest groups dominated congressional tariff-making in the nineteenth century, an "important *strategic* component" existed.[9] Executive branch leaders guided tariff policy in a fashion that supported state interests. Judith Goldstein, however, points out that the United States "did not get what was in her objective best 'interest' not because of a lack of power but because of domestic institutional, ideational, and social constraints." Agriculture exerted its own interests against those of the state. "Once institutionalized," says Goldstein, these protectionist tariff policies were extremely difficult to "uproot."[10]

Adding one more layer of explanatory complexity, I. M. Destler notes that the strategic policy of the members of Congress on trade is quite deceptive. Objective voting patterns do not always reveal real trade preferences. "Members of Congress find their interests well-served by a system of power-sharing that gives them ample opportunity for initiative and visibility but allows the buck to stop elsewhere."[11] This certainly describes the behavior of the Congress towards the North American Free Trade Agreement (NAFTA) expressed in the vote. Institutions do matter. But analysts of international political economy must also probe the attitudinal and behavioral reality both *above* institutions across states and time, and *below* institutions manifested in the strategic subtleties of the voter and the political representative.

Variables in the Party-Trade Relationship

Clearly political party is an intermediate variable; government posture toward free trade is the dependent variable. The principal independent variable which operates through political party upon trade orientation is interest group pressure. Richard E. Caves finds the interest group model a better explanation for tariff protection in Canada than either a model which maximizes votes for the government on a geographic basis or a model that posits a unified government position favoring nationalism.[12] Interest groups, augmented by the legal status of the Political Action Committee (PAC) in the United States but underwritten everywhere by substantial sums of money used at election time to support or punish the individual candidate, provide the action center of moves toward greater free trade or greater protectionism as Schattschneider long ago posited.[13]

While the most important interest groups are surely identifiable across polities, the unambiguous direction of their activity is sometimes tough to fathom. In the Stolper-Samuelson theorem, protectionism favors the scarce factor of production being used most intensely by a state's import-competing industries which suffer from foreign competition. While some early studies have supported that assessment, other more recent empirical studies have not.[14] On theoretical grounds, it is little wonder that this should be so in terms of interest group behavior. For the factors of production do not separate easily into the Ricardian categories of capital, labor and land. In reality, capital and labor in the disadvantaged industries jointly lobby for protection; and capital and labor in the export and import industries jointly lobby for trade liberalization. There is no solidarity along pure factor lines. To argue that protection favors the scarce factor of production is to assert a homogeneity of political position with respect to "labor" or to "business" that frequently does not exist.

Business today may support free trade, but business often is and has been resolutely opposed to trade liberalization. Moreover, some sectors of business, notably "big business," may support freer trade, while other sectors, such as "small business" or "import substitution industries" or certain "labor-intensive businesses," may vigorously oppose liberalization.

Public choice interest group models have explored the importance of concentration of lobbying effort and geographic location.[15] J. J. Pincus finds that in contrast to the conclusion of the theory of public goods that small, concentrated groups would lobby most effectively, in Congress where a majority vote is needed it is a disadvantage to be too narrow or local.[16] But Cheryl Schonhardt-Bailey concludes that free trade lobbying in nineteenth century England benefitted from a geographic concentration of the core export industry, cotton textiles, and a deconcentration of the broader export sector to provide some breadth.[17]

Three generalizations emerge about the dependent variable in the contemporary setting. First, organized labor opposes freer trade. This is so for at least two reasons. Trade liberalization threatens jobs in the very manufacturing industries in which organized labor is strongest, namely the more labor-intensive industries. The fact that freer trade causes job loss that is highly visible is a problem for unions. No matter that freer trade may also create jobs elsewhere, jobs that are higher paying and more rewarding to the worker. These jobs are often delayed in generation and often are not as easily claimed for membership by the union that originally lost jobs to competition from abroad. Freer trade thus *potentially* reduces the size of labor unions. Since membership loss undermines the strength of the union, freer trade is an enemy of union organization as it presently exists.

Second, agriculture normally opposes free trade, particularly where it tends to be a high-cost producer internationally. Agriculture is one of the very few industries that corresponds to virtually perfect competition. No individual farmer affects price; hence each maximizes output. Overproduction results, causing downward pressure on price. Farmers quickly understand that freer trade, while potentially generating new markets for their products abroad, also generates new competition at home from imports which forces them to work harder to expand output in the face of declining price. In the modern period farmers world-wide have used their electoral power to resist trade liberalization.

A partial exception to this rule may be found in Western Canada where more prosperous farmers perceived that free trade with the United States would reduce their dependency on Central Canada. While they would face increased competition from American agricultural exports, they would more than offset these losses by gains from importing manufactured goods and services from the United States at much lower cost than those produced in the smaller, protected and hence less efficient market of Canada. They also realized that supports and subsidies are not as viable a policy in a small country like Canada as in the United States or the European Community. The logic of this rationale for free trade, undoubtedly replicated in many places around the world (including the pre-Civil War United States) nonetheless often escapes the hard-pressed individual farmer.

Third, the multinational corporation in whatever field of manufacture or services is probably the major source of support for freer trade at present. Supposedly the consumer should be the strongest proponent of free trade, because the consumer benefits most from a larger variety of imports at lower cost, but it is an unreliable proponent. Neither organized nor broadly aware of its political leverage, the consumer seldom registers much political impact even in a country like the United States where that impact can rather easily be transferred to government. But the multinational corporation with its global orientation and desire for larger markets is, mainly through its trade associations, currently the most powerful and effective proponent of freer trade.

Three Primary Explanations for Party Attitude on Trade

How does a political party acquire its orientation toward freer trade? One explanation is that attitude toward free trade is intrinsic to the political party itself. As the party changes in organization, composition, or ideological orientation, its stand on trade liberalization changes also. A second explanation is that attitude toward free trade is associated with the nature of the party constituency. As the nature of that constituency and its support for political party changes, so the position adopted by the party on freer trade is likely to change. Finally, a third explanation holds that the position on free trade assumed by a party is a function of which party is governing. In this incumbency-based view, party attitude is based on the responsibilities of governing and of representing the polity abroad. Once elected to government, the reigning political party does what it must on trade, that is, for the most part to support liberalization. And in the adversarial atmosphere of the modern democratic polity, opposition parties then adopt the position on freer trade that remains to them, which usually involves a stronger dose of protectionism.

While these three explanations may complement each other, they also are conceptually and behaviorally distinct. A theory of party and trade ought to be able to rank them as to importance and to show why one explanation for trade orientation is more important than the others for a particular polity in a particular interval of history. Ideally, they will account for the party flip-flops observed historically regarding trade liberalization in North America.

Party-level Explanation

The political party itself, its ideological orientation, is the source of trade disposition in this explanation. Following Charles Kindleberger and Peter Gourevitch, the impetus to trade reform in the nineteenth century was ideology.[18] The Manchester Liberals were convinced that free trade was good for England as well as for the world. These ideas led to the repeal of the Corn Laws and the reduction of food prices for the urban classes. The tariff reductions were of course opposed by the rural squirarchy with as much vigor as they were defended by the political parties representing urban England. However, while the Conservative, Liberal, and the Socialist parties embodied the trade orientation per se, it was the independent influence of idea, of economic ideology, which persuaded the member of each party to adopt a particular stand.

Political parties in nineteenth century England, and in America and Canada, thus assumed a position on trade that had a strongly ideological flavor. This ideology was debated in schools and churches as well as in union halls and around boardroom tables. The ideology of trade liberalization became the basis of classical (and neo-classical) trade theory, further entrenching it as an identifiable source of policy initiative. But that ideology was deeply imbedded in the British Liberal Party, more than any other, and had its corresponding adherents in the Canadian Liberal Party and the American Democratic Party of the century. No less, the ideology of trade reform appealed to some of the utopian Socialists in Britain and to American populists and Canadian prairie radicals. Without the ideology of trade liberalization, the political parties could not have mounted a shared challenge to the old high tariff order with its encrusted traditions of rural privilege and constrained electoral behavior. Liberalization of the vote went hand in hand with liberalization of the international trade order in the minds of most reformers.

As party ideology changes, party positions regarding trade shift over time as well. In the United States, Hamilton and Jefferson symbolize the two wings of the political spectrum, namely, the Northeastern industrial and commercial establishment, and the Southern and Western plantation and small free-hold agricultural classes. Throughout the pre-Civil War period, the propensity for high tariffs on manufactured goods was kept in check by the Jeffersonian ideology of low tariffs such that imports of manufactured goods and other items would not destroy the profits from the export of tobacco, cotton, and other agricultural commodities. After the Civil war, the victorious North canceled the Reciprocity Treaty of 1854 with Canada that had allowed some free trade in agricultural goods and other commodities, re-instituting high tariffs on all goods.

Populism, epitomized by the critical election of 1896, espoused low tariffs and an end to tariff subsidies that made tools and other farm implements more expensive. The Progressive Reformers with a more urban orientation also supported freer trade but for different reasons, envisioning tariffs as a way that big business had to enrich itself at the cost of labor. Thus the ideology of political reform in the United States carried with it a propensity for trade liberalization. The Democratic party, adopting the ideology of reform, also assumed the banner of freer trade. Freer trade became identified with the interests of labor and of consumers. Tariffs were associated with the interests of capital and of big business through the 1920s.

At some point in the post-1945 period, ideology regarding free trade flip-floped for the U.S. political parties, shaping party positions. The Republican Party became the protagonist of free trade. The Democratic Party, supported by organized labor, farmers, and professional groups, shifted toward an anti-free trade posture. The party-level explanation for these shifts is that Republican Party ideology increasingly stressed open markets, reduced government intervention in markets, and a global trade orientation; the Democratic Party ideology stressed "fair trade" rather than free trade and managed trade arrangements rather than open, multilateral trade. Protectionism inside some circles of the Democratic Party came to be equated with jobs. Retaliation was equated with reciprocity and with forcing foreigners to "play by the same rules" as Americans. Within a few decades, the two American political parties had swapped ideological orientation toward trade liberalization.

Ideological shifts in Canada followed a surprisingly similar pattern. At the end of the nineteenth century, the Liberal Party was the champion of free trade. Although the defeat of the Laurier Government in 1911 on the free trade issue with the United States marked Liberal Party policy for decades, the party continued to stress an ideology that was quite supportive of multilateral free trade throughout the King years and much of the post-1945 interval. The Conservative Party adopted the opposite ideology of protectionism that was often equated with Canadian nationalism and the building of the Canadian nation, just as the old high-tariff National Policy of Sir John A. Macdonald had been equated with accelerated economic growth through the creation of a sheltered domestic market.

But with the Mulroney Government in 1984, this ideological preference shifted. Under Pierre Trudeau, the Liberals had already adopted an anti-free trade policy with the United States, later modified to include sector free-trade which in effect remained quite protectionist in character (only those sectors in which Canada was already competitive would be opened to sectoral free trade). After the unpopularity of the Foreign Investment Review Agency (FIRA), the National Energy Program (NEP), and other Liberal protectionist measures, the Conservative Party became the chief exponent of free trade in Canada. Conservatism and support of bilateral and multilateral free trade became synonymous in the minds of most Canadians. The ideology of free trade had flip-flopped in Canada, much as it had in the United States, with each political party taking the position of the opposite party on free trade by the mid-1980s.

In this party-level explanation of free trade orientation, ideology is at the foundation of the trade liberalization outlook. As Stephen Magee and Leslie Young argue, Republicans prefer low inflation at the expense of unemployment, Democrats low unemployment at the expense of greater inflation, even though these macroeconomic preferences may get in the way of their respective tariff preferences.[19] John T. Williams confirmed that for the party-differences model he tested, Democrats did favor short-term expansion and growth, Republicans inflation-averse policies.[20]

When the ideology of the party on free trade shifts, so does the party position on foreign trade matters. Since long-terms shifts in ideology and party position on trade liberalization changed in both Canada and the United States (and reciprocally for both major parties in each country), the thesis appears compelling that ideology and party politics greatly affect how political party members will vote on foreign trade issues.

Constituency-level Explanation

According to this interpretation of trade preference in the democratic polity, everything is determined by how constituencies behave.[21] This is illustrated for Canada by the findings of G. K. Helleiner for the period 1961-70. He shows that labor seeks protection because of the increased flow of low-wage products from the newly-industrializing countries. Likewise he shows that multinational corporations like free trade because they need markets and investment outlets abroad that are unencumbered by trade and investment barriers.

When a constituency changes its behavior either regarding its support for free trade or its support for a political party which has free trade as one of its planks, then the political party itself will adopt a new orientation toward the free trade issue. In 1954 Congressmen from Southern textile areas who had favored the traditional Democratic Party policy of low tariffs began to feel pressure for higher tariffs from the expanding Southern textile industry that feared foreign competition.[22]

Historically big business involved large enterprises located in a single country, enterprises that nonetheless traded abroad and met foreign competition in domestic markets. Firms primarily located in a domestic market, but subject to foreign competition in trade, easily favored protectionism. Protectionism created monopoly profits for them in their home market where they made the majority of their income. Big business historically in North America, with only rare exceptions, thus supported the anti-free trade position.

Organized labor historically also favored liberalized trade. Tariffs redistributed income from labor to capital. This distortion in income distribution was compounded by the reality that the worker felt the brunt of the tariff. Workers had to pay more for imported goods they consumed when purchased either from import-competing industries at home or from importers of goods from abroad. Organized labor could not support "exploitative" trade arrange-ments and thus favored trade reform instead. Farmers found themselves in a similar situation and encouraged trade liberalization to lower the cost of their inputs.

Given these past constituency preferences, of big business on the one hand and organized labor and farmers on the other, it is scarcely surprising that business tended to be protectionist in the Northeast manufacturing areas of the United States and in the industrial heartland of Ontario. With the defeat of the South in the American Civil War, the pro-free trade agricultural south was defeated as well, and merchants and manufacturers in New England and New York wanted to end the 1854 Reciprocity Treaty with Canada.

Conversely, the Populist Movement and the Progressive Movement that followed it, the former stemming from the efforts of the agricultural West, the latter from workers in the cities, each favored a reduction in tariffs on manufactured goods. This attitude carried over into the policies of the Democratic Party, which each group tended to support. Franklin

Delano Roosevelt was the first president to transform this sympathy into major tariff reductions in the aftermath of the Great Depression. But the electoral base that made much of this trade reform possible came from the old populist and progressive tradition.

Hence the Republican Party came to be known as the high tariff party, while the Democratic Party earned the reputation as the party favoring trade liberalization. Neither categorization was entirely true. Taft, for example, experimented with a tariff reduction treaty in 1911 to the chagrin of much of his party membership. Moreover, farmers who voted democratic nonetheless learned the benefits of subsidies for their agricultural goods. But in the main, the constituencies that voted for or against trade liberalization tended to transmit these preferences directly to the political party that most readily listened.

In Canada the pattern was quite similar. Sir John A. Macdonald toyed with free trade, but neither Britain nor the United States seemed interested. The National Policy was self-consciously oriented toward the interests of business in Canada. The Conservative Party enjoyed the unswerving support of this constituency. High tariffs earned revenue for the federal government. They also enabled business to earn enormous revenue that was translated into campaign funds at election time.

The Liberal Party reflected the preferences of labor and the farm vote as well as the important Quebec constituency. Laurier's effort to conclude a free trade agreement with the United States in 1911 was an effort to respond to the interests of those outside the business community in Canada who lamented the cost of high tariffs to themselves and to their regions. While perhaps not so stridently supportive of free trade as their American counterparts, Canadian labor and the farmers in the West understood where the burden of a high tariff policy rested. The Liberal Party tapped this resentment for its own electoral purpose throughout much of the late nineteenth and early twentieth centuries.

In the more recent period, parties in both Canada and the United States flip-flopped on trade reform because the respective constituencies changed their attitudes on trade liberalization. Big business became multinational in scope. It recognized the meaning of interdependence. In order to obtain lower tariffs abroad, Americans and Canadians would have to be prepared to lower their own tariffs. Capital was highly mobile. It could take advantage of situations where the prospects for economic growth were greatest. Tariff reductions spurred economic growth. Gradually, large manufacturing and service firms in the United States and Canada came around to the view that trade liberalization and faster economic growth were partners. The free trade position, normally advocated through their powerful trade associations, became the objective of the biggest firms, provided that trade reform was broad-based.

Simultaneously in both countries, organized labor and the farm vote were becoming much more protectionist. Labor perceived that industry was moving outside North America to lower-wage rate countries, and feared the "hollowing out" of home industry and the loss of jobs. Organized labor transmitted these fears to the New Democratic Party and the Liberal Party in Canada and, with the farming community, to the Democratic Party in the United States. Each of these parties responded to the new anxieties that their traditional voter constituencies felt.

Organized labor by the last third of the twentieth century found itself in a particular bind. Free trade seemed to open the economy to fierce competition from abroad (even though this competition would make itself felt eventually whether through tariff walls or not). The consequence for organized labor was downward wage pressure and/or job loss. The latter was far worse for the union because it meant smaller unions, lower dues revenue, and less political clout for the union. Hence preference for or against the tariff seemed a decision about institutional survival. No other avenues seemed open to labor. The onslaught of technological change and pressure from the low-wage trading countries abroad was an unmitigated threat to its existence. Organized labor thus changed its position on free trade. In the 1970 battle over protectionist legislation in the Congress, this flip-flop was apparent. "Intense union pressure for protection," says Pietro S. Nivola, "split northern Democrats."[23] But the Liberal and Democratic parties, dependent upon organized labor for votes, changed their orientations toward freer trade.

Perhaps the greatest test of these contemporary party flip-flops on free trade came with the North American Free Trade Agreement among the United States, Canada, and Mexico. Predictably, organized labor in both countries (ironically in all three countries) was the most opposed to the agreement. Labor will feel the greatest pressure for adjustment from free trade. Change is painful for organized labor because although new jobs may be created elsewhere in each economy, labor unions will lose specific jobs immediately, never to be regained. From the perspective of the labor union, free trade is a zero-sum loss. For about the same but inverted reasons, liberalized trade is a gain for large multilateral business. Hence the Conservative and Republican parties felt support from their principal constituencies for freer trade with Mexico; the Liberal, New Democratic, and U.S. Democratic parties all felt a great deal of pressure to reject the free trade agreement, the first of its kind to open competition directly between a low-wage poor country and high-wage rich countries.

In short, from the constituency-level interpretation of party impact upon trade policy, party has a brokerage function and ideology is quite secondary. Industries that lose market share press for protection. Industries that lay off workers and are forced to cut costs abruptly apply for protection. More organized industries try harder to protect.[24] As the constituency base of the party changes, and as the trade attitudes of its constituency change because of their own changed economic circumstance, the winds of change blow across the party outlook of trade. That outlook changes course. Causation moves from constituency to voting behavior to a change in party outlook, and back.

Party flip-flops are the result; flip-flops of business and organized labor are the cause. But if one follows causation here one step further back historically, perhaps a deeper cause is change in the nature of the world market structure. The critical beginning of the flip-flop occurred when North American business moved from the confines of the national market-place to the world market, from the status of national firm to multinational firm. The multinational firm needed markets open worldwide, and it traded home-based protection for international openness. Labor opposed protectionism for the national firm because that meant a transferrence of welfare from labor to capital, from worker to firm. But when business went multinational, labor shifted to a protectionist position in hopes of safeguarding jobs, of preventing or slowing down the "export" of low-wage jobs to other countries where North American multinationals were now located. The switch from national production to international production was the hinge around which the interest group and party flip-flops could occur.

In all parties under the period of study for the United States, Canada and Mexico, a massive shift in trade attitude for organized labor and for business has occurred. This shift is quite logical in terms of specific economic interest of each grouping if not for the polity as a whole. In general, labor has become more protectionist and business has become more supportive of freer trade. This attitude change suggests that the real origin of change in party voting behavior on trade policy came at the constituency level. Without full attention to the changing interests of the respective constituencies, no model of party-trade interaction can possibly hope to explain trade outcomes.

Incumbency-focussed Interpretation

According to this interpretation, parties do not have innate, ideological positions regarding trade liberalization. Or, at any rate, their stated prior-to-election positions on free trade are subject to deep modification. This is born out by the finding of John MacArthur and Stephen V. Marks that returnees to Congress are more likely to submit to protectionist pressure than those who were defeated or chose not to run again (lame ducks).[25]

Nor, in this view, is the constituency-level explanation compelling. The critique is not that constituencies fail to hold views about free trade, or that these constituencies fail to try to influence political parties and government to accept their view. According to the incumbency-focussed explanation for trade orientation, the problem regarding the constituency-level argument is that it is not strong enough to affect how governments ultimately and actually behave on free trade matters.[26]

In the incumbency-focussed explanation, governments respond in favor of trade liberalization because they must. The national interest is at stake. Regardless of constituency desires, or political party rhetoric, the party in power supports trade liberalization because the trend in the twentieth century has been toward opening up markets on a multilateral basis. "The gains from trade are so large," that small states especially "are constrained to remain open."[27] Party centralization and even the form of representation (ie. proportional representation) are affected by the international trade imperative.[28] To oppose this trend toward multilateral trade liberalization is to isolate oneself. This is the opposite of the thesis put forward by Jan Tumlir that political executives are increasingly intervening on the trade process at the cost of freer trade.[29] No polity can afford an autarkic policy in the late twentieth century and still serve its citizens. Hence regardless of prior, party position, or set of constituency preferences, the governing political party still adopts the prevailing orientation toward increased free trade, either regional or universal. What determines party position on trade, according to the incumbency-focussed interpretation, is whether the party is in power.

By negation, the party or parties out of power are anti-free trade, the political turf left to them. If the party in power is pro-free trade, by the terms of response and counter-response in the adversarial proceedings of elections and parliamentary debate, the parties out of power must take the opposite trade position, namely the more protectionist stand.

The incumbency interpretation allows as well for other reasons why parties out of power adopt the more protectionist stand. They may be closer to the voter or to electoral constituencies that are dissatisfied with the government's official trade policy. They may also be more accessible to interest groups attempting to change trade legislation, at least in democratic systems where the opposition party or parties can actually block legislation proposed by the governing party or coalition. Interest groups which attempt to hold the status quo against impending legislation that opens markets will fully realize how much easier the task of negating legislation is than finding positive support for it. This task of negation, moreover, will be far easier among the members of the opposition party than among the members of the governing party, on average, whatever the local constituency preferences of each member.

The incumbency thesis readily explains the contemporary party positions of all of the governments in North America. Prime Minister Mulroney campaigned initially on an anti-free trade platform, but once elected, he fought hard for a free trade agreement with the United States. John Turner, the Liberal Party candidate, fought against free trade as did Edward Broadbent, the New Democratic Party candidate, even though Turner personally was far closer to free trade as an issue when not involved in politics (and when he was a minister in the governing Liberal Party during the late 1960s) than Prime Minister Mulroney himself. A plausible hypothesis, albeit a counterfactual, is that if John Turner had been Prime Minister when the opportunity for a free trade agreement with the United States emerged, the Liberal Party would have championed free trade for Canada and the Progressive Conservatives in a shadow role would have opposed it. Indeed, the effort to inch toward free trade through the sectoral proposals, although still protectionist and unacceptable to the United States, may be interpreted as a way of preparing the Liberal Party constituency for the fuller free trade gambit should the opportunity arise once the party was in power. But victory for the Progressive Conservative Party left the Liberals no choice but to continue their anti-free trade role in opposition.

Similarly, the incumbency thesis is to some extent borne out in the United States. There can be little doubt that Presidents Reagan and Bush supported the notion of universal and regional free trade, notwithstanding voting records in Congress which passed much protectionist legislation including the super-301 legislation to be used for retaliatory purpose. Likewise the Democrats were on record as being less convinced of free trade, especially the free trade agreement with Mexico, than were the Republicans. Yet if the Democrats had been in power in the 1980s instead of the Republicans, again a counterfactual and therefore difficult to substantiate, would they have adopted a posture toward the Uruguay Round or toward NAFTA much different than that of Reagan or Bush? It is hard to imagine that a U.S. government, whichever party was in power, would have turned its back on freer trade in the 1980s.

As far as Mexico is concerned, the governing party was the controlling element in determining the country's trade posture. Inasmuch as the PRI has lately been the only party to lead Mexico, it is perhaps not useful to speculate what the opposition parties might do, or might have done, if they were in power. Nonetheless, even the more leftist parties, were they in power, probably would distance themselves from constituencies like organized labor and the peasantry, now very opposed to an opening of trade with the United States.

In sum, everywhere in the late twentieth century we see the pressure in the governing party to accept freer trade. The party in power takes this liberalized view of trade because it must express the national interest. The opposition parties are stuck with what is left strategically and electorally, namely, opposition to free trade, at least in detail if not in concept. The party in power must deal with other governments who are themselves moving toward a tighter international regime of freer trade and commerce. Opposition parties take the more local interest and the more parochial position on free trade because that is the reciprocal position of the governing party, the position that the dynamic of politics has left to the parties out of power and in the posture of critic.

Towards an Explanatory Model of Party Position and Trade

The only hope to unravel the complex politics of the party-trade flip-flop in North America is to use a multi-causal model having at least limited feed-back potential. The dynamic of the party-trade relationship is too complicated for the primary sources of causation, in isolation, to explain outcomes consistently across polities and across time. We therefore propose the following model as an instrument for sorting out why and when the major political parties in North America changed their orientations toward free trade. But the model also ought to be able to place political party in the larger societal and political context as a source of explanation regarding protectionism and trade liberalization.

Such a model, if applied cross-sectionally at various times in the evolution of each country's trade policy, should unearth much other valuable information about how trade policy gets generated and implemented. Whether one's interest is in learning how political party operates in a significant area of external policy-making, in understanding the relative importance of political party and other variables such as institutionalization in the trade policy process, or in ascertaining why protectionism gains support within the democratic polity, the following explanatory model (Figure 10.1) may be of assistance. In short, although the independent variables and the dependent variable in this examination are very specific, the model itself can be used to explore quite a diverse set of more generalized questions and hypotheses, some of which we propose at the end of this discussion.

Political party (1) is an intermediary variable between interest groups (A) and governmental trade policy (B). Interest groups try to influence government directly (C), especially in Canada where power is more concentrated in the Cabinet and in the Prime Minister's Office (PMO) than in the United States. Interest groups also operate through political

FIGURE 10.1 Political Party Orientation Toward Freer Trade (North America)

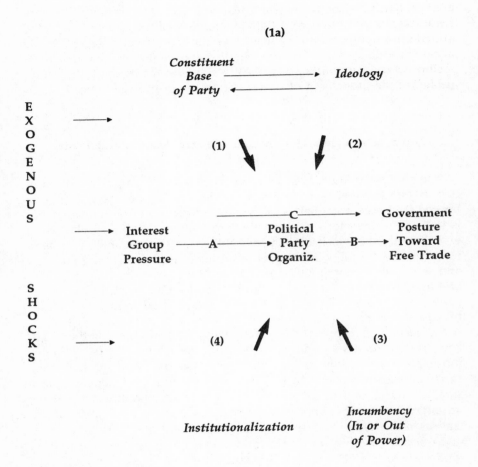

Source: Conceptualized by the author. Political party mediates between (A) interest groups and (B) government posture toward free trade. Interest groups also influence (C) government policy directly. Also impacting on policy are (1) constituent base, (2) ideology, (3) incumbency, and (4) institutionalization. Ideology affects constituency base (1a) reciprocally. Exogenous shocks such as economic booms and recession accelerate or decelerate change.

party leaders and the heads of relevant Congressional committees (U.S.) to influence elections and crucial governmental decisions on trade. In fact, in a democracy, this is the primary linkage (A-B): interest groups to political parties to governmental trade outcomes. R. E. Baldwin provides empirical support for at least part of the argument in this linkage: party affiliation, import-sensitive industries, and union contributions all have a statistically significant association with protectionism.[30]

But other factors affect this linkage. At least four sets of complex influences impinge on the interest group-party-trade linkage.

The constituent base of the party (1) is important, since that base has interests which it expects to have defended. When the interests of the constituency change, or the constituency itself changes, party support for protectionism or free trade will also change.

Ideology (2) has a political life of its own, especially if reinforced by an intellectual edifice such as liberal trade theory, or by a set of constituency values such as "conservatism" or "liberalism." J. Michael Finger calls this the "American ideology of trade and protection," or the benefits and costs of protection versus an open international trade order.[31] Ideology is a motivational force. Without ideology, a political party has much more difficulty in spurring its members to make the sacrifices necessary on behalf of a specific trade policy. Ideology is no substitute for strategy, but it augments the strategy of the party leadership.

Whether a political party is in or out of power is extremely relevant to the kind of trade policy that it advocates. Incumbency (3) carries with it responsibility and exposure to cosmopolitan external influences that are seen as affecting the whole of the polity. Conversely, the party out of power is subject to all kinds of local interest group pressure and a more parochial outlook on trade matters. The political turf left to it, in the adversarial atmosphere of politics in the democratic polity, is that of opposition, and in recent years this has meant opposition to the more liberalized trade policies of the governing party.

Institutionalization (4) has received much attention from contemporary writers on protectionism and with justification. Michael Mastanduno, for example, has shown that depending upon whether the State Department and Defense Department are given the lead in shaping a policy on trade in semiconductors or whether Commerce and the Trade Representative's Office are given the lead, the outcome in trade terms is likely to be very different.[32] Thus institutions are a screen through which all trade policies must pass. The nature of the screen, its mesh size, and its material composition all could influence governmental decision-making on trade. Judith Goldstein warns that "the norms and institutions of fair trade" coexist with "their liberal counterparts."[33] That is why I. M. Destler warns against trying to find ways to halt "conflict among policy perspectives" other than keeping the trade policy group in the Executive Branch small and focussed.[34] Nonetheless, the underlying party base will determine whether a particular institution in the Executive Branch is successful in its handling of larger trade policy, and even regarding whether it is given responsibility to take the lead in trade policy formulation. Bear in mind the difference that the Conservative Party made in Canada in determining the nature and role of the foreign investment screening agency housed in the federal bureaucracy. Institutions can make a difference in trade policy formulation and implementation, but only if they are allowed to do so by the political process.

This model shows further causal complexity. Interest group pressure can affect governmental posture toward free trade by going directly (C) to the principal policy-makers in the Executive. This establishes an important second path of influence over trade, and a reciprocal set of influences operate between the constituent base of the party and ideology (1a). This reciprocal interaction is long-standing. Certain constituents such as organized labor have an affinity for certain types of ideology that will affect the ability of a political party to shape trade policy.

What sets trade liberalization in motion historically? What elicits waves of protectionism world-wide? The role of *conditioning* variables, although exogenous (as shocks to the system), must be included as critical causal linkages. At critical moments on the world stage, trade policy, like other foreign policy, is subject to the shoves and jolts of massive structural change within the international system.

As Helen Hughes notes, broad cultural attitudes toward government intervention change and are contagious.[35] Large-scale liberalization, argues Max Corden, results from an ideology of free trade or "patently bad experiences that are believed to be associated with controls."[36] The coincidence of the Smoot-Hawley Tariff and the Great Depression is the quintessential example. But the aftermath of major war, the prospect of political or economic isolation (e.g., the 1846 Reciprocity Treaty with the United States as a consequence of the Repeal of the British Corn Laws leading to British free trade and Canadian isolation), or a long economic boom, may also stimulate tariff reform. Arye L. Hillman has attempted to model how foreign and domestic influences come together in terms of campaign contributions.[37] But the exogenous forces that catalyze trade liberalization, or its opposite, may be less direct and material but no less instrumental than influence upon elections.

This model suggests five general hypotheses. Operationalization may suggest empirical tests for the many linkages in the model.

Hypothesis I. Political parties in the United States and Canada have flip-flopped on trade liberalization in the twentieth century. For the United States, this flip-flop is examined in terms of election platform statements by Uslaner and is discussed critically by McKeowan. For Canada, these patterns of exchange are documented in the Liberal Party and Conservative Party by McDowall. More complex patterns of change, acting as a control on this analysis, are found in Canada's New Democratic Party discussed by Owram, and in the Quebec party structure assessed by Martin. Although both Vega-Canovas and Story detect profound shifts in party postion toward trade by Mexico's ruling PRI party, nothing like the complete exchange of party positions observed for other North American political parties is evident within Mexico.

In short, the hypothesis is that these party flip-flops on trade liberalization are deeply-rooted and of great consequence for the manner in which trade policy is made in both of these countries.

Hypothesis II. In differing historical intervals, the party-based, constituency-based, or incumbency-focussed interpretations of the party-trade relationship will find more, or less, compelling support. Causal explanation is therefore dynamic. Although the factors that explain governmental trade policy are internal to the polity, and are political, they are not static. This dynamic quality of the model is captured through repeated cross-sectional empirical tests.

Hypothesis III. When a confluence of internal factors reflected in the linkages in this model act together across polities in a particular interval, a new trading regime is born. It is thus possible to go from the internal workings of the model to the external shifts in the international trading regime. While the dominance of one or other polity, in terms of the causal linkage illustrated here, may be helpful to the emergence of international trading regimes, it is the simultaneous flow of the internal forces in a number of polities that ensures transformation of the regime.

Hypothesis IV. In the most recent period, the incumbency-focused interpretation concerning the formulation of trade policy is the most convincing. This hypothesis suggests that although political parties continue to be the purveyor of trade attitude within the democratic polity, the impact of the leader of the governing party is increasingly central. More and more commonly, the president or prime minister, drawn from the governing party, adopts an outlook favoring liberalized trade at the regional and global levels, sometimes dragging a reluctant political party along with him or her.

Hence, interdependence among the principal trading states, driven by ideological impulse (liberal trade theory), observed practice (conviction of firm managers), and technological change, all are pushing governments toward a continued opening of the international system to trade.

Hypothesis V. Despite the political party flip-flops regarding freer trade, the NAFTA vote in Congress will continue to reflect a distinct and significant role for political party. While the contemporary position of the Republican Party will be essentially pro-free trade, and that of the Democratic Party will be anti-free trade, political party will play a significant role in determining the outcome of the Congressional vote together with other important variables.

A corollary perhaps is that the next most important variable may be the constituency, particularly organizations such as the Businessman's Roundtable on the one hand, and the AFL-CIO (U.S.) or the public service unions (Canada) on the other. These interest groups continue to wield important influence. In the age of brokerage politics today, ideology, that is, the ideological face of political party, is held to be somewhat less significant than other variables in explaining trade outlook. The model ought to be used to test this supposition.

But the cohesion of the political parties concerning trade in North America has not been lost. If anything, the role of political party on trade issues is becoming more delineated. The flip-flop in trade orientation did not destroy the efficacy of party in Congress; it made possible a continuing role for political parties in the making of trade policy.

Internal determinants of party and interest group will, nonetheless, always act as the causal instruments of trade liberalization. Despite current progress, the perpetual liberalization of the world trading system is never guaranteed. Charles Lipson probes the evolution of domestic efforts, for example, to protect enterprize when external regimes fail to do so.[38] Trade liberalization is a consciously learned and implemented set of policies inevitably subject to hesitancy and even on occasion reversal.

Conclusion

Concluding our study of the relationship between political parties and trade in North America, this theoretical assessment contrasts three types or levels of explanation: (1) the political party as the source of trade policy, (2) constituents, including interest group activity, as the stimulus to reform, and (3) incumbency of the governing party and its adoption of a free trade outlook that expresses the perceived national interest as the explanation for trade policy. Each type of explanation for the formation of party attitude toward trade policy has some validity. Each goes part way in accounting for the profound flip-flops that have accompanied the relationship between political party and trade in North America. A more encompassing model of all of these relationships could sort out the relative strengths of each type of explanation. If applied to separate historical intervals, the mix of explanation will be seen to change.

Today the dominant force in trade is the governing party in power. It reflects the interests of the country as a whole. It brokers those interests inside Congress or Parliament. It mediates between local stakeholders and external pressures for trade liberalization stemming from the international community, globally through GATT or within regions.

The big policy issues that will affect the political party-trade relation are the effort to achieve U.S. economic resurgence, the strategy adopted to overcome the federal and trade deficits, and the outcome of Quebec nationalism. Trade policy will tilt toward greater liberalization or greater protectionism, toward a global or regional emphasis, based on how each of these matters is handled. Whether the Democrats and the Liberals continue the path of global trade liberalization, for example, instead of again resorting to more protectionist policies, depends on how the United States and Canada cope with the larger challenges facing them. Whether the governing party in Mexico City retains its momentum in the drive for greater economic openness depends to quite an extent on how responsive its immediate neighbors are to its trade and investment overtures.

The model of trade-party linkage proposed here shows how multi-faceted and subject to slippage trade policy can become. Pressure points involve constituency change, ideological shifts, incumbency factors, and the effects of institutional screening of trade policy. Ultimately the theoretical and historical analysis can become a clue to policy prediction and prescription. Perhaps such an explanatory model of how political party has affected trade policy-making in North America can assist in the judgments necessary regarding the future path of North American trade.

In sum, analysts wishing to identify the future likely trend of trade policy would be well-advised to study the attitudes of the political parties in North America toward trade. When combined with the larger issues of unity, fiscal responsibility, and economic reform, these political party positions become a kind of early warning mechanism. Political party is a bellwether for the evolution of the possible, as well as the probable, in all future trade initiatives.

Notes

I would like to thank John Meehan for invaluable research assistance in preparing this article.

1. Stephen Krasner, "State power and the structure of international trade," *World Politics*, Vol. 28, No. 3, April 1976.

2. Robert Gilpin, *The Political Economy of International Relations* (Princeton, NJ: Princeton University Press, 1987).

3. Robert E. Baldwin, "The New Protectionism: A Response to Shifts in National Economic Power," in Dominick Salvatore, ed., *The New Protectionist Threat to World Welfare* (New York: Elsevier, 1987), pp. 105-106.

4. Robert O. Keohane, *After Hegemony: Cooperation and Discord in the World Political Economy* (Princeton, NJ: Princeton University Press, 1984).

5. E. E. Schattschneider, *Politics, Pressures and the Tariff: A Study of Free Enterprise in Pressure Politics as Shown in the 1929-1930 Revision of the Tariff* (New York: Prentice-Hall, 1935), pp. 288-295.

6. Charles P. Kindleberger, "The Rise of Free Trade in Western Europe," *The Journal of Economic History*, Vol. 35, No. 1, 1975.

7. See G. K. Helleiner, "Transnational Enterprises and the New Political Economy of U.S. Trade Policy," *Oxford Economic Papers*, Vol. 29, No. 1, 1977, pp. 102-116.

8. Peter Katzenstein, *West Germany's Semisovereign State* (Philadelphia, PA: Temple University Press, 1987), p.7. Peter Gourevitch claims that political regimes do not matter much. A republicanized or democratized Germany would have adopted the same policies, he thinks, as did the Kaiser's Germany. A monarchist France would have favored the same high tariffs as a Republican France, or for that matter, a "Bourbon, Orleanist, or Bonapartist" France. This thesis counters that of Katzenstein, and seems to make some rather strong assumptions about comparability of outcomes across regimes within each historical time-period. Peter Alexis Gourevitch, "International Trade, Domestic Coalitions, and Liberty: Comparative Responses to the Crisis of 1873-1896," *The Journal of Interdisciplinary History*, Vol. 8, 1977, pp. 281-313.

9. David A. Lake, "The State and American trade strategy in the pre-hegemonic era," in G. John Ikenberry, David A. Lake, and Michael Mastanduno, eds., *The State and American Foreign Economic Policy* (Ithaca, NY: Cornell University Press, 1988).

10. Judith Goldstein, "Creating the GATT rules: Politics, Institutions, and American Policy," in John Gerald Ruggie, ed., *Multilateralism Matters* (New York: Columbia University Press, 1993), pp. 201-232.

11. I. M. Destler, "U.S. Trade Policy-making in the Eighties," in Alberto Alesina and Goeffrey Carliner, eds., *Politics and Economics in the Eighties* (Chicago, IL: University of Chicago Press, 1991), pp. 251-281.

12. Richard E. Caves, "Economic Models of Political Choice: Canada's Tariff Structure," *Canadian Journal of Economics*, Vol. 9, No. 2, 1976, pp. 278-300.

13. E. E. Schattschneider, *Politics, Pressures and the Tariff* (New York: Prentice-Hall, 1935).

14. Finding support for the theorem is Beatrice N. Vaccara, *Employment and Output in Protected Manufacturing Industries* (Washington, D.C.: Brookings Institution, 1960). Finding no support is Giorgio Basevi, "The United States Tariff Structure: Estimation of Effective Rates of Protection of United States Industries and Industrial Labor," *Review of Economics and Statistics*, Vol. 48, 1966, pp. 147-60. Rejecting the argument on empirical grounds is John H. Cheh, "A Note on Tariffs,

Nontariff Barriers, and Labor Protection in United States Manufacturing Industries," *Journal of Political Economy*, Vol. 84, 1976, pp. 389-94.

15. Jonathan J. Pincus, *Pressure Groups and Politics in Antebellum Tariffs* (New York: Columbia University Press, 1977); William A. Brock and Stephen P. Magee, "The Economics of Special Interests: The Case of the Tariffs," *American Economic Review, Papers and Proceedings*, Vol. 68, 1978, pp. 246-250.

16. J. J. Pincus, "Pressure Groups and the Pattern of Tariffs," *Journal of Political Economy*, Vol. 83, 1975, p. 757.

17. Cheryl Schonhardt-Bailey, "Lessons in Lobbying for Free Trade in 19th-Century Britain: To Concentrate or Not," *American Political Science Review*, Vol. 85, No. 1, 1991, pp.37-40.

18. Charles Kindleberger, *The World in Depression* (Berkeley: University of California Press, 1973); Peter Gourevitch, *Politics in Hard Times: Comparative Responses to International Economic Crises* (Ithaca: Cornell University Press, 1986).

19. Stephen P. Magee and Leslie Young, "Endogenous Protection in the United States, 1900-1984," in Robert M. Stern, ed., *Trade Policy in the 1980's* (Cambridge, MA: MIT Press, 1987), pp. 148-195.

20. John T. Williams, "Manipulation of Macroeconomic Policy," *American Political Science Review*, Vol. 84, No. 3, 1990, p. 777.

21. G. K. Helleiner, "The Political Economy of Canada's Tariff Structure: An Alternative Model," *Canadian Journal of Economics*, Vol. 10, 1977, pp. 318-326.

22. Robert A. Dahl, *Pluralist Democracy in the United States: Conflict and Consent* (Chicago: Rand McNally, 1967), p. 409.

23. Pietro S. Nivola, "Protectionism in U.S. Trade Policy," *Political Science Quarterly*, Vol. 101, No. 4, 1986, p.588.

24. Wendy L. Hansen, "The International Trade Commission and the Politics of Protectionism," *American Political Science Review*, Vol. 84, 1990, p. 31.

25. John MacArthur and Stephen V. Marks, "Constituent Interest vs. Legislator Ideology: The Role of Political Opportunity Cost," *Economic Inquiry*, Vol. 26, No. 3, 1988, pp. 461-470.

26. See David A. Lake, *Power, Protection, and Free Trade: International Sources of U.S. Commercial Strategy 1887-1939* (Ithaca: Cornell University Press, 1988); Stephen D. Krasner, *Defending the National Interest: Raw Materials Investment and U.S. Foreign Policy* (Princeton: Princeton University Press, 1978).

27. Ronald Rogowski, "Trade and the Variety of Democratic Institutions," *International Organization*, Vol. 41, No. 2, 1987, pp. 203-224.

28. Ibid., pp. 218-219.

29. Jan Tumlir, *On Protectionism*, pp. 38-55.

30. R. E. Baldwin, *Political Economy of U.S. Trade Policy* (New York: New York University Center for the Study of Financial Institutions, 1976). See also Bruno S. Fry, "The Public Choice View of International Political Economy," *International Organization*, Vol. 38, No. 1, 1984, pp. 210-211.

31. J. Michael Finger, "Ideas Count, Words Inform," in R. H. Snape, ed., *Issues in World Trade Policy* (New York: St. Martin's Press, 1986), p. 269.

32. Michael Mastanduno, "Do Relative Gains Matter? America's Response to Japanese Industry Policy," *International Security*, Vol. 16, Summer 1991, pp. 73-113.

33. Judith Goldstein, "Ideas, Institutions, and American Trade Policy," in Ikenberry, Lake, and Mastanduno, eds. *The State and American Foreign Economic Policy*, p. 216.

34. I. M. Destler, *Making Foreign Economic Policy* (Washington, D.C.: The Brookings Institution, 1990), p. 227.

35. Helen Hughes, "The Political Economy of Protection in Eleven Industrial Countries," in R. H. Snape, ed., *Issues in World Trade Policy*, p. 234.

36. W. Max Corden, "Why Trade is Not Free: Is There a Clash Between Theory and Practice?," in Herbert Giersch, ed., *Free Trade in the World Economy: Towards and Opening of Markets* (Tuebingen: J.C.B. Mohr-Paul Siebeck, 1987), pp. 1-19.

37. Arye L. Hillman, *The Political Economy of Protection* (Chur, Australia: Harwood Academic Publishers, 1989), pp. 90-92.

38. See Charles Lipson, *Standing Guard: Protecting Foreign Capital in the Nineteenth and Twentieth Centuries* (Berkeley: University of California Press, 1985).

11

The NAFTA Vote and
Political Party: A Partial Test

Charles F. Doran

Trade treaties normally do not stir much political emotion. On the evening of the NAFTA vote, however, much of Washington expectantly awaited the outcome. At stake was not only a regional trade agreement, but quite possibly the subsequent outcome of the global Uruguay Trade Round of talks. Bill Clinton's foreign policy was on line as well. Not since the U.S.-Canada Free Trade talks, which had dominated a Canadian federal election in 1988, had a free trade agreement so excited public attention.

After its passage in Congress, the NAFTA continued to send political shock waves through the region. The Zapatist National Liberation Army revolting in the southern Mexican state of Chiapas made no mistake about its intended target, NAFTA. Analysts could point to widening income gaps in Mexico (16 percent of the population categorized as falling in "extreme poverty,") gross unemployment, failed agricultural plans, inadequate social services, and an unresponsive political system.[1] No matter, the Zapatistas themselves blamed their revolt on the specifics of the NAFTA, on tariff reductions in corn which would leave this local industry in ruin against imports from the north that were three times more productive.

Everywhere in the United States, Canada, and Mexico the same themes of opportunity mixed with pain and adjustment to new competition greeted the proponents of trade liberalization. Seldom in North American experience had the fears of trade liberalization been so widespread and so violently expressed.

In this political context, the NAFTA vote in the U.S. Congress can be seen as an event that was pivotal. Everyone knew this at the time. Specialists anticipated passage after a hard fight.[2] But not until the final day before the vote was the outcome guaranteed, and then only after an unprecedented last Presidential surge of patronage and suasion. So, in trade terms, the NAFTA vote was a kind of "critical election." It was a test of the themes articulated throughout this book regarding the impact of political change on economic outcomes, of party unity as a mediating variable, indeed, of the party flip-flop thesis on trade matters writ large.

How central was political party to the process that yielded a freer trade outcome? Which of the levels of explanation for the passage of trade legislation outlined in the prior multicausal model was most at work, the level of the constituency including interest groups, the level of incumbency regarding which party is in power led by a committed president, or the level of the political party itself as a source of cohesion and identity regarding trade matters? Simply put, is it the identity of the party itself that counts, or is it the constituents and interest groups which the party represents, or the fact of whether or not a party is in power that will be most determinative of how the elected members of Congress will vote on trade legislation?

A Test of Party Centrality

Has political party lost importance regarding trade matters? Walter Dean Burnham writes that a loss of identity for parties could well lead to a "dissolution of the parties as action intermediaries in electoral choice."[3] Reasons abound for this decline of party in a media age where candidates are less in need of a political party at election time. Public office-holders and the organized membership may have separate "bases for claiming policy-making authority," according to Leon Epstein, and these bases may conflict.[4] Moreover the machines are gone that in the past promoted party discipline, and in the view of James L. Sundquist, individual politicians like freedom of maneuver.[5]

If party strength is on the wan, does the historical flip-flop in party position toward free trade indicate that political party is now a spurious variable in the explanation of how trade policy is made? Alternatively, have the president and prime minister essentially taken over all functions regarding trade liberalization in the United States and Canada, respectively, thus destroying the significance of political parties on these matters?[6]

In trying to offer a preliminary answer to these questions, we examine the critical U.S. Congressional vote on NAFTA. Given the complexity surrounding NAFTA, this is not an easy test of the various hypotheses in the theoretical model. But because of this more complex situation, this test is in some ways an even stronger affirmation of party than that provided in the simpler context. Here the incumbent party did not merely assume a free trade orientation, allowing the opposition party, the Republican Party, to take the electoral turf that was left to it. Each party retained its own position concerning free trade despite the pressures associated with whether it was the governing party (the majority party in Congress) or was in opposition.

The U.S. Congressional vote was the bellwether event concerning the entire NAFTA process. Canada and Mexico had already indicated their predisposition to support the agreement, and the votes in favor of NAFTA already existed in the U.S. Senate. But up until two weeks prior to the vote, the outcome was tilted against NAFTA in Congress. Thus, at least in terms of arena, the Congress would determine the success or failure of regional trade liberalization in North America. Congress voted at 10:42 PM on November 17. While 102 Democrats voted for NAFTA, 258 plus one independent voted against. Exhibiting a majority on the opposite side of the issue, 132 Republicans voted for and 43 voted against. The apparently effortless victory of 234 votes in favor, as opposed to 200 against, was quite misleading.

Although some 23 percent of the Republican Congressmen defected, the Republican Party in opposition stuck to its party pledge in favor of free trade. Although the Democratic Party was the majority party in Congress, and the Democratic President led the struggle for passage, most of the members of the Democratic Party still voted the party line against free trade. This analysis offers preliminary evidence that the strength of political party was scarcely spurious as an explanation for the vote outcome.

Close observation of the Congress as early as the summer of 1993, and assessment of the analytical literature on Congressional roll call voting, suggested five variables within the model of the trade-party relationship as relevant to an empirical exploration, using correlation and regression analysis, of how Congress would vote.

1. Considered most important to the vote was political party itself, the party identification (ID) variable. Each party had taken a strong position on NAFTA, a position that was clearly identified with the respective party label. Would Congressmen vote the party line? Party ID was recorded as a zero (Democrat), one (Republican) or 2 (Independent). When a Democrat voted against the agreement, or a Republican voted for it, party identification was upheld.

2. Highlighted in the final week by the televised debate between Vice-President Gore and Ross Perot, the "Perot factor" seemed paramount. Among the events leading to the NAFTA vote, the debate was considered

a high-point of public interest and "education" about NAFTA. Perot threatened to challenge any member of Congress voting for NAFTA through a candidate from his party in the upcoming Congressional elections. Percent of popular vote for Ross Perot in each Congressional district in the 1992 presidential election was the actual indicator used in the regression equation.[7] When a Congressman voted against NAFTA and the percentage who voted for Perot in his or her district was high, then the Perot factor was upheld.

3. Nothing rang louder in U.S. ears than Ross Perot's phrase about a "giant sucking sound" of U.S. firms and jobs being pulled into Mexico. Reflected in polls, press accounts, and discussion was the deeply-felt fear that plants from the northern "Rust Belt" would move south of the border where labor costs are anywhere from one-fifth to one-seventh less than elsewhere in North America. The same fear that Canadians, during the debates prior to the U.S.-Canada free trade agreement, had regarding the United States as an investment haven, now U.S. citizens along the northern border had concerning NAFTA and Mexico. Hence this variable was indexed as geographic distance from Mexico, assuming that those furthest from Mexico geographically would feel themselves most vulnerable and would be most opposed to the regional free trade agreement for that reason.[8]

4. Organized labor was the chief interest group opposing NAFTA, for reasons directly related to the fear of investment diversion and job loss in the United States. In trade discussions, "jobs" are the single most sensitive issue from a political perspective. Emotions understandably ran high as econometric models reported "estimated job losses" of up to 690,000 while others reported up to 300,000 jobs "gained." Of course, jobs lost are politically more visible than jobs gained so far as labor unions are concerned. Competitive pressures already were causing the loss of U.S. jobs, and trade liberalization would only speed up the process. The jobs to be affected most were blue-collar. An index based on the reported blue-collar vote in each Congressional district was thus used to tap the influence of organized labor in opposing NAFTA.[9]

Given the strong stance taken by the trade union movement against free trade of all kinds, and particular against this agreement which they suspected would open the United States and Canada to the full brunt of low-wage competition, the AFL-CIO and other labor unions lobbied hard against the NAFTA. Business organizations like the Businessman's Roundtable were, of course, equally supportive of NAFTA. But the effectiveness of this campaign to dissuade the members of Congress from voting for NAFTA was measured by the fact that the second and third ranking members of the Democratic Party leadership, Congressman Bonier and Congressman Gephardt, were opposed to passage.

Assessment of the multi-causal model (generated prior to the NAFTA vote) suggested that constituency and interest group variables would be the second most important variables in the model after party identification, while ideology in the age of brokerage politics would contribute to explanation but would be less statistically important.

5. Ideological orientation seemed relevant to the NAFTA vote in Congress, since liberals appeared to have doubts about free trade and many conservatives supported trade liberalization. Yet this relationship was complicated by the existence of Pat Buchanan conservatives who also opposed the trade initiative. This split of ideological position against the agreement, bringing together the opposite ends of the ideological spectrum and the opposite wings of each party, against the agreement, suggests a kind of populist reaction opposing free trade. The Perot factor picked up some of the same influence. But how strong was this populist force? Did such populism affect only a few members of Congress on trade, or was this influence pronounced enough to shape Congressional behavior broadly?

If both ends of the ideological spectrum convincingly opposed NAFTA, then a non-linearity would exist with liberals and conservatives opposing and moderates supporting the agreement. A quick test for such a non-linearity is to divide the membership into two samples, one composed of conservatives, the other of liberals, and then determine whether the signs of the resulting regression lines are opposite. Such a finding would indicate non-linearity, and non-linearity of this kind would indicate a populist political influence at work. On the other hand, mixed responses at either end of the ideological spectrum would probably yield the generally anticipated finding that the more conservative members of Congress, on average, will display a propensity to vote for NAFTA, the more liberal members "everything else being equal" will not.

In this test, the ideology variable is the summed percentiles of "conservative" votes by each member in the "economic," "social," and "foreign" categories during the 1992 Congressional year.[10] Since the 103rd Congress which voted for NAFTA included many new members who were not able to be scored based upon past voting record, the scale was adjusted slightly.[11]

When the vote for and against an issue is close, as it is here, ordinary least squares yields good results even with a bivariate dependent variable, and it is far more interpretable than allegedly more "statistically" appropriate techniques such as logistical regression.[12]

As Table 11.1 reveals, bivariate correlational findings do reinforce the selection of variables. Although the correlational coefficients are not terribly high, possibly in part because of the dichotomous character of the dependent variable, the vote for or against NAFTA, they are meaningful and show the predicted sign for directionality. Political party shows a correlation of .38 with the NAFTA vote. Correlation for the blue-collar vote is small but positive. A -.25 correlation between geographic distance from the Mexican border and the NAFTA vote is correct in sign and magnitude, suggesting that the northern members of Congress worried that their constituents feared the regional trade outcome. Ideology correlated with the Congressional roll call at the second highest level with an r of .32. The Perot variable showed a direct influence on the Congressional vote. Thus all of these variables, seen in bivariate terms, appeared relevant to the outcome of the NAFTA vote. None was excessively intercorrelated with any of the others, indicating that each pretty much tapped a separate dimension of Congressional roll call behavior. Multicollinearity among these independent variables was not likely to be a problem.

But as Table 11.2 shows, the mutivariate regression findings tell quite another story. Given that a substantial amount of variance in the overall equation remains unexplained, some volatility may exist in the coefficients. So the experienced political scientist advances interpretation cautiously under these circumstances. If statistical significance, however, is used as a bench-mark of validity, then the findings here can be regarded as reliable given the closeness of the vote.

Most of the variance is explained by three variables, party identification, distance from Mexico, and political ideology, in that order. Party affiliation is more important than any other single variable. The strength of the party identification variable was tested through a series of separate tests, including separation of the freshman members from the rest of the Congress, and a sub-division of the Congress into conservative

TABLE 11.1   Possible Influences on the NAFTA Vote (Bivariate Correlations)

	Vote	Party	BlueCol.	D.Mex.	Ideol.	Perot
NAFTA Vote	1.000	.345	.061	-.252	.320	.130
Party ID	.345	1.000	.015	-.006	.469	.256
Blue Collar Vote	.061	.015	1.000	-.002	.098	.158
Distance from Mexico	-.252	-.006	-.002	1.000	-.125	-.128
Ideology	.320	.469	.098	-.125	1.000	.232
Perot Factor	.130	.256	.158	-.128	.232	1.000

(n=234)

Source: Calculated by the author.

Table 11.2 Impact of Political Variables on NAFTA Vote in Congress (Regression)

	Beta Weights[a]
Party ID	.269*
Blue-Collar Vote	.043
Distance from Mexico	-.231*
Ideology	.163*
Perot Factor	-.013
Variance Explained (R^2) (n=434)	.204

[a]Beta-weights reported here are for ordinary least squares equation.
*Statistically significant at the .001 level

Source: Calculated by the author.

and liberal factions. Party ID holds up well under all of these separate tests, revealing its underlying potency. Throughout a variety of tests, party ID virtually always is the most robust single indicator in the face of all control variables, at least considered individually, regarding the NAFTA vote in Congress.

According to the multiple regression results, a number of the bivariate correlations between independent and dependent variable were spurious, that is, falsely interrelated. This occurred for both the Perot factor and the blue-collar constituency. This was not the case with party ID. Likewise, political ideology was a more robust influence than anticipated by the prior theoretical discussion. Conservatives tended to support trade liberalization while, regardless of party ID or other factor, liberals tended to reject regional trade liberalization.

Now if we step back from the empirical findings on the NAFTA vote for a moment, so as to ask ourselves what all of this means politically, the conclusions are instructive. Each of the plausible causes of Congressional vote behavior on NAFTA *appeared* to be borne out by the bivariate correlations. But in multivariate terms, the interest group explanation of labor union impact, indexed by the blue-collar vote, has little relevance, counter to the supposition of the theoretical model. This finding may mean that the lobbying effort of organized labor was rather seriously offset by the equal but opposed influence of business. On the other hand, the matter of fear of plant closures along the northern border of the United States, indexed by geographic distance from Mexico, is shown to correlate inversely with the NAFTA roll call and with some vigor in both bivariate and multivariate terms.

Thus, distance from Mexico (the greater the distance, the less the support for NAFTA) was a factor in Congressional thinking about trade liberalization involving Mexico. Members of Congress in the Northeast and northern Midwest were aware that voters in their districts were worried about shifts of firms toward lower wage areas south of the border. Conversely, southern Congresspersons were much more content with NAFTA because voters in their districts thought they might benefit from additional trade with Mexico and were more confident that their own firms could compete with Mexican industry.

Political ideology, either when examined for the Congress as a whole, or when treated by ideological grouping, or when considered without the first-term members (who had yet to establish their ideological credentials in terms of roll call behavior), always has a demonstrated bearing on the NAFTA vote in the bivariate analysis. More conservative members tended to vote for NAFTA, more liberal members against. There was no trace of a non-linear effect. Populism may have been present. As the historical case studies pointed out, nineteenth century populism supported trade liberalization. Perhaps modern-day populism is a more complex phenomenon regarding trade orientation. In any case, populism was insufficient to offset traditional liberal and conservative political tendencies regarding trade liberalization. Hence the "Perot factor," which at first glance through the bivariate results looked important, in the multivariate analysis was washed out by other issues. When the final vote was recorded, members of Congress either ignored the Perot impact, disbelieved it, or allowed themselves to be more deeply motivated by other considerations.

Likewise, political ideology, treated in multivariate terms, was an influence on the NAFTA vote in Congress. The more conservative members of Congress were more likely to support trade liberalization than the more liberal, although there is some evidence that regionally within the United States this effect is less significant. Other more extensive analysis may yield other findings. Yet, in a rather concise model, where each variable is required to explain a statistically significant amount of variance in the dependent variable, the NAFTA vote, these results hold meaning. This first cut at explaining the NAFTA vote demonstrates that political ideology was linear, was important, and was not easily washed out by other considerations, especially, we suspect, on the liberal end of the political spectrum.

What this analysis also shows is the well-know observation that bivariate analysis is often quite misleading. Despite reporting only bivariate results, the *Congressional Quarterly (CQ)* came to the right conclusion when it observed that Perot "apparently did not" have a major impact on the vote.[13] It came to the wrong conclusion, however, about the significance of union pressure, as likewise occurred here in the bivariate analysis. In contrast to our earlier hypothesis, and to the conclusions of *CQ*, our multivariate findings show that the effect of party identification withstood the impact of union influence as an independent factor on the NAFTA vote. Perhaps the hard-pressure, but countervailing tactics of organized labor and of big business simply enabled some members to vote their own preference.

A Test of Party Unity

One more argument is the degree to which each political party voted as a unit. Evidence employed here is the "party unity score," which indicates the extent of political cohesion. The party unity score has two elements. First is the percent of roll-call votes in which one party's majority opposes a majority of the other party. Second, is the percentage of time that a Democrat or Republican votes with the party when it is in opposition. Party voting has declined significantly from its unusually high level at the beginning of the century. In administrations of the post-war period, the percent of votes in which a majority of each party opposed one another leveled to around 40. On the second measure, for either Democrats or Republicans, percent voting with their party in opposition to the dominant party rarely reached 70 percent.[14]

By these comparative standards, the NAFTA vote showed above-average party unity in both parties (despite effective arm-twisting of the president against the will of his own party). Regarding the party majority score, a majority of Congressional Democrats did indeed vote against a majority of Republicans, something that has happened in the recent past, with the exception of two Kennedy-Johnson years, much less than half the time.

Regarding percentage of the vote against (in opposition to) the president, the meaning of "opposition" is a little clouded, since the opposition Republican Party in Congress was voting with the Democratic president. Nonetheless, on the NAFTA vote, the Republican Party far exceeded the average party unity score. The Republicans' score was 75 percent, much higher than the average of any post-war Congress. Moreover, even though the Democrats were seriously divided on the trade liberalization issue, they still mustered an impressive party unity score of 60 percent.

The scores for trade liberalization thus must be regarded as above average. Set against the historical declines in party unity scores in the twentieth century, these scores may even be regarded as something of a resurgence for party unity. Despite a major battle over the future of trade policy surrounding NAFTA passage, then, neither political party fell apart or lost its sense of mission or identity.

Presidential Leverage

But it would be too facile to leave the analysis here, that is, confirming the salience once again, in spite of historical flip-flops of orientation, of political party in matters of trade liberalization. There is one more piece to the puzzle of the NAFTA Congressional vote that is evident in these results but only by implication. Bill Clinton's hand is omnipresent throughout. Without a strong executive, the NAFTA vote could not have been won. The hypothesis of the prior multicausal model regarding the relative importance of incumbency, although not tested directly here, has strong circumstantial support.

Thus those like I. M. Destler who argue that trade liberalization is an *executive branch* phenomenon have a point. The political party in power feels compelled to acknowledge the need for executive leadership in the national interest and in the interest of U.S. foreign policy leadership world-wide. This is true even when, need we say in particular when, the party in power is itself opposed to trade liberalization as the Democratic Party in this instance clearly was.

Put more sharply in political terms, if Clinton had not acted very strongly in support of NAFTA by twisting the arms of reluctant members of his own party to support the agreement, the measure would have failed. Indeed, if the Republicans had been in power, despite their extraordinary support for the agreement, probably an insufficient number of Democratic votes could have been found to pass the trade measure in the Congress. In fact, if all 175 Republican members of Congress had supported NAFTA, something even a Republican president could not have guaranteed, another 93 Democrats would have been needed in support of the trade agreement. That is only 9 short of what Clinton squeezed from his own party, notwithstanding all of the suasion and largesse available to the White House. A Republican president could not have gotten enough Democratic votes. In all probability, a Republican president could not have persuaded Congress to pass the NAFTA legislation.

So the situation of a Democratic president, facing down opposition to this form of trade liberalization, supported by a majority of the Republican members of Congress, is perhaps the only way the legislation could have been passed.[15] This conclusion provides convincing support for the argument that trade liberalization is also very much an executive branch effort, not only in conception and implementation, but in enactment as well.

Explaining the NAFTA Vote

The historical and critical research contained in this volume was stimulated by the speculation that political parties in North America have recently flip-flopped on trade. This idea gained support as this inter-disciplinary group of scholars began to examine the historical conditions, the mechanism, the limits, and the consequence of the flip-flop for the initiation of trade liberalization policy in the United States, Canada, and Mexico. The hypothesis of the long-term flip-flop was validated. What is more, the fact that a similar historical process had occurred among two of the dominant political parties, in both Canada and the United States, suggested that perhaps we were observing a fundamental shift in the politics of international economy.

The theoretical chapter explored the origins of trade liberalization policy within the democratic policy, and the causal underpinnings of the flip-flop, in particular the question regarding which level of analysis is responsible for the exchange of party outlooks on trade. A striking conclusion emerges. All three levels of analysis interact to account for the flip-flop phenomenon. It is analytically possible, in a static sense, to attribute cause to individual levels of analysis. But in dynamic terms, the separation into levels of analysis regarding causal interpretation is shown to be fallacious. A complete explanation can only occur through the use of a fully dynamic multicausal model employing feedback loops and all three levels of assessment simultaneously.

NAFTA epitomizes this complex, multi-level causal interpretation involving party politics. Some evidence exists in support of each of the sub-models. Interest group pressure was present, even though just prior to the vote, it seems to have been less important than other factors. Support for the incumbency theory of trade policy making is scarcely open to dismissal given Bill Clinton's performance, and the power of the pork barrel, in the last hours of the NAFTA vote. But institutional factors turn out to have been very significant as well, perhaps in the last analysis most significant as a source of explanation in trade policy behavior.

In sum, political party is a strong indicator of the outcome of the NAFTA vote in Congress. But so are other variables that move with or against political party as an explanator. Through each long-term flip-flop in party position, the integrity of the party regarding free trade is preserved. But only by taking completely into account the actions of both a strong executive and coherent political parties can the outcome of the NAFTA vote be fully understood.

Indeed, our final conclusion remains undiminished in its intensity. Political party is of compelling importance when considering trade issues in the United States, and perhaps also in Canada, and in other democracies. If by some oddity of circumstance, President Clinton had not been so committed to NAFTA, and many contemporaneous observers thought his show of support came perilously late, the significance of party would have been made even more clear during the actual vote. The Republicans would have largely supported NAFTA; the Democrats would have largely opposed it. The only difference here is that, without executive branch intervention, partisan impact on the vote with respect to trade liberalization probably would have been even more pronounced than it was.

Our findings generally support the prudent conclusions of Charles O. Jones a decade ago:

> Though congressional parties appear weak when compared to their counterparts in other political systems, still it must be acknowledged that they continue to play a role at every stage of the legislative process. Certainly no other grouping is as pervasive in congress as that of the political party.[16]

In short, a prevailing lesson of this analysis, and of this book, is that in trade matters, despite long-term historical shifts in orientation toward the electorate on the increasingly vital issue of trade liberalization, the role of political party is enduring and germinative.[17]

NAFTA and the Future of Trade Policy
in North America

More than an end, NAFTA is a beginning.[18] It is the beginning of a profound shift toward a recognition of two things in trade policy. First, regional trade blocs now vie with global trade liberalization for the determination of industrial structure that stretches beyond the nation-state. Second, the Third World can now become a full partner with the industrialized countries in the fruits of regional economic partnership. Neither of these NAFTA achievements was slight or easy.

Passage of the Uruguay Round of trade initiatives signalled that the latest global effort at trade liberalization under the sponsorship of the GATT still had life and impetus. Tariffs would fall virtually to zero. Services and intellectual property rights would gradually come under the liberalization umbrella. Even subsidies would receive new definition. But significant as these achievements were, they did not erase the outlines of industrial structure in North America carved out by the NAFTA.

Just as the European Union created an economic identity with a regional focus for hundreds of millions of people, and ASEAN did the same for South East Asia, so NAFTA did for North America. In each case, the regional grouping was as much a recognition of past reality as it was a framework in which to shape future trade policy. Each grouping was composed of countries that increasingly had more trade and commercial interactions among themselves than with the rest of the world. This oddity of interdependence, coming at the end of the twentieth century, could not have been predicted. Who would have guessed that in the era of vastly reduced freight rates and vastly increased communications, Germany would export more goods inside the European union than outside it, that Japan would invest more heavily within Asia than in other regions, or that Canada would be the most important trading partner of the United States. In an era of far-flung multinational corporate empires, regionalism is the unlikely benefactor of heavy cross-border flows of goods and services that stay close to home.

Paramount is the question whether these new regional groupings, including NAFTA, will create more, or will divert more, trade and investment. The answer need not be the same for both trade and investment, although for reasons that involve the nature of contemporary trade, the tendencies are likely to move together. Most trade today is investment-driven. This means that most trade is intra-firm and intra-industry, not just Japanese trade as some critics think, but all trade including that of most U.S. multinationals. Since foreign investment drives trade, it follows that if investment becomes prone to diversion because of regional influence, so trade may become diverted. The effect of the Auto-pact, the Canada-U.S. Free Trade Agreement, and finally the NAFTA itself on automobile investment and the flow of cars and spare parts ought to be a warning of these trends. But whether, in a larger context, NAFTA will begin to bend the curves of trade inward into the North American region has yet to be determined.

The second result of the NAFTA, the meshing of the South with the North, of the less-developed and the developed, of the poor and the rich, took a great deal of political courage all around. That the NAFTA was so pilloried in all three countries was a good sign. This mutual hostility showed that the benefits were not concentrated in a single country, nor were the costs. The American steel worker was as afraid of the consequences of free trade as the Mexican peasant, though protest may have found different channels. Greater market efficiencies may accelerate overall incomes, while those who must adjust always do so with trepidation. But that countries with such diverse average per capita incomes as the United States and Mexico possess can contemplate market integration is, in the end, one of the most hopeful economic lessons of the twentieth century. Such integration means that the neo-classical trade notion of an ever-expanding "pie" of goods and services accessible to rich and poor alike is a reality in North America far sooner than will be the case where North and South do not meet so directly and intensely.

"Deepening" through policy harmonization, and "widening" through the addition of new members starting with Chile, will give to NAFTA the same dynamic quality evident for other regional efforts. Which trend will dominate within NAFTA is not the most interesting question. Each will feed off the other, promising benefits that can only come from scale and standardization. By regionalizing these dual processes, change will come far faster than through global liberalization that must "average out" so much more divergency.

What both of these trends, deepening and widening, indicate is that trade and investment regionalism is an open-ended process. It is highly practical and pragmatic. It is a process, though economic in substance, which is overwhelmingly political in direction. Regionalism is the politician's answer to the businessman and the economist.

Finally, NAFTA reveals how deeply political the making of trade policy is within the contemporary democracy. Maastricht, the unleashing of the European Union, repeatedly was ratified by majorities of only one or two percent. Inside Canada, Mexico, and the United States, a majority of the electorate might have rejected NAFTA if it had been put to them in a referendum. Does this mean that trade liberalization is anti-democratic? Probably not. Elected representatives, where democracy works (and in different ways where it does not), have an opportunity to lead and to act in a mode which they believe will eventually be proven best for their own society and polity. Electorates can always reverse these decisions in future contests.

Political party remains a principal vehicle, not only for coalescing opinion on trade liberalization, but for conditioning and shaping trade policy. As the NAFTA vote in the U.S. Congress poignantly shows, trade liberalization is the product of a vigorous and enlightened executive and a supple but enduring political party reality.

Notes

I wish to thank Andrew Parasiliti and Dahlia Stein for insightful and highly competent assistance.

1. *Economist,* January 15, 1994, p. 19.

2. Charles F. Doran, Briefing, Subcommittee of the Western Hemisphere, House Foreign Affairs Committee, U.S. House of Representatives, November 10, 1993; see Charles F. Doran, "Combining Regional and Global Trade Liberalization North American Style," paper presented at the conference "Toward a North American Community?" University of Calgary, Alberta, Oct. 14-16, 1993, for a forecast of the chances of passage of NAFTA and/or the Uruguay Round. Also published in Spanish as "La Liberación de los Comercios Regional y Mundial al Estilo de América del North," *Comercio Exterior,* Vol. 44, No. 1, January 1994, pp. 19-29.

3. Walter Dean Burnham, *Critical Elections and the Mainsprings of American Politics* (New York: Norton, 1970), pp. 130-131; Martin P. Wattenburg, *The Decline of American Political Parties: 1952-1988* (Cambridge: Harvard University Press, 1984, 1990); John Ferejohn, "On the Decline of Competition in Congressional Elections," *American Political Science Review,* Vol. 71, 1977, pp. 166-176; Frank J. Sorauf, *Party Politics in America,* 4th ed. (Boston: Little, Brown, 1980); Morris Fiorina, "The Decline of Collective Responsibility in American Politics," *Daedalus,* Vol. 109, 1980, pp. 25-45.

4. Leon Epstein, *Political Parties in Western Democracies,* pp. 289-290, quoted in Malcolm E. Jewell, "Linkages Between Legislative Parties and External Parties," in *Legislatures in Comparative Perspective* (New York: David McKay, 1973), p. 222.

5. James L. Sundquist, "Strengthening the National Parties," in A. James Sundquist, *Elections American Style* (Washington, D.C.: Brookings Institution, 1987, p. 213.

6. In some ways this "level of analysis" problem can as usefully be expressed in terms of the power of the respective branches of government to initiate trade policy and therefore ultimately to control its implementation. See William West and Joseph Cooper, "Legislative Influence vs. Presidential Dominance: Competing Models of Bureaucratic Control," *Political Science Quarterly,* Vol. 108, Winter 1989/90, pp. 581-606.

7. "1992 Election: District Vote for President," *Congressional Quarterly,* 7 August 1993, pp. 2185-2192.

8. The variable "Distance from Mexico" was scaled from 1 (closest to Mexico) to 10 (farthest from Mexico), based upon arbitrary lines drawn across a map of the United States with Mexico as origin.

9. The "Percent Blue Collar" variable is coded as the percentage of the labor force (16 years and older) in each district employed in the following three industries: agriculture, forestry, fishing and mining; construction; manufacturing. Data is drawn from U.S. Census Bureau, "103rd Congress--Labor Force Characteristics: 1990."

10. These categories and ratings are drawn from the National Journal's *Almanac of American Politics: 1994.* Scores range from 0 to 99 in these ratings, with the higher scores being the most conservative. Note that for statistical reasons, most maximum percentiles are less than 99. Michael Barone and Grant Ujifusa, *The Almanac of American Politics: 1994* (Washington, D.C.: National Journal, 1993).

11. New members with no voting record are ranked as "00." Those members who received the most liberal rating based upon their past voting record according to the National Journal's *Almanac*, a "0," are ranked as "01."

12. See L. Marvin Overby, Beth M. Henschen, Michael Walsh and Julie Strauss, "Courting Constituents? An Analysis of the Senate Confirmation Vote on Justice Clarence Thomas," *American Political Science Review*, Vol. 86, No. 4, Dec. 1992, pp. 997-1003.

13. Jon Healey and Thomas H. Moore, "Clinton Forms New Coalition To Win NAFTA's Approval," *Congressional Quarterly*, November 20, 1993, p. 3183.

14. Charles O. Jones, *The United States Congress: People, Place, and Policy* (Homewood, IL: The Dorsey Press, 1982), p. 235, presents a table of party unity scores for the period 1961-1980.

15. George Ingram, Director of International and Environmental Affairs for the U.S. House Foreign Affairs Committee, has argued that the fact that NAFTA was initiated by a Republican president bound the Republicans to the measure. He does not believe they would have responded in the same positive way to a measure initiated by the Democrats. See also George M. Ingram, *NAFTA: Evaluating the Arguments* (Washington, D.C.: Foreign Policy Institute, The Paul H. Nitze School of Advanced International Studies, Johns Hopkins University, 1993).

16. Charles O. Jones, *The United States Congress*: p. 223.

17. See also Alberto Alesina, John Londregan and Howard Rosenthal, "A Model of the Political Economy of the United States," *American Political Science Review*, Vol. 87, No. 1, March 1993, p. 26; Ken Killman, John H. Miller and Scott E. Page, "Adaptive Parties in Spatial Elections," *American Political Science Review*, Vol. 86, No. 4, December 1992, pp. 929-937.

18. See the section "¿Nace una Nueva Norteamérica?" in *Observador Internacional*, Vol. 1, No. 20, February 1994, pp. 32-45, in particular the essays by Michael Hawes, "Construyendo una Nueva Casa," pp. 40-42, and Charles F. Doran, "Más allá del TLC: La emergente comunidad norteamericana," pp. 43-45.

About the Book

The NAFTA Puzzle: Political Parties and Trade in North America explores the political background of trade liberalization culminating in the signing of the historic North American agreement more than a decade after the North America Accord idea had been outright rejected. Experts from Canada, the U.S., and Mexico examine how each political party grappled with trade as the constituent base, interest group pressures, and ideologies shifted over broad time periods. The book treats each of Canada's long-standing national parties, the Republican and Democratic parties in the U.S., and Mexico's PRI historically, concluding that North America's principal parties have flip-flopped on the trade liberalization issue. *The NAFTA Puzzle* details the congressional vote in the U.S. and brings us all the way up to the Zapatista uprising in Mexico, ending with a discussion of the significance of NAFTA for overall trade liberalization and the future of trade and commercial relations on the continent.

About the Contributors

Charles F. Doran is the Andrew W. Mellon Professor of International Relations at the Paul H. Nitze School of Advanced International Studies (SAIS), Johns Hopkins University, Washington, D.C. He is also Director of the Center of Canadian Studies and Co-Director of the North American Studies Program at SAIS.

Gregory P. Marchildon is Assistant Professor of Canadian Studies and Economic History at the Paul H. Nitze School of Advanced International Studies (SAIS), Johns Hopkins University, Washington, D.C. During the duration of this project, he was Acting Director of the SAIS Center of Canadian Studies.

Pierre Martin is Assistant Professor of Political Science, Université de Montréal, Montreal, Quebec.

Duncan McDowall is Professor of History at Carleton University, Ottawa, Ontario.

Timothy J. McKeown is Associate Professor of Political Science at University of North Carolina, Chapel Hill, North Carolina.

Douglas Owram is Professor of History at University of Alberta, Edmonton, Alberta.

Dale Story is Professor and Chair, Department of Political Science, University of Texas at Arlington, Arlington, Texas.

Eric M. Uslaner is Professor of Government and Politics, University of Maryland, College Park, Maryland.

Gustavo Vega-Canovas is Academic Coordinator of the Program on Mexico-United States Studies, Center for International Studies, El Colegio de Mexico, Mexico, D.F.